Accessing Capital Markets through Securitization

Frank J. Fabozzi, Ph.D., CFA
Editor

Published by Frank J. Fabozzi Associates

This publication is designed to provide accurate and authoritative information in regard to the subject matter covered. It is sold with the understanding that the publisher is not engaged in rendering legal, accounting, or other professional services.

ISBN: 1-883249-92-9   **3 2280 00753 2120**

Printed in the United States of America

Table of Contents

Contributing Authors

Bradley Adams	Capital Markets Saxon Mortgage
Albert E. Avery	Towson University
Anand K. Bhattacharya	Countrywide Capital Markets Inc.
Peter J. Elmer	FDIC
Frank J. Fabozzi	Yale University
Lina Hsu	Prudential Securities Inc.
Bharat A. Jain	Towson University
Shane A. Johnson	Louisiana State University
Brent M. Lockwood	Havenwood Capital Markets, LLC
Jojy Vaniss Mathew	eBizTeka, Inc.
Cyrus Mohebbi	Prudential Securities Inc.
David Mond	Greenwich Financial Services, LLC
Kenneth P. Morrison	Kirkland & Ellis
Phillip R. Pollock	Tobin & Tobin
Glenn Schultz	Banc One Capital Markets, Inc.
Michael E. Shaff	Jeffers, Shaff & Falk, LLP
Daniel Singer	Towson University
Joseph F. Sinkey Jr.	The University of Georgia
Craig S. Stein	Schulte Roth & Zabel LLP
Shlomo C. Twerski	Schulte Roth & Zabel LLP
Paul N. Watterson Jr.	Schulte Roth & Zabel LLP
Thomas Zimmerman	PaineWebber

Chapter 1

Market Innovation in Securitization and Structured Finance

Daniel Singer, Ph.D
Professor of Finance
Towson University

INTRODUCTION

A revolution is in process. Financial institutions, processes, and products are in a state of continuing flux. Innovation is the order of the day. Market mechanisms in financial markets increasingly displace administrative solutions to the problem of allocating scarce capital. These innovations have encouraged visceral competition in sanctuary after sanctuary of monopolistic privilege and gentlemen's agreements.

Securitization and structured finance are techniques of financial engineering that have been at the cutting edge of these changes. Securitization and structured finance facilitate disintermediation in financial markets. These mechanisms permit the transformation of traditional asset classes into new forms of financial assets that provide improved risk-return outcomes, increasing the potential value of the assets to both buyers and sellers. Yet, securitization and structured finance are more than passive instruments of defined properties, they represent conceptual juggernauts that are rapidly changing the face of financial markets.

FORCES OF INNOVATION

Financial markets, assets, and processes appear to be evolving at a breathtaking pace. Each day seems to call forth innovation. Innovation that is driven by an interactive process between:

1. technological changes that extend what it is possible to know through advances in computerization and communication;
2. the breakdown of traditional market boundaries between different kinds of financial assets;
3. the breakdown of traditional regional and national boundaries in financial markets;

4. an increasing governmental proclivity towards market solutions, which translates into increasing deregulation;
5. increasing concentration among financial institutions; and
6. increasing potential volatility in global capital markets.

Collectively, these factors are combining to create increasingly competitive, efficient (fast) and rational (price driven) financial markets.

This dynamic context exacerbates competitive pressures forcing financial institutions to innovate at a breakneck pace. Much of the pressure to innovate is initiated by non-financial institutions seeking to rationalize their own capital structures or simply attracted by the extraordinary profits possible. Financial institutions attempt to move within this dynamic milieu towards a risk-return posture consistent with their underlying preferences and values. The traditional financial system with commercial banks serving as portfolio lenders, thrifts gathering funds for the mortgage market, and clearly demarcated equity and debt markets creates large pricing discontinuities in the financial markets — discontinuities that spell exceptional profits for those able to move quickly. In an era of erratic yield curve movements and continuing global uncertainties, competition is continually eroding the traditional profitable activities financial institutions have historically engaged in. Profit is found in innovation in today's financial markets.

The dynamic of continuous competitive pressure stimulating additional innovation which in turn erodes existing product and geographic boundaries even further reduces traditional opportunities for profits. Financial institutions are then pushed feverishly into increasingly exotic innovative behaviors that attempt to find additional profits in the unexplored arenas where such discontinuities may be found. These innovative behaviors involve the creation of new classes of assets that add real value by allowing financial institutions and investors to better manage their risk-return exposure.

One direction these innovative behaviors have taken is to create new types of financial assets, particularly assets that have been securitized and structured. These new asset classes are created through the transformation of traditional financial asset classes (loans, mortgages, bonds, and leases) into derivative securities. Derivative assets created through the process of securitizing or structuring are simple in concept, but can become bewilderingly complex in practice.

TWO FORMS OF ASSET TRANSFORMATION

Securitization

The mechanics of securitization involves taking individual financial assets, combining these assets in a single pool, and then issuing securities based on that pool. Securitizations may create either pass-through securities (an investor in is entitled to a *pro rata* share of any cash flow) or multi-class collateralized obligations (a format in which differentiated asset classes — or tranches — are created). Securitization pools may have a passive cash flow structure (based on relatively predictable cash flows requiring only administrative management) or a market-driven cash flow structure (based on less predictable cash flows requiring active management).

Though securitization is most often thought of in the context of commercial banking, any business can securitize their financial assets and almost any financial asset can be securitized. Securitization is attractive to the owners of financial assets because it:

1. reduces risk through increased diversification;
2. reduces risk through the reduction of information asymmetries;
3. reduces transaction costs;
4. provides increased leverage; and
5. can allow the securities issued to be tailored to the needs of specific investor classes.

Capturing these advantages can bring exceptional rewards to those bold enough to overcome the resistance to change.

Structured Finance

The mechanics of structured finance involves the transformation of a financial asset whose value is dependent on one set of events to an asset whose value is dependent on another set of events. Structured finance typically transforms the classic financial assets of loans, mortgages, bonds, and equities through a process that changes their risk and yield characteristics, frequently by combining them with forwards, futures, options, or swaps.

This transformation creates value by altering the risk-return characteristics of the original asset. This process involves combining the original asset with other assets (forward contracts, futures contract, swaps, and options) whose combinatorial properties create a new type of asset — an asset whose risk-return properties may be entirely different than that of the underlying original asset(s).

A simple example of a structured financial transaction would be a conventional loan by an U.S. bank to a German national demarcated in euro that was combined with a forward contract to sell a corresponding amount of euro. Return is reduced along with the elimination of foreign-exchange risk. Other combinations can be used to ameliorate interest rate risk, inflation risk, market risk or even random catastrophic risk. The possible permutations of financial assets whose characteristics can be altered structurally are enormous.

MARKET INNOVATION FOR FINANCIAL ASSETS

The demand for and supply of financial assets can be reconciled administratively or by market forces. The nature of this reconciliation process is illustrated in

Exhibit 1. Historically, administrative market linkages were utilized because of information asymmetries among market participants and the existence of an array of institutional and regulatory barriers.

The innovative use of asset securitization and structured finance are propelling the use of market mechanisms to allocate scarce capital because they make it possible to decompose specific idiosyncratic financial assets into commodity-like securities that can be parsed into any form desired by savers and investors. This is disintermediation. The implications of this concept are profound for the financial system as we currently know it.

Exhibit 1: Demand and Supply of Financial Assets

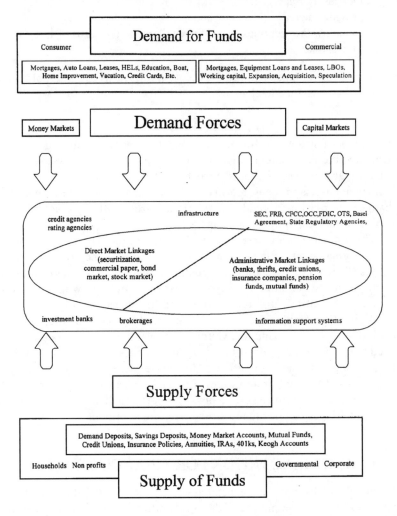

Historically, banks and other financial institutions have functioned as intermediaries between saver/investors and borrowers, i.e., provided a mechanism that administratively linked the needs of savers with those willing to pay a price for short- or long-term funds. The essence of this linkage involved creating an environment that encouraged individuals to save or invest and provided sufficient information to determine the creditworthiness of those desiring funds. Discipline in providing these linkages was enforced by tying the cost of funds to the quality of investments made within a profit maximizing organization. The stability of this system was supported by an elaborate web of government regulation and oversight whose function was to protect the integrity of the system and prevent financial panic.

Asset securitization and structured finance represents a sea of change in this way of doing business. Asset securitization and structured finance thus represent mechanisms that can link savers and investors directly through the market. Administrative intermediaries are relegated to a support role necessary to satisfy the requirements of the market for standardization. Money and capital markets become increasingly rational and gain in efficiency.

The result of this change in financial markets is that the traditional commercial banks as a portfolio lender are becoming extinct. Bill Gates was prescient in 1992 when he stated that "banks are dinosaurs." It's simply not efficient for banks to fund their own originations on a permanent basis. The traditional market boundaries specified by Glass-Steagall between commercial banks, investment banks, insurance companies, other financial institutions, and non-financial organizations have largely dissolved. Banks engage increasingly in non-bank activities and non-bank institutions increasingly behave as banks. Capital and money markets have globalized at a withering pace. Citibank can now claim to "be able to be competitive in any market, anywhere in the world."

Securitization and structured finance are techniques that provide for this type of transformation of assets within given institutional and legal frameworks. The increasing use of securitization and structured finance techniques create additional pressure to modify the existing institutional and legal framework to facilitate further change.

The impact of these powerful forces is not merely expressed in the dynamic of capital markets, but on the institutional infrastructure in which the forces of supply and demand meet. Laws governing the behavior of commercial banks, thrift institutions, credit unions, pension funds, mutual funds, insurance companies, mortgage companies, other financial institutions, tax laws and accounting conventions are changing rapidly in response to these pressures.

Change in these markets is accelerating. As profits are garnered by finding innovative and creative ways to circumvent existing regulatory and legal barriers in order to bring borrowers more directly into contact with investors, political pressure is generated to further weaken the regulatory and legal supports to existing administrative linkages. This all contributes to a complex and somewhat chaotic set of financial markets that is nevertheless very exciting and full of opportunity.

Continuing innovation in creating market-driven financial assets is fostered by the interaction of market forces and technology. Vehicles for this innovation include securitization and structured finance. The engine for innovation is the classic interplay of lenders and borrowers, each seeking a competitive edge to maximize their own advantage. Technology provides the chassis for these forces to express themselves. Technology in the form of advances in computerization and communication.

Computers have enormously increased our capacity to know and assimilate data. Information that was once the prerogative of the community bank can now be known for large and heterogeneous pools of assets. Moreover such data can be kept current and instantly disseminated to all interested parties. This erosion of information asymmetries has contributed substantially to the effectiveness of the market mechanism in this arena.

The high-octane fuel for this vehicle is the self-interest of the participants. What a powerful driving force to have shattered the complacent, bureaucratic world of commercial banking, intertwined as it was with the political and regulatory environment. In the nature of human beings, not all banks welcomed this change. Yet, the opportunities for gain, which could be obtained by a rationalization of the system, were too large to be ignored. More change has been initiated from within the system than without.

Testimony to the strength of these forces has been the wave of consolidation and diversification that has transformed the financial community. The Travelers-Citicorp, Bank America-Nations Bank, Wells Fargo-Norwest, mega mergers reflect this qualitative change in the nature of financial markets. The impetus for this type of depth and breadth is to effectively contain the market forces being unleashed by asset securitization and structured finance within a given organization. For such firms, the alternative to an imposing market presence is to be dominated by such market forces and experience an erosion of profits from the unrelenting, visceral forces of competition.

The much larger set of regional and community banks have also played a role in the evolution of these markets. BankBoston acquires Robertson-Stephens investment banking unit, not to get into another line of business, but because the imperatives of securitization and structured finance have forced the integration of the traditionally separate banking and underwriting areas. Smaller banks seek out small market niches that they, in their boutique status, are capable of defending. In so doing they facilitate this process either directly (e.g., by specializing in some facet of loan origination) or indirectly (e.g., by providing specialized services which the market mechanism can't yet provide).

THE PROCESS OF ASSET SECURITIZATION

The securitization process is illustrated in Exhibit 2. The process has many variants, but its essence is always to create market linkages between borrowers and investors (thereby bypassing traditional administrative linkages).

Exhibit 2: The Securitization Process

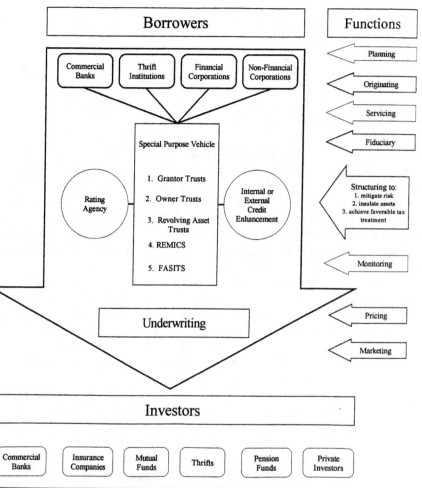

Creating Asset Pools

While historically, most asset securitizations have been for assets originated within the banking community, that is changing. Note that the catalytic agent that creates securitized assets can be a commercial bank, thrift institution, financial corporation, or non-financial corporation. Non-financial corporations (e.g., GE Capital and GMAC) are particularly aggressive innovators in using securitization and structured finance techniques. As the processes of securitization and structured finance become increasingly standardized, smaller non-financials will become increasingly active in this area. The size of an organization does not constitute a barrier to initiating these processes as financial assets may be accumulated from a variety of sources to create an asset pool.

Commonly securitized financial assets today include residential mortgages, commercial mortgages, high LTV mortgages, home equity loans, small business loans, credit card balances, automobile loans and leases, equipment loans and leases, distressed bonds, tax liens, etc. These assets are accumulated in a pool which is transferred to a special purpose vehicle (SPV) or special purpose entity (SPE), which most commonly takes the form of a trust. The form of the trust depends on the types of assets going into the trust and the purpose of the securitization. The trust then issues securities that are rated, underwritten and then sold to the investing public or placed privately.

Special Purpose Vehicles

The transfer may either be a straight sale from the originating institution(s) to the SPV or a financing. When the transfer takes the form of a straight sale, the SPV (and the owners of its securities) has no recourse to the originating institution and the originating institution removes the assets from its balance sheet. When the transfer is characterized as a financing, the SPV (and the owners of its securities) would have recourse to the originator of the assets. Under a financing, the assets remain on the balance sheet of the originator.

It is also important that the SPV be constructed in such a way as to be considered bankruptcy remote. This attribute means that if the originating institution goes bankrupt, its receiver will not be able to claim the assets transferred to the SPV. This attribute reduces the risk to the purchasers of the securities issued by the SPV.

The SPV issues securities in two basic forms: (1) the pass-through security and (2) the collateralized obligation. The pass-through security gives each investor a pro-rata share of any cash flow (both interest and principal) generated by the mortgage pool. The collateralized obligation takes a multi-class format with the pool being divided into a number of different creditor classes or tranches. These tranches typically have widely varying risk-return characteristics which increases their appeal to different sectors of the investment community.

Cash Flow Structures

The cash flow structure associated with securitization pools may be considered passive or active. Passive cash flow structures have values that are relatively predictable and flow from pools that require only administrative management. In contrast, active cash flow structures have values that are market driven and thus require more active management.

Passive Structures

Historically (that is to say, dating from the late 1970s through most of the 1980s), most securitizations had a passive cash flow structure. A frequently used metaphor to describe this structure has been that of a "waterfall." The waterfall is the cash stream derived from the securitization pool, flowing regularly and predictably through the various tranches of the securitization. Much of the energy in forming this type of securitization was directed towards reducing the uncertainty surrounding the cash flow from the collateralized assets. Credit enhancements in the form of over-collateralization, guarantees by investment-rated third parties, senior-subordinated tranches, and cash reserve or spread accounts were the order of the day. The largest uncertainty in this structure had to do with difficulties in forecasting prepayments.

Active Structures

Market value structures have emerged because a tremendous reservoir of funds exists in financial institutions whose existing regulatory structure prohibits them from investing directly in less than investment-grade securities. Securitization can create new classes of investment-grade assets based upon pools of more speculative assets (junk bonds, emerging market bonds, and distressed loans) which allow such institutions access to these opportunities. Proper packaging of the assets to secure the necessary credit ratings for particular tranches allows such regulatory constraints to be transcended.

The key factor in the market value structure is that its ultimate value to all investor classes is dependent on the future performance of the manager and/or changes in the market value of the underling pool of assets. In the face of such potential volatility, investor's struggle over understanding the risk-return attributes of a given asset class. Such uncertainty and its attendant difficulties have not diminished the rapidly growing popularity of this securitization format. Market value securitizations are becoming more widely used, even as they become increasingly complex, incorporating endless permutations of hybrid and synthetic securities in an increasingly leveraged environment.

STRUCTURED FINANCE PROCESSES

As defined above, structured finance is a process for creating derivative securities. This process transforms an asset whose value is dependent on one set of events to an asset whose value is dependent on another set of events. This process involves combining the original asset with other assets (forward contracts, futures contract, swaps, and options) whose combinatorial properties create a new type of asset, whose risk-return properties may be entirely different from that of the underlying original assets.

It is unfortunate that derivatives have pejorative connotations of high risk. This is not inherently true. In the majority of cases, derivatives are used to ameliorate risk. Indeed, in modern finance, derivatives are essential to managing risk. As witness to the debacle in Orange County and the difficulties between Bankers Trust and Procter & Gamble on this topic, the greatest risk associated with derivatives appears to be the failure of the participants to understand the attributes of the security created.

In its simplest form, a 20-year debenture with a fixed coupon interest payment is subject to considerable uncertainty with respect to its value at any point in its life. Such uncertainty results from the possibility of default, of changes in interest rates, of changes in inflation, or of changes in the underlying tax and regulatory structure. This risk can be managed through a swap for a series of Treasury bills. The contract which embeds this swap effectively creates a new security, a derivative (i.e., its value is derived from the combined values of the underlying securities).

Although the forms of futures, forwards, swaps and options look very different, they each represent an attempt to anticipate the value of an asset over time and have fundamental similarities. Charles Smithson and Clifford Smith have characterized these instruments as the "building blocks" of financial engineering.[1] The connotation of this term is that forwards, futures, swaps, and options are all interchangeable components, that can be "sliced and diced" in ever changing permutations to achieve a desired risk-return outcome. They are, the building blocks of structural finance.

New Organizational Forms

Another response to the push for innovation is to develop organizational structures that can support the new products and behaviors without the encumbrances of traditional legal or regulatory constrictions. These would include hedge funds, conduits, and derivative product companies.

Hedge Funds

Hedge funds are private partnerships formed to implement the investment purposes of its partners. Hedge funds have been very active buyers of securitizations and structured financial products. The sophisticated demand by some hedge funds has accelerated the innovation of structured financial products.

Conduits

Conduits are stand-alone organizations (although they may be subsidiaries of larger financial institutions) whose function is purely to accumulate financial assets and resell them through securitization to the general public. Conduits are most commonly used to originate and finance fixed-rate residential and commercial mortgages.

Conduits have certain disadvantages and advantages relative to their traditional competitors, commercial banks and thrifts). Their advantages lie largely in their flexibility to ramp up or down in the face of rapid change in the highly cyclical real estate market. This gives conduits a lower cost basis over the cycle and allows them to innovate and segment their market according to market conditions.

A risk to conduits is that at any time their inventory of mortgages may deteriorate in value due to a rise in interest rates or a deterioration in market conditions for that type of property. Capital to carry the mortgages during the process they are originated or accumulated prior to being securitized is provided from

---

[1] Charles W. Smithson and Clifford W. Smith, *Managing Financial Risk: A Guide to Derivative Products, Financial Engineering and Value Maximization* (Homewood, IL: Irwin Publishing, 3rd Ed., 1998).

warehouse lines of credit. This has the effect of giving the conduits a competitive disadvantage over traditional portfolio lenders as a result of their higher cost of funds. This also has the effect of making the conduits subject to margin calls (or even outright denial of credit), which can create severe liquidity problems in times of market volatility.

Conduits typically do not have their own servicing platforms. This means they will not be able to capture the servicing revenues associated with mortgages they originate, contributing to their inherent instability.

Derivative Product Companies

Turmoil in the international financial markets during the late 1980s and early 1990s created the need for a stable platform from which to create a variety of derivative securities. Derivative Product Companies (DPCs) were created in response to this need. The idea was to isolate the platform from the normal ups and downs of larger financial organizations, to capture certain tax advantages, and to escape certain regulatory constraints. DPCs presently originate, intermediate, and/or guarantee a wide variety of derivative products.

DPCs may be unstructured or structured (enhanced). Unstructured DPCs get an investment grade credit rating either from their parent companies or their own capital. The problems referred to above occurred when the credit rating of the parent company of these subsidiaries was downgraded. This resulted in a downgrading of the credit ratings of the DPCs and the subsequent reduction in the value of the securities they had issued, even though the inherent value of those securities remained unchanged.

Structured DPCs derive their credit through financial and credit support structures, independently of their parent companies. These credit and financial support structures attempt to eliminate value at risk through hedging activities and the use of an automatic workout process.

SUMMARY

Securitization and structured finance are techniques of financial engineering that have fostered innovation in capital markets. These techniques have encouraged the substitution of market mechanisms for administrative procedures in allocating scarce capital. The result has been increasing disintermediation for the commercial banking system and an increasingly efficient market.

Securitization and structured finance both add value to financial assets by transforming the asset's risk-return properties. The derivative securities created through these processes confer substantial benefits on all participating parties. Institutions originating the financial assets gain both a greater access to capital and a lower cost of capital. Investors gain through higher returns and the availability of preferred risk-return profiles.

Chapter 2

Securitization Basics

Daniel Singer, Ph.D
Professor of Finance
Towson University

INTRODUCTION

A securitization takes place when a special purpose entity (SPE) or special purpose vehicle (SPV) takes ownership of a pool of financial assets and issues securities based on the expected proceeds from those assets. The issued securities created from the securitization are derivative in nature. Banks, mortgage companies, indeed any organization, may originate the loans or other financial assets, but these are passed to the special purpose vehicle where securities based on the value of this loan are sold to investors. The key to the success of a securitization lies in the ability to predict the performance of the underlying pool of assets.

To be perfectly clear about what a securitization is, it is necessary to understand what it is not. Ownership of participations in securitized asset pools issued by special purpose entities is not the same as owning the underlying financial assets. Banks traditionally make loans from liquid assets in their portfolios that are created by deposits in the bank and secure these loans with a claim on assets or income. The bank is said to intermediate between borrowers and savers. In contrast to the owner of a beneficial interest in a securitization, a bank (or other originating entity) has a direct claim on the financial asset securing the loan. The key to the success of this process lies in the bank's ability to judge the creditworthiness of its borrowers and link this to the cost of credit.

Securitization thus represents a form of disintermediation because it allows for direct market contact between borrowers and investors.

TYPES OF SECURITIZATIONS

While securitizations may reflect either a true sale or a financing by the originator, the advantages to the originator are generally better when the securitization is treated as a true sale — indeed, much of the process is directed towards making sure that the transfer of assets from the originator to the SPV will be legally construed as a true sale.

Securitizations may create either pass-through securities or collateralized obligations. Pass-through securities are characterized by all asset classes receiving a pro-rata share of any cash flows (both interest and principal) from the underlying pool of assets. The certificates issued in this format represent an undivided beneficial ownership in a pool of loans. A variant of the pass-through is the pay-through, where the certificates represent a debt obligation of the SPV, rather than ownership of the underlying pool.

Collateralized obligations take a multi-class format with the pool being divided into a number of different creditor classes or tranches. These tranches typically have widely variant risk-return characteristics. Collateralized obligations may be further differentiated into those with cash flow structures and those with market value structures. The difference between these two structures is a matter of degree. Cash flow structures are expected to produce relatively predictable, but still uncertain, revenue streams (e.g., a pool of seasoned, conventional residential mortgages). Market value structures, in contrast, must be actively managed and their revenue streams will be influenced by the quality of management and future economic conditions (e.g., a pool of distressed bonds).

The tranches of a securitization will generally be ordered from the less risky to the more risky. The value of each tranche will be determined by the claim on the cash flows proceeding from the pool of assets. An attempt is generally made to place as much of the pool as possible in investment grade tranches. Here the relative lack of credit risk permits the application of a discount rate that maximizes the value of that portion of the cash flow. Tranches also may be structured to receive various combinations of principal and/or interest in some predetermined priority to create desirable risk-return characteristics.

For example, while prepayment risk is always present in a securitized pool of mortgages, that risk may be minimized for some tranches and increased for others. Planned amortization class (PAC) and non-accelerating senior class (NAS) tranches are often used to transfer prepayment risk to other classes.

Tranches may be structured in an IO (interest only) or PO (principal only) format. POs and IOs tend to be quite volatile in nature and sensitive to underlying economic changes, particularly changes in the interest rate. POs tend to increase in value as interest rates decline — i.e., the cash is realized more quickly than anticipated in the original pricing of the security. IOs tend to decrease in value as interest rates decrease — the cash flow is diminished by prepayments. While some investors may prefer IOs and POs as speculative investments, they can prove very useful as hedging instruments within a larger portfolio.

The "Z" tranche accrues interest on the unpaid principal amount. The payment terms in this tranche provide for interest on the unpaid interest at a rate equal to the bond's yield, thereby eliminating reinvestment risk. Thus a Z bond is similar to a zero coupon bond.

A securitization may frequently have a residual tranche whose function is to "clean up" any residual profits from the pool or absorbs any unanticipated losses. These residual tranches are often privately placed because of their extreme volatility. Depending on how it is structured in the SPV, an originator who holds a residual tranche can imperil the true sale status of the securitization.

ELEMENTS OF THE SECURITIZATION PROCESS

The Underlying Securities

The first requirement in a successful securitization is that the trustee is able to perfect a security interest in the underlying pool of assets. In general this can be done through appropriate Uniform Commercial Code Filings, title amendments, mortgage liens, and so on. This requires careful and detailed documentation and continuous monitoring. A perfected interest in the underlying assets should not be automatically assumed.

The second requirement is that the transfer of assets from the originator of the asset to the trustee be a true sale rather than a financing. This is important should the originating institution go into bankruptcy and the receiver attempt to attach the assets. The general requirements for a true sale would require that:

- the obligation represents a bona fide and arm's length transaction
- the secured parties are not insiders
- the grant of a security interest was made for adequate (fair market value) compensation
- the transaction was undertaken within the ordinary course of business without intent to defraud creditors
- the security agreement conforms to governing laws and regulations

If the seller or originator of the assets were a bank, Federal Bankruptcy Code would not apply. If a bank becomes insolvent, the FDIC would act as the receiver for the institution. The FDIC has the power to ask for a judicial stay of all payments and the voiding of any contract. While the FDIC has suggested it would not seek to void a true sale of assets, this issue is not fully resolved at present.

Where the pool of financial assets to be securitized represents a sub-set of a larger pool, care should be taken to examine the methods by which assets were selected for securitization. This is important because selection procedures may impact pool performance. Pool selection may be random in order to approximate the characteristics of the larger pool or stratified by a variety of characteristics (e.g., age, geographic location, payment history, etc.) in order to create a pool with specific performance attributes. The details for asset selection should be specified in the pooling and servicing agreement between the trustee and the originator.

Special Purpose Vehicles

SPVs may be described as the linchpin of the securitization process. An SPV is the operating mechanism for a securitization. Above all SPVs must be functional. Aside from providing the organizational framework for the securitization, it is important that SPVs be constructed to achieve favorable tax treatment and to insulate the assets from the originator's creditors. Favorable tax treatment is most often accomplished with a trust, although similar ends can be accomplished with C Chapter incorporation.

Most SPVs are organized as trusts where the trustee has a fiduciary responsibility to the certificate holders (beneficial owners). The specific responsibilities of the trustee will be delineated in the trust agreement. The trustee monitors the performance of the asset pool and is charged with the responsibility for addressing problems associated with poor pool performance or default.

Grantor Trusts
Grantor trusts are most often used in pass-through securitizations. Grantor trust certificate holders are generally treated as beneficial owners of the assets and taxed as if the certificate holders actually owned the underlying securities. Grantor trusts must be passively managed and may not issue multiple classes of securities.

Owner Trusts
Owner trusts allow for more active management and the creation of multiple classes of securities. For tax purposes, a properly structured owners trust will be treated like a partnership allowing profits to pass through the entity without paying federal income tax. The assets in an owner trust are typically secured by a lien of indenture through which notes are issued. The beneficial ownership of these notes are then represented by the certificates that can be used to form the various asset classes.

Revolving Asset Trusts
Revolving asset trusts allow groups of financial assets which do not have a fixed amortization schedule (e.g., revolving credit card accounts, and home equity credit lines) to be sold to a trust. This may be either in the form of a single sale to a single trust (the *stand-alone trust*) or a series of sales to a trust (a *master trust*). This structure allows active management, pass-through tax protection, and multiple asset classes.

Cooperatives
The function of a cooperative is to facilitate the business interest of its members. This allows a SPV in the form of a cooperative to finance the receivables of its members (and to a limited extent, its non-members). While not commonly used, this format yields great flexibility to the SPV and confers upon it significant tax advantages. Even though cooperatives are subject to corporate tax, they are allowed to deduct patronage dividends from its revenue stream. Patronage dividends are those that are distributed on the basis of the business done with the cooperative. If all profits are distributed in this manner, there will be no tax liability.

C Corporations
An SPV may take a corporate form that is clearly taxable, if its taxable net income can be minimized through a structure that matches its income with its

expenses. The corporate format may offer more flexibility in structuring debt issues to meet investor preferences. A corporation may issue preferred stock. Also, a corporation may be used repeatedly for multiple filings. These advantages increase the potential profit of a corporate format.

REMICS

Strictly speaking, a REMIC (*Real Estate Mortgage Investment Conduit*) is not an SPV, but a tax status that can apply to a qualified SPV whose pool of financial assets are mortgages. REMIC status provides a simplification of the legal, regulatory, and accounting obstacles surrounding the issuance of multiple asset classes to investors and removes the threat of double taxation at the federal level. It currently provides the most common format for multiple-class mortgage-backed securities.

Under certain circumstances a REIT can hold an interest in a REMIC as if it were real estate. This provision significantly broadens the range of assets a REIT can invest in. This provision is applicable only where the REMIC's holdings are capable of passing the requisite REIT income and asset tests.

FASITS

As the advantages of REMICS, which were created in 1986 and further extended in 1992, became apparent the concept was extended to other asset classes with the creation of the FASIT (*Financial Asset Securitization Investment Trust*). This format is also not an SPV but a tax status that can apply to a qualified SPV. FASIT status provides a simplification of the legal, regulatory, and accounting obstacles surrounding the issuance of multiple asset classes to investors and removes the threat of double taxation at the federal level.[1]

A problem with the corporate format is that care must be taken to ensure that the corporate debt (manifesting itself in payments to investors) is a bona fide indebtedness for tax purposes. If asset classes receive variable payments depending upon the performance of the pool, the IRS might construe such "debt" as equity and disallow the deductions for tax purposes.

Credit Enhancement

Credit enhancement is inherent in the process of creating multiple asset classes and may be further augmented through a variety of internal or external measures.[2]

A tremendous advantage of the securitization process is that it allows a heterogeneous pool of assets to be split into several homogeneous asset classes (tranches) which allow credit risk to be more effectively predicted. For example, a given pool of assets may have an unknown, but potentially high, default rate

---

[1] For a more detailed discussion of FASIT, see Phillip R. Pollack and Michael E. Shaff, "FASIT Flexibility Applied to Subprime Securitizations" in this book.

[2] For a more detailed discussion of credit enhancements, see Lina Hsu and Cyrus Mohebbi, "Credit Enhancements in ABS Structures" in this book.

that prevent it from obtaining an investment grade credit rating. Splitting the beneficial owners of the pool into senior/subordinate asset classes would allow the senior classes (who receive priority with respect to payment of principal and interest) to receive an investment grade rating. Of course, this will leave the subordinate classes even more exposed to credit risk. Depending upon the specific characteristics of the pool and tranches, the securitization may make the pool itself intrinsically more valuable by allowing investors to more precisely express their risk-return preferences.

Internal Mechanisms

A variety of *internal credit enhancements* can be implemented. The purpose of each of these is to increase the certainty associated with the expected cash flows associated with a particular tranche. These would include (1) a senior/subordinated class structure, (2) overcollateralization, (3) excess spread, and (4) cash collateral accounts.

A pool may be over collateralized if $400 million of financial assets is sold to the trustee to support a pool with a nominal value of $350 million. The originator would often take ownership of a residual tranche under this circumstance. The extra assets in the pool serve as a buffer to defaults in the more senior tranches.

Where the yield from the pool is greater than the coupon, servicing charges, and any reserves for losses, this "excess spread" may be reserved against deficits in expected cash flows. With the termination of the special purpose vehicle, any unused portion of the excess spread may revert to the originator. This reversion must be carefully structured to allow the originator to initially qualify for sales treatment. The excess spread may also revert to other parties to the securitization.

Cash collateral accounts take the form of a segregated trust account funded at the initiation of the securitization. These funds will be used to cover deficits in principal, interest, or servicing expenses. At the termination of the trust, any residual funds will be returned to the organization that initially funded the account.

External Mechanisms

The simplest form of *external credit enhancement* would be a third-party letter of credit. Such letters of credit may cover all or a portion of potential losses. A third party must have sufficient credit standing to support a prospective credit rating (i.e., an AA party letter of credit cannot support an AAA credit rating). A similar type of credit enhancement may be obtained in the form of surety bonds with respect to principal and interest.

A securitization may provide credit enhancement in the form of recourse to the originator of the financial assets. This form of credit enhancement is more likely to be interpreted as a financing rather than a true sale on the part of the originator. Under this circumstance, the securities could not have a higher credit rating than the originator.

Servicing

Servicing a securitization is frequently a profitable activity for the originator. A pool servicer must monitor the performance of the pool, see that the contractual performance of the parties to the pool is performed satisfactorily, and administer cash flow. Servicers prepare monthly information reports (often containing very specific detail), remit collections to the trust, and process payment to the trust's various asset classes (the trustee has the direct responsibility for the cash disbursements). The reports prepared are typically distributed to the investors, the trustees, the rating agencies, and the external credit enhancer, if any. This function is so critical that the pooling and servicing agreement will normally require the use of an approved backup servicer.

Underwriting

Underwriting is the name traditionally given to the process of selling securities by an investment bank (or syndicate of investment banks and stockbrokers). The function of an investment bank is to purchase the securities and re-sell them. If the sale is to the general public, the investment bank must insure that the process of the sale conforms to SEC regulations. If the sale is in the form of a private placement, the regulatory requirements are noticeably less stringent. The investment bank (or syndicate) is compensated by a variety of fees and the spread between the price it pays for the securities and the price it sells them for. For this compensation, the investment bank (or syndicate) usually bears the risk that, in the time lag between its purchase and sale of the securities, the price of the securities may fall.

A contributing factor to the failure of the banking system in the early 1930s was the fact that large commercial banks also functioned as investment banks. In the face of the stock market crash of 1929, banks which had large unsold stock portfolios became insolvent as a result. The remedy to this situation was a more highly regulated banking environment. In particular, the Glass-Steagall Act (The Banking Act of 1933), prohibited commercial banks from underwriting most securities. Under the 1956 Bank Holding Company Act, bank holding companies (BHCs) were permitted to own investment banking subsidiaries under Federal Reserve regulation.

The importance of this for the securitization process is that MBCs often find it advantageous to have their investment bank subsidiary securitize financial assets originated by their commercial bank subsidiary. Indeed, this practice has become so common that it often appears seamless to the investor. The wisdom of combining the originating function and the underwriting function within the same organizational umbrella is less than clear since the two functions are inherently different and would provide checks and balances to the process for the investor were these functions completely independent.

Under Federal Reserve regulation this has not been a problem to date. The current underwriting market appears quite competitive with independent investment banks competing effectively with the investment bank subsidiaries of BHCs. Competition is essential to preserving the integrity of this process. The recent trends toward consolidation in the industry are interpreted by some observers to be a harbinger of a less competitive market context.

Traditional underwriting can be either on a competitive bid or negotiated basis. Where the catalytic agent in a securitization is the originating institution (either a bank or a large corporation), the competitive bidding process has been very effective in lowering underwriting spreads. Where the catalytic agent for the securitization is an investment bank, the underwriting spread tends to be negotiated and wider. This is particularly true where the securitization involves an innovative or creative approach to creating the asset pool.

As the risk to the underwriter is proportional to the length of time the securities purchased from the issuer are expected to be held, the significance of the time lag generated by the intricacies of the SEC registration process is large. For this reason, shelf registrations are utilized when possible. Under Rule 415, the requirements of registration may be shortcut by filing an amendment to its detailed SEC filing containing only details about the specific security being offered.

THE SIMPLE MECHANICS OF SECURITIZATION

The following examples are intended as generic illustrations of the basic principals of securitization. As such, they lack the nuances that characterize actual securitization problems.

Pass-Through Securitization at a Commercial Bank

Insight into the essence of the securitization process can be gained from the consideration of a pass-through securitization at a commercial bank, one of the most common types of securitization outstanding.

Assume a bank assembles a pool of 1,000 FHA/VA new mortgages with an average size of $100,000, an initial stated maturity of 30 years, and a coupon of 7%. The capital required by the bank to back these assets when the mortgages are held in its portfolio would be $4 million (where the risk-adjusted value of residential mortgages is 50% and the risk-based capital requirement is 8%). The bank would support the $100 million asset with $106.6 million of demand deposits ($96 million adjusted for the 10% reserve non-interest bearing reserve requirement for demand deposits) and $4 million of required capital.

If the bank's marginal cost of funds were 5.5% (including the cost of the FDIC insurance premium), its operating margin on the portfolio would be 1.5%. The bank also gained whatever points were associated with originating the mortgages. From the bank's perspective, keeping its portfolio under the circumstances indicated in Exhibit 1 nets it a $2.5 million gross return on its required capital of

$4 million. However, the continued holding of these mortgages exposes the bank to a higher duration gap, creating the possibility of significant losses if interest rates rise. In addition, in the absence of excess reserves, the use of such funds for this purpose precludes the bank from lending funds for other purposes. Also, if the mortgages reflect concentration in a particular geographic region that is sensitive to industry shifts or economic fluctuations, the default risk associated with the pool is likely to be higher than if the pool of assets reflected greater diversity.

The securitization is initiated by the bank removing the package of mortgages and transferring them to a SPV. This process is illustrated in Exhibit 2. As an approved lender, the bank is eligible for GNMA guaranteeing (for a fee) the timing of interest and principal payments on the bonds issued from the asset pool. The SPV issues bonds through an underwriter and the value of the bonds reflects a pro rata share of principal and interest due. The $100 million pool is priced to yield 6% (a small premium to comparable government bonds at the time the bonds are sold).

The purchaser of these securities bears little default risk as a result of the FHA/VA/GMNA guarantees and owns a security isolated from any risk associated with the originating institution. The primary risks borne are the risk of prepayment (effectively a call option for the borrower) and interest rate risk. The pricing structure of these securities will compensate investors for that risk plus a premium over straight government bonds.

The difference between the 7% earned by the original mortgages and the 6% paid to the SPV bondholders is divided between the bank which for 0.5% retains the right to service the mortgage pool and 0.5% to GNMA (for timing insurance) and underwriting fees. Current accounting rules allow the bank to capitalize the anticipated profit from servicing the mortgage pool. The net effect of the securitization to the bank is (1) the elimination of $100 million of loans requiring $4 million of capital, (2) the infusion of $100 million cash (from the proceeds of the bond sales), (3) a reduction in its duration gap and (4) freedom from whatever default risk might have been associated with the portfolio. The bank has earned a profit from the transaction and is free to lend again.

Exhibit 1: Commercial Bank Impact of Securitization (in million of $)

	Without Securitization	With Securitization
Portfolio value of mortgages	$100.0	$0
Supporting deposits	106.6	0
Required reserves	4.0	0
Origination fees	1.0	1.0
Gross spread (7%-5.5%)	1.5%	0
Value of servicing*	1.4	1.4
Capacity to create new mortgages	0	100.0

* Assuming 75% amortization rate and capitalization factor of 10%

Exhibit 2: Steps in the GNMA Pass-Through Securitization

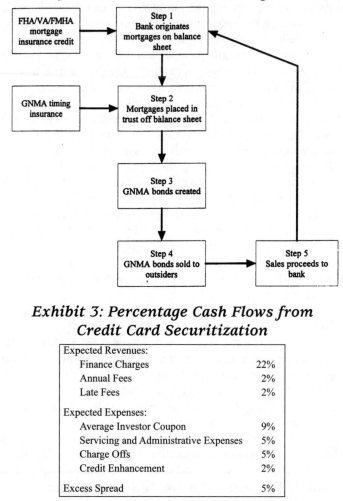

Exhibit 3: Percentage Cash Flows from Credit Card Securitization

Expected Revenues:	
Finance Charges	22%
Annual Fees	2%
Late Fees	2%
Expected Expenses:	
Average Investor Coupon	9%
Servicing and Administrative Expenses	5%
Charge Offs	5%
Credit Enhancement	2%
Excess Spread	5%

SECURITIZATION OF CREDIT CARD BALANCES

A credit card company has as its primary asset a $5 billion portfolio of credit card loans. As a result of a recent expansion, it lacks the cash reserves to support further expansion. Its debt/equity ratio stands as high as is considered prudent. Under current volatile market conditions, the sale of additional stock is not seen as enhancing shareholder wealth. The credit card company has a BB credit rating.

The process of this securitization is illustrated in Exhibit 3. The securitization begins with the random selection of a $1 billion pool of credit card receivables from its total pool of receivables. The average finance charge is 22% in the selected pool. This pool is transferred to a SPV in the form of a revolving asset trust using a sales treatment. While the format of the pool may be constructed to either maintain its present size through refreshment or be self-liquidating, the decision is made to create a pool which maintains its present size for five years (through asset replenishment if necessary and referred to as the *lockout period*) and then becomes self-liquidating (referred to as the *principal amortization period*).

The revenue and expense flows associated with this securitization are presented in Exhibit 4.

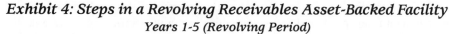

Exhibit 4: Steps in a Revolving Receivables Asset-Backed Facility
Years 1-5 (Revolving Period)

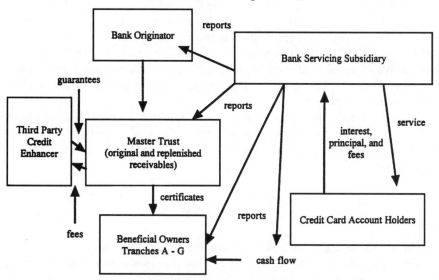

Years 1-10 (Revolving and Amortization Periods)

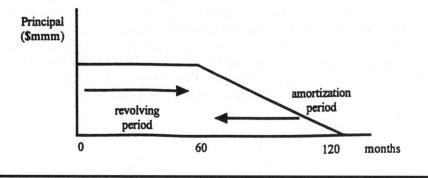

Exhibit 5: Credit Card Tranche Structure

Class	Credit Rating	Size ($000,000)	Maturity	Yield
A (IO)	AAA	500	1-5 years	LIBOR
B (IO)	AA	300	1-5 years	LIBOR + 25bp
C (IO)	A	200	1-5 years	LIBOR + 50bp
D	A	500	5-10 years	8.0%-9.0%
E	B	300	5-10 years	9.5%-10.5%
F	C	200	5-10 years	12.0%-15.0%
G	(Residual IO)	1 - 10 years	indeterminate	

Following verification of the characteristics of the pool (default rates, prepayment rates, etc.), and following consultation with rating agencies and the underwriter, the decision is made to divide the pool into seven tranches (Exhibit 5) using a senior/subordinate structure, differentiated by the level of default risk and maturity. A soft bullet (principal funds are paid as received) will be used to pay principal after the first five years. This is done in order to make the securities as attractive as possible to investors by providing them with their preferred risk-return combination. The seven tranches of the securitization pool will be structured as seen in Exhibit 5.

As a result, the credit card company replaces $1 billion of its illiquid credit card portfolio with cash proceeds from the sale of these assets and is now free to use this money to expand its business, pay down its debt, or for any general corporate purpose.

SUMMARY

Securitization occurs when a pool of financial assets is created and then transformed into a set of derivative financial assets with superior risk-return characteristics. In this process the originator of the original financial assets may be able to remove these assets from its balance sheet if the requisites of a "true sale" to a SPV are met. The SPV would normally take the form of a trust, the particular vehicle depending on the types of assets being securitized, the intentions of the originator, and the degree of asset management required. Care must be taken to formulate the SPV in such a manner that it is remote from any bankruptcy claim attempted by the asset originator and that it avoids taxation at this level. The beneficial interests arising from the securitized asset pool may then be organized into a series of tranches with a variety of risk-return attributes.

Chapter 3

The Anatomy of a Securitization

Brent M. Lockwood
President
Havenwood Capital Markets, LLC

David Mond
Partner
Greenwich Financial Services, LLC

Frank J. Fabozzi, Ph.D., CFA
Adjunct Professor of Finance
School of Management
Yale University

INTRODUCTION

Securitization is defined as a transaction that isolates financial assets from the credit of the originator and enables the originator to obtain financing through the capital markets based upon the quality of the assets, rather than the originator's overall credit. The originator is the entity originating the underlying asset being securitized. Often the originator's primary business creates the underlying asset.

There are several compelling reasons financial institutions securitize their assets. These include:

- Securitization can assist institutions originating these assets by reducing their cost of funds.
- The securitization process can complement or offer an alternative to current funding sources.
- Securitizing assets can reduce credit and interest rate risk for the institution originating the loans and, more importantly, allow for off-balance sheet financing.

While almost any asset can be securitized, the most commonly securitized are traditional assets such as mortgage loans (standard and home equity loans), credit card receivables, auto loans, student loans, SBA loans, and commercial mortgage-backed loans.

The steps to accessing the capital markets using securitization are

- Planning the securitization
- Forming a team
- Developing a special purpose/bankruptcy remote corporation
- Servicing the assets
- Credit enhancing the structure
- Marketing the securities created

The purpose of this chapter is to provide an overview of the steps listed above.

PLANNING THE SECURITIZATION

More often than not institutional investors, although very sophisticated, know very little about the origination of the underlying asset. Investors will rely on information provided by the investment banker and the rating agencies and make their investment decision accordingly. Understanding what goes into the decision making/due diligence process will assist the seller/securitizer in achieving a successful transaction.

When deciding upon the structure and credit enhancement the seller must consider the investor. The investment banker will offer suggestions regarding the structure. The investment banker operates as a facilitator, and will deal directly with the originator, rating agencies, and the end investor. The originator is looking for the lowest cost of funds for its assets. The investor is looking for the highest return given the type of collateral, credit rating, and maturity of the securities.

The first step in undertaking a securitization is to hire an investment banker who is often a broker/dealer or a commercial bank. The investment banker plays a major role in developing the securitization process. The financial institution should consider the investment banker the project manager.

The investment banker's primary responsibility is to structure, market, and distribute the securities to the end investors. In addition, the investment banker will offer continued support for the transaction long after settlement by providing information regarding the underlying assets and by developing a secondary market for the existing securities for investors and the originator. The investment banker will continuously monitor the capital markets looking for a more efficient execution for the issuer. The investment banker can often reduce the originator's cost of securitization. The investment banker will assist the issuer by coordinating the activities between the rating agencies, legal counsel, accounting firms, and trustees.

The investment banker is responsible for marketing and distributing the securities. The investment banking firm will develop a plan to introduce the issuer and the transaction to the investor base. An investment banking firm must have an experienced staff that will give it the ability to develop a plan to market the transaction in an efficient manner. The dealer will look for features that will keep the cost of issuance down while at the same time attract investors. Distinguishing features can relate to the prepayment speed, loss severity, geographic concentration of the underlying collateral. Getting the originators story out properly will reduce the costs and assist in the financing of future transactions.

The financial institution or issuer should designate a securitization manager. The senior management at a financial institution should have a clear understanding of which risks and responsibilities are transferred to other parties and which will remain with the issuer/originator. Proficient issuers and servicers of asset-backed securities typically assign responsibility for managing the securitization process to a single individual or department that understand the issues, and has the authority to make changes when needed.

FORMING A TEAM

Securitizations are complex. There is no substitute for an experienced staff, working together with responsible leadership. There are, aside from the in-house or specialized finance people required for a securitization, a need for five separate areas of expertise. In effect a relationship with the following needs to be created:

- attorneys
- accountants
- rating agencies
- underwriters
- trustee agent

Attorneys

Securitizing assets is a legally intense process. To securitize assets the originator will need experienced legal counsel.[1] The sale or purchase of the assets will require a *purchase agreement* that, among other things, sets forth the *representations and warranties* offered by the seller/originator of the assets. The attorneys will create a *servicing agreement* since all assets will need to be serviced after their purchase by the originator or another highly qualified servicer. Finally, documents need to be created to describe how cash flows are divided among the security holders. The net is that there needs to be a good number of terms negotiated and corresponding documents created. The good news is that many of these documents have already been written and their form (as well as substance) can be cannibalized. However, only the typically larger law firms have complete templates from which to work.

---

[1] For a more detailed discussion of the role of attorneys, see Kenneth P. Morrison, "Observations on Effecting Your First Asset-Backed Securities Offering," Chapter 5 in this book.

Accountants

A successful securitization will require a *comfort letter* from an accounting firm attesting to the veracity or accuracy of all numerical information placed in either the prospectus or the private placement memorandum. The way this is typically accomplished is that a copy of the deal's payment schedule, underlying collateral, average life and yield tables are supplied to the accountants for verification. In turn, the accountants reverse engineer the deal according to the deal's payment rules. Following those rules and using the same collateral that actually supplies the cash flows for the deal, the accountants reproduce the yield and average life tables that investors have relied on to make their investment decisions. A deal is considered "tied out" if the accountants produce the same analysis as the original deal structurers did. At this point, the accountants issue a comfort letter stating that the analysis has been sampled and conforms to accepted analytical techniques.

Rating Agencies

Although not necessary if the issuer is going to issue a non-rated deal, most deals in fact are issued on a rated basis. In order to earn a rating, the issuer must submit information about the collateral to a rating agency so that the rating agency can determine how much subordination or credit enhancement is required to create AAA securities, AA securities, and so on. The rating agencies will not only look at the specific collateral but they will review the originator's internal processes and ability to originate and service (if the issuer will also be servicing) the collateral. The idea is that the collateral should meet certain requirements and security holders should be able to assume that those levels are maintained over the security's life. The originator typically pays a fee to a rating agency to rate a particular deal.

Underwriters

Similar in purpose to the rating agencies, underwriters work on behalf of the purchasers of the collateral. When a purchaser buys a pool of collateral, it needs some assurance that the assets purchased have been fairly represented. This assurance is provided by an underwriter who reviews loan files and underwriting standards, examining on a sampled basis to see if the underwriting standards stated by the seller have been adhered to. This is basically the only chance that the buyer of a pool of assets has to review the pool and reject those assets that do not conform to or are perceived as not up to the standards of the rest of the pool.

Trustee Agent

The trustee agent is the entity that safeguards the assets after they have been placed in a trust, receives the payments due to the security holders, and provides periodic information to the security holders. The information is provided in the form of remittance reports that may be issued quarterly, monthly or whenever agreed to by the terms of the prospectus or the private placement memorandum.

DEVELOPING A SPECIAL PURPOSE/BANKRUPTCY REMOTE CORPORATION

The majority of small/medium-sized originators do not have an investment- grade rating. In order to achieve an investment-grade rating on the securities two steps must be taken. The first step is to create a bankruptcy remote entity. The collateral must be isolated, that is taken off the balance sheet of the originator. The security interest must be "perfected" in order that the investor's interest remains secure. The sale must be a true sale not a transfer of assets to insure that a true transfer of ownership is made. This is accomplished by establishing a *special purpose entity* (SPE) whereby the collateral is sold to a bankruptcy remote corporation designed to isolate the collateral.

The second step is placing the assets in a trust. The assets are sold to the SPE. Once this occurs a trustee is named. The trustee safeguards the assets that have been placed in trust. The trustee receives the payments due to the security holders and provides periodic information as outlined in the indenture.

SERVICING THE ASSETS

In order to obtain and maintain an investment-grade rating it is critical that an experienced servicer is engaged. The servicer's primary responsibility is to collect the payments from the borrowers and disburse the funds to the trustee for the investors. The rating agencies and the investment banker will demand that the servicer be experienced in the collection, monitoring, and disbursement of funds within this structure. Often the seller/originator for a fee will continue to service the assets placed in the SPE. Before the seller is approved, the rating agencies will review the servicer's experience in collecting and disbursing of funds. Depending upon the results of their findings, the rating agencies may require that the seller have a backup servicer in place. The backup servicer will be an experienced servicer who will take over the servicing role if the primary servicer falters. The seller may also elect to have a qualified third-party servicer in the transaction.

CREDIT ENHANCEMENT

To achieve an investment-grade rating on a proposed transaction the issuer must submit information about the collateral to a rating agency. The rating agency will determine how much subordination or credit enhancement is needed to achieve an investment-grade rating. Rating agencies will not only look at the specific collateral, they will review the originator's internal processes such as underwriting and servicing (if handled internally). The investors in asset-backed transactions rely on the rating agencies to perform the analysis, monitor the issuer, and monitor the securities created.

In order to be awarded an investment-grade rating on securities, some form of credit enhancement must be provided. The way credit enhancement works is some third party is either paid a fee (or an insurance premium) or earns extra yield on a security in the structure to assume risk. There are two forms of credit enhancement – external and internal. *External credit enhancement* involves third-party guarantees such as insurance, a letter of credit, or a guarantee by the issuer. *Internal credit enhancement* includes overcollateralization, senior-subordinated structure, and reserves. Deals will often have more than one form of enhancement.

It is critical for the issuer to examine each form of credit enhancement prior to issuance to determine the enhancement mechanism or combination of enhancement mechanisms that is most cost effective. Over time, due to changing market conditions, the least expensive form of enhancement today may not be the least expensive in a subsequent securitization transaction.

Why doesn't an issuer simply seek a AAA rating for all the securities in the structure? The reason is that there is a cost to doing so. The issuer must examine the cost of credit enhancing a structure to obtain a AAA rating versus the reduction in the yield (i.e., the increase in price) at which it can offer the securities due to a AAA rating. In fact, in general the issuer in deciding to improve the rating on some securities in a structure will evaluate the trade-off associated with the cost of enhancement versus the reduction in yield required to sell the security.

Credit enhancement mechanisms are discussed in more detail later in this book.[2] Here we will provide a quick look at third-party guarantees, overcollateralization, and senior-subordinated structures.

Third-Party Guarantees

Perhaps the easiest form of credit enhancement to understand is a letter of credit or guarantee. In this form of enhancement, an insurance provider agrees, for a fee, to guarantee the performance of a certain amount of the assets in the pool that underlie the securities issued. If, for example, a loan in a pool of loans goes into default and the asset is sold at a loss resulting in a partial payoff of the outstanding loan balance, the bondholders would be in a position not to recover the principal outstanding for that loan. To provide AAA type protection to the security holders, an insurance provider will pay the difference between the loan payoff amount and the amount due to the security holders, thereby absorbing the loss. The fee for this service will vary as the perceived riskiness of the collateral changes. The rating agencies decide on the creditworthiness of the insurance provider and the extent of the insurance provider's performance guarantee to determine the credit rating of the security.

Perhaps the biggest perceived disadvantage to this form of credit enhancement is so called *event risk*. The AAA security holders can enjoy AAA status only as long as the enhancement provider retains its AAA credit status. If the credit enhancement provider is downgraded, the securities are typically downgraded as well.

---

[2] See, Lina Hsu and Cyrus Mohebbi, "Credit Enhancements in ABS Structures," Chapter 4 in this book.

Overcollateralization

One form of internal credit enhancement is overcollateralization or OC accounts. In this form of credit protection, the rating agencies determine how risky the underlying pool of assets is and decide on an appropriate level of OC. This results in less securities being issued versus the face value of assets in the pool. For example, if there are $100 million of loans in a pool and the issuer wanted to employ an OC to achieve AAA rating for the securities to be issued, the issuer would obtain from the rating agencies an indication as to how many securities they could issue versus the $100 million par value of loans in the pool. Depending on the characteristics of the loans and their perceived creditworthiness, the rating agencies might allow $95 million of par value of securities to be issued. This means that cash flows for $100 million par value of loans flow into the trust but only $95 million par value of securities need to be paid. The cash flows from the extra $5 million of loans can either flow into a reserve account where the flows are reserved until such a time as they are needed to cover losses or the funds are used to retire senior securities early. If a $1 million loss is realized by the pool of loans, there will still be enough cash flows from the other loans to insure that the AAA senior bonds receive their payments. After all the securities have been retired, the remaining funds in the reserve account and any remaining collateral is distributed to the residual holder.

The cost of such an arrangement is implicit in the price paid for $100 million par value of collateral versus the proceeds of issuing only $95 million par value of securities and any proceeds recognized for the residual account. In effect, it is a present value equivalent of the performance guarantee enhancement described above.

Senior/Subordinated Structure

Another form of internal credit enhancement is the senior/subordinated structure. This involves the subordination of some tranches for the benefit of attaining AAA rating for others. The way this is performed is to submit the collateral to a rating agency which in turn decides how many AAA securities can be issued, how many AA, and so forth down to a non-rated or first loss security. A structure can have simply two tranches, a senior tranche and a subordinated tranche. Or it can have several subordinated tranche in addition to the senior tranche.

For example, suppose that a senior/subordinated structure for $100 million of collateral is as follows:

Tranche	Rating	Percent	Par value
A	AAA	85%	$65 million
B	AA	7%	$20 million
C	BBB	5%	$10 million
D	NR	3%	$5 million

Tranche A is the senior tranche. The subordinated tranches are B, C, and D. Tranche D is the first loss tranche.

The mechanism for recognizing losses is as follows. As a $1 of loss on collateral is realized, that loss is first applied to the non-rated piece, tranche D. When the NR piece has no balance, the next dollar of loss is applied to the C tranche, and then the D tranche. After all the subordinated or junior bonds are paid off or wiped out due to losses, the losses are shared equally among the remaining senior bonds.

The cost of this form of credit enhancement is based on the proceeds for selling the securities which is, in turn, determined by the demand for the securities. The lower rated tranches are affected by the yields demanded by investors for the various tranches. The higher the perceived risk of the security (i.e., the more likely the security is to recognize a loss) the more yield is demanded and the lower will be the price received. The proceeds for the sale of all the securities has to be compared to the cost of the pool of loans and again is in effect the present value of the insurance provided by a third-party guarantor illustrated earlier.

One of the perceived advantages of internal credit enhancements such as overcollateralization and the senior/subordinated structure is the lack of event risk that accompanies the external credit enhancement (i.e., a third-party guarantee). The assets in the pool provide all credit support and investors are at risk only due to the performance of those assets.

MARKETING THE SECURITIES CREATED

The final step is the marketing of the securities created. How does one originator maximize the proceeds received for its assets used as collateral for a securitization while another originator is relegated to selling its assets in an anonymous form to conduits? There are plenty of reasons including volume of assets sold. One key feature is to market the assets with a story so that investors can distinguish between the originator's assets and those of other originators.

Distinguishing features can relate to speed at which assets prepay, likelihood at which the assets are expected to default, geographic dispersion (or concentration), among other features. The key is to focus on a feature and produce information, reports, etc. so that investors can appreciate the feature and eventually pay a premium for that feature. Conversely, if there is no special feature surrounding the collateral, that too can be a selling point. The collateral should trade no worse than generic collateral, because that is what it is.

Part and parcel with marketing the securities is structuring the deal to take advantage of current investor interests. Structures can include tranches created with different exposure to prepayments, resulting in securities with different average lives and varying degrees of interest rate exposure. This is referred to as "prepayment tranching." The creation of senior/subordinated structures provides investors with a choice of different exposure to credit risk. This is referred to as "credit tranching."

CONCLUSION

In this chapter we provided an introduction to the asset securitization process and the participants that play an important role in the process. The specifics change due to market appetites, new regulations, and accounting practices or even market innovations. There are many dynamic aspects to securitization, but much of the process involves using techniques that have been well established during the past 20 years.

CONCLUSION

Chapter 4

Credit Enhancement in ABS Structures

Lina Hsu
Managing Director
Financial Strategies Group
Prudential Securities Inc.

Cyrus Mohebbi
Managing Director
Financial Strategies Group
Prudential Securities Inc.

INTRODUCTION

A key element in ABS transactions is the credit enhancement associated with the structure. Credit enhancement levels are determined by the characteristics of the underlying collateral, historical delinquency and default statistics, underwriting guidelines, and the industry outlook regarding the robustness of future cash flows. Credit enhancement could either involve a third party enhancement or utilize a self-insurance feature generated from the cash flows. Most transactions have structures utilizing a combination of internal and external credit enhancement techniques. The selection of enhancement tools is based on minimizing the all-in issuance cost and creating marketable securities. A description of the various credit enhancement tools is discussed in this chapter.

EXTERNAL CREDIT ENHANCEMENT

Third party credit enhancement tools in ABS securitizations include insurance provided by bond insurers, corporate guarantees, and letters of credit.

Insurance

Within the genre of external credit enhancement, the most common technique is a guarantee provided by insurance companies. Companies such as Municipal Bond Investors Assurance (MBIA), Financial Guaranty Insurance Co. (FGIC), AMBAC

Financial Group, or Financial Security Assurance (FSA), are able to insure up to triple-A ratings. These entities typically insure investment-grade-rated (triple-B minus and above) cash flows to higher ratings desired by the issuer or the underwriter for an upfront fee and/or an on-going fee. Other insurers insure non-investment-grade-rated (double-B plus or below) cash flows to higher ratings depending on the claims- paying ability of the insurers. The higher the desired insured rating or the lower the stand-alone cash flow rating, the higher the fees. Insurers are able to insure cash flows to higher ratings as they are required by rating agencies to reserve a certain amount of capital for each insured transaction to protect bondholders against any losses on the underlying assets due to credit defaults, standard and special hazards, fraud, and bankruptcy up to the amount sustainable by the desired rating. Investors are guaranteed timely payment of interest and eventual payment of principal.

Issues guaranteed by insurers are subject to the credit standing of the insurers as the insured rating is dependent upon the claims-paying abilities of the insurer. Insurance may provide coverage for the entire issue or specific classes within the issue.

Fannie Mae (FNMA) and Freddie Mac (FHLMC) have also ventured into the insurance business in limited asset types, such as home equity loans. However, both agencies have very stringent sets of guidelines and are very selective in the quality of the collateral which is insured.

Typically, investors prefer bonds to be insured if the underlying asset is risky, new to the market, the sector which the asset belongs to has headline risk, or the issuer is not well-capitalized. Among bond insurers, non-triple-A insurers are not broadly accepted by investors.

Corporate Guarantees

Similar to an insurance policy, a *corporate guarantee* protects bondholders from losses due to default, bankruptcy, fraud, and standard and special hazards of the underlying assets, with full recourse to the guarantor. The rating of the security is directly affected by any upgrade or downgrade of the guarantor as the highest rating an insured security can obtain is the rating of the guarantor. Corporate guarantees could be issued for the entire transaction or specific classes. Unlike an insurance policy, a corporate guarantee is generally provided by an entity associated with the issuer of the guaranteed securities. Sometimes a parent company provides a corporate guarantee for a certain security in a bond issue of its subsidiary. A corporate guarantee can be applied to a bond issue regardless of its underlying rating.

Letter of Credit

A *letter of credit* (LOC) is an insurance policy issued by a financial institution whereby the institution is obligated to reimburse losses up to a specified amount. Similar to bond insurance and corporate guarantees, a LOC provider cannot provide any enhancement with a rating above its own rating; therefore any downgrades of the LOC provider will directly impact the rating of the insured securities. With the scarcity of higher rated banks, which have been traditional providers of LOCs, this method of credit enhancement is infrequently used.

INTERNAL CREDIT ENHANCEMENT

One major drawback of most third-party enhancement tools is that the insured classes are often susceptible to the risk of downgrades of the credit enhancement provider. Internal credit enhancement removes third-party risk because a part of the actual cash flows from the underlying assets are used to credit-enhance the structure. Internal credit enhancement tools include the creation of subordinated classes, turbo structures with overcollateralization, and spread account.

Senior-Subordinated Structures

In general, senior-subordinated credit structures are created with a single or multiple subordinated credit classes depending on subordination levels required by rating agencies. The credit structure is designed to have classes pay pro-rata and/or sequentially, with losses allocated first to the outstanding junior classes. Typically, credit enhancement levels determined by rating agencies are also affected by the paydown rules of principal and interest in the deal structure, in addition to the characteristics of the collateral. Senior-subordinated structures are commonly used in transactions with asset types such as B&C mortgages, home-equity loans, manufactured housing loans, commercial-mortgage loans, credit card receivables, franchise loans, small business loans, equipment lease receivables, aircraft lease receivables, and ABS CDOs, to name a few.

Generally, a structure with pro-rata-paying credit tranches receives a higher subordination level than one with credit tranches that pay sequentially. This is because the subordination level of the senior classes of a sequentially-paying credit structure increases over time whereas the subordination level remains the same for a pro-rata-paying credit structure in the absence of defaults. Hence, if the same credit enhancement level were to be assigned to a pro-rata-paying credit structure versus a sequentially-paying structure, the credit support for the former would erode much faster in the event of defaults.

Another alternative senior/subordinated structure encompasses a *shifting-interest feature*. This shifting interest structure is commonly used in most non-conforming type mortgage-backed transactions. The structure is designed such that all prepayment amounts that would otherwise be allocated to the subordinated class are paid to the senior classes. This feature slows down the amortization of the junior pieces and increases the subordination level of the senior classes as the deal amortizes. The amount of prepayment shifted from the subordinated classes to the senior classes is reduced as the deal ages subject to meeting certain delinquency and loss tests. A modified version of the shifting-interest structure includes a senior-support class, also referred to as the triple-A mezzanine class, where the triple-A mezzanine class has payment characteristics of a subordinated class.

Overcollateralization

Another type of commonly used internal credit enhancement is *overcollateralization*. Overcollateralization credit enhancement structures utilize the excess spread, which is the amount of excess interest cash flow after payment of all fees and bond coupon expenses, to pay down the principal of the structured bonds. This payment structure, also known as a *turbo structure*, accelerates the principal paydown of the bonds, thereby creating an overcollateralization cushion for losses.

Overcollateralization provides a higher collateral-to-bond balance ratio in a structure. In case of losses, the bonds are protected from any write-down first by excess spread, which provides extra cash flows for payment of bond interest and principal, then by the amount of overcollateralization.

If more than one asset group is included in a transaction, such as fixed-rate and adjustable-rate loans home-equity loan groups, excess spread from one group is first used to enhance the bonds created from cash flows from the same group. Any excess spread is then used to enhance the bonds created from other collateral groups. This type of enhancement is known as *cross-collateralization.*

Depending on the amount of excess spread available at the inception of the deal, an initial deposit may not be required for the transaction. In cases where an initial deposit in the form of overcollateralization is required at the inception of the deal, the overall proceeds received by the issuer will be reduced.

Issuers may use overcollateralization for internal credit enhancement along with bond insurance. Generally, the usage of overcollateralization brings the cash flows to an investment rating causing the resultant securities to be eligible for insurance by a major bond insurer in order to obtain a triple-A rating. A major advantage of the usage of overcollateralization is that issuers are allowed to retire securities faster, thereby reducing their cost of funds. Another interesting feature of an overcollateralized structure is that principal windows of bonds in such transactions are usually tighter than the collateral since interest cash flows are used to pay down bond principal. As a result, more short average life and tight window bonds can be created which improves the execution of the transaction, particularly in an upward sloping yield curve environment.

Spread Accounts

An alternative to overcollateralization as credit enhancement is through the application of one or more spread accounts. Similar to the overcollateralized structure, a *spread account* is built up to some predetermined levels specified by the rating agencies through excess spread in the transaction. Unlike the overcollateralized structure, the excess spread is accumulated in an account as cash and reinvested as short-term eligible investments. Depending on the structure, a spread account could be created for all bond classes or be specifically used to credit enhance certain classes. Like the overcollateralized structure, the build-up of the spread account can be designed for the cash flows to obtain a triple-B minus rating. Based upon this internal credit enhancement, the cash flows are then eligible to be insured by a bond insurer. Issuers typically choose an overcollateralized structure over a spread account structure because of the advantages discussed above.

CONCLUSION

Most issuers use a combination of different types of credit enhancement tools, either internally or externally, to obtain the most proceeds for the lowest cost of funds. In general, internal credit enhancement enables the transaction to be independent of any risks external to the collateral. However, a structure with only internal credit enhancement such as a senior/subordinated structure could be extremely expensive for first-time issuers or exotic asset types since rating agencies tend to adopt a conservative stance in such cases. Additionally, subordinated classes have less investor appeal for first-time issuers due to the paucity of data and lack of name recognition. Internally enhanced structures are best applied to well-capitalized issuers or servicers with tier-one and stable asset types. Tier-one asset types include large bank credit card, bank and captive finance company prime auto loans, and Sallie Mae products.

Chapter 5

Observations on Effecting Your First Asset-Backed Securities Offering

Kenneth P. Morrison
Partner
Kirkland & Ellis

INTRODUCTION

This chapter is addressed to the concerns of financial personnel and inside counsel at a company that is undertaking its first asset-backed securities offering. It offers the perspective of seasoned outside counsel to many such companies on this process, and it assumes that the company is in the initial stage of the transaction, having selected an investment banker and received a term sheet describing the proposed transactions, but not otherwise having started on the securitization process.

The purpose of this chapter is twofold. First, we want to share with you some of our observations on the process of completing an asset-backed securities (sometimes herein referred to as "ABS") offering. Many companies that are undertaking their first ABS offering do not realize at the outset the kinds of issues and problems that they will confront. For many companies, an ABS transaction represents a new level of frustration, self-inspection, and scrutiny by outsiders. If you understand in advance the potential pitfalls and how the process will differ from other capital raising transactions, the experience should be a much more positive one for you and your organization.

Second, we want to outline the key legal activities that will need to be performed by company counsel in an ABS offering. Cost is an important issue here. Managing the process effectively, including through the appropriate allocation of work between inside counsel and outside counsel, is fundamental to accomplishing the offering on an efficient basis.

In this chapter it is assumed that your company is intending to securitize receivables such as auto loans and that your company is the originator of these loans. However, most of the observations contained in this chapter are applicable to ABS transactions generally.

BACKGROUND

As a starting point for our discussion of your anticipated ABS offering, we offer a few general observations about ABS transactions.[1]

There are a number of common structures used to securitize assets such as auto loans. You might be considering both a "wrapped" term ABS issuance that will be underwritten and sold in the capital markets and a "warehouse" facility that will be funded by a group of banks. You may intend to have each of these facilities rated by one or more rating agencies.

In the wrapped term structure, your company as originator would establish a special purpose, bankruptcy remote subsidiary (an "SPC"), which acquires a fixed, liquidating pool of receivables from the originator; the SPC then sells the receivables to a trust, which in turn issues asset-backed notes to an underwriter or placement agent for resale directly to investors. A monoline insurer issues a guaranty policy — also known as a "wrap" — that guarantees repayment of principal and interest on the asset-backed notes. The SPC in this term structure — we will sometimes refer to it as the "term SPC" — retains the residual interest in the assets transferred to the trust through a subordinated certificate.

In the warehouse facility, your company would establish another SPC. This "warehouse SPC" would acquire receivables from time to time from your company. Rather than sell those receivables to a trust, the warehouse SPC will borrow directly from the banks to fund its acquisition of the receivables. The SPC will continue to accumulate receivables until it has a sufficient pool to effect another securitization; it will then sell those receivables back to your company, which will then effect another securitization with the term SPC.

ABS offerings can have a number of advantages over the alternatives of unsecured corporate medium-term notes and secured or unsecured revolving credit borrowings, including the following:

- a higher credit rating for the asset-backed securities than your company can presently achieve for its own debt
- on- or off-balance sheet accounting treatment, as desired
- a new source of funding in the marketplace for your company
- lower interest expense

Your investment bankers will explain the structure of the proposed ABS programs to you in great detail and cover such essentials as rating agency review, necessary levels and types of credit enhancement, expected all-in costs, and periodic information reporting requirements. Typically, you will receive a copy of the time and responsibility schedule conveniently prepared by them; we have assumed that their schedule allows for eight weeks from the date that outside counsel begins drafting the documentation to the closings on the two facilities.

---

[1] The appendix to this book provides a glossary of terms.

PREPARING FOR THE ABS EXPERIENCE

As the transaction begins, we will need to consider a number of high priority legal items, including:

- identifying any legal or contractual impediments to effecting the securitization and resolving them
- understanding the receivables
- understanding your company's servicing procedures and policies
- identifying and drafting the necessary agreements
- identifying any problematic legal opinion issues

Each of these items is important and requires almost immediate attention, and each is discussed in greater detail below. But there is another item that, although less obvious, is the first topic we should discuss: the nature of the first-time securitization experience.

What Every First-Time Issuer Should Know About Securitization

Experience tells us that, early on in an ABS offering, a corporate officer's head is spinning in anticipation of completing the offering. The officer may be wondering why he or she did not get on this bandwagon earlier, given the obvious company benefits of a highly rated financing that will be off-balance sheet and that, to boot, will be done in eight weeks.

It should come as no surprise to you to learn that it probably will not be that easy. There are some common issues and problems in ABS deals that you should understand from the outset, because they will almost certainly come up here.

Timing

The time and responsibility schedule allows eight weeks to finish the offering. That is an ambitious timeline. There are a great many variables and players in these transactions, and a problem with any one of them could result in an extension of the timetable. Rating agency review, bank and monoline insurer selection and internal credit approval, and the obtaining of any necessary consents from your existing lenders are all factors that are largely outside of your control. Even factors which are more controllable, such as the pace at which documents are drafted and reviewed and the data reporting systems that need to be established, can and often do take longer than expected.

Indeed, it could be counterproductive to try to move so quickly. As discussed below, there is a definite additional cost to pushing too hard to get a deal closed. Duplication of effort and costly mistakes caused by overwork can offset the perceived benefits of a fast transaction.

Costs

Cost is undeniably a big concern in ABS deals. After all, a principal reason for undertaking an ABS offering is often the desire to obtain a lower cost of funds. It is a hollow victory at best if the benefits of the lower interest rate (lower than obtainable through a more conventional financing) are offset by a substantially higher expenditure for legal and other fees and expenses.

This issue is a sensitive and central one for all of us. Any suggestion that costs may be higher than budgeted is not something that you will be happy to hear. Nonetheless, this issue should not be ducked just because it is unpopular. Costs in these transactions can end up exceeding the amounts budgeted.

The basic cause of cost overruns is "unanticipated problems," which covers a multitude of topics. Although hope springs eternal,[2] we have seen few first-time securitizations that have not encountered unanticipated problems resulting in cost overruns. Our best advice is that the company should "expect the unexpected." No one can know exactly what problems will come up, but you can be sure that some problems will in fact come up, despite everyone's best efforts. While those involved in the transaction will work very hard to anticipate and eliminate problems before they occur, the prediction stands that something will arise that will require extra effort to resolve. In large part, the point of this chapter is to alert you to the types of problems that we have previously confronted. Our experience tells us that it is best to build some cushion for these kinds of difficulties into your internal budget.

Front-End Loading

Unfortunately for a first time ABS issuer, there are a great many one-time costs associated with the initial ABS transactions. The process of learning about the company's origination and servicing procedures (and, if necessary, revising or recasting those procedures), designing and documenting the structure that is appropriate for the company's securitization, establishing the special purpose subsidiaries, passing muster with the rating agencies, and assuring that the securitization can be accomplished without violation of other contracts and laws to which the company is subject generally need not be repeated for follow-on offerings. To some degree, however, some of these costs (such as designing and documenting the structure and passing muster with the rating agencies) will also be incurred for each new structure and other costs (such as learning about the company's origination and servicing procedures) will be incurred for each new asset that is securitized. For finance companies and banks, the good news is that subsequent offerings can be completed at a fraction of the cost of the first one.

Rating Agency Approval

Another significant variable in the ABS process is the requisite rating agency approval. Except for sales of receivables to a select few of the established multi-seller conduits, approval by rating agencies must, as a practical matter, be

---

[2] Alexander Pope, *An Essay on Man* (1733-34. Epistle I, 1. 95); *cf.* Thayer, Ernest L., *Casey at the Bat* (1888) *reprinted* in *The Illustrated Casey at the Bat* (1987).

obtained prior to or at the closing. The market plainly puts a lot of reliance on the rating agencies' imprimatur on an offering, because the public investor or trader that has the patience (or, in all likelihood, the time necessary) to read the transaction documents has yet to be found.

Obtaining rating agency approval is no mean feat. The rating agencies are thorough and cautious, and they can be idiosyncratic. Rating agency bashing is popular sport in asset-backed circles, but it must be admitted that the rating agencies have a difficult assignment. They are provided with reams of data and documents and are put under a lot of time pressure. It is reasonable to assume that at any given time the average rating agency analyst has more deals than fingers. Even the best intentioned analyst may have so many deals ahead of yours that delay is inevitable.

Other participants in the ABS process are only too happy to seek to hold the rating agencies to a standard of consistency that few law firms or investment banks would welcome. Once a concession is made in one transaction, it will spread quickly throughout the industry as others demand it. Similarly (and particularly troublesome for clients), outside counsel will often strongly resist rating agency demands for legal opinions on novel issues. Speaking from experience, outside counsel does not want to go beyond the established practice. Unfortunately, counsel can be put in the position of receiving an opinion demand at the eleventh hour — literally, perhaps, on the night before a closing — and that puts counsel in a very difficult situation. The result can be a great hue and cry over very arcane issues, much to the chagrin of the company's expectant officers. Fortunately, this type of problem has subsided in recent years, as rating agencies (and counsel) have learned to anticipate and handle these issues further in advance.

Fortunately, there is some competition for your rating agency dollar. While Standard & Poor's and Moody's enjoy a preeminent position in the marketplace, Fitch and the former Duff & Phelps (now acquired by Fitch) proved themselves capable in the ABS arena, and they are winning many assignments. Fitch, in fact, is particularly strong in auto ABS.

The rating agencies, to different degrees, realize that it is good business to be open with their customers about the process, and they are continuously refining their approach and trying to maintain consistency. They are very active in publishing their criteria, and each of them has published at least one write-up outlining their views on the securitization of the asset type you seek to securitize. Nonetheless, lapses and reversals do occur, and you are well advised to be prepared for the possibility.

Data Keeping Requirements
You may not appreciate the onerous data keeping requirements that can be part of many ABS offerings. After all, the existing public debt that your company has issued requires little more than semi-annual interest payments and an annual officers' certificate. If your company is a public company, you will already be making Securities Exchange Act of 1934 quarterly and annual filings, and you may figure that the existing controller's staff will be more than adequate to track a few extra items.

But you must be aware that a non-recourse deal, which essentially relies solely on the collectibility of its receivables,[3] is a very different proposition from one that is predicated on your company's corporate creditworthiness. Asset-backed transactions, particularly those involving originators/servicers who are not A-1/P-1 rated, can require substantial monthly reporting obligations. Often, the company will find itself in the position of having to dedicate one person on the treasurer's or the controller's staff to the ABS reporting function, particularly when there are multiple ABS issuances outstanding.

Independent Directors and Other Aggravations of Bankruptcy Remoteness, Non-Consolidation, and True Sales

The distinguishing characteristics of rated asset-backed securities transactions include the "bankruptcy-remote" SPC, including the emphasis on keeping the SPC and its assets out of a bankruptcy proceeding of your company (were one to occur) by avoiding "substantive consolidation" of the SPC and your company and by effecting a "true sale" of receivables from your company to the SPC. These companion legal concepts are the basis on which your company can structure a transaction that will be given a higher credit rating than your company currently has.

Legal Issues

Here we will digress briefly to describe the purpose of these legal constructs. In brief, the goal of the securitization is to minimize the risk to the purchasers of the asset-backed securities that their cash flows will be impaired by an insolvency or bankruptcy of your company. Should your company become a debtor in a Chapter 11 proceeding, for instance, those cash flows would be impaired if the bankruptcy court could impose the "automatic stay" to prohibit collections on the receivables from being used to make payments on the asset-backed securities. The court would have the power to impose the automatic stay on any asset that would be part of your company's bankruptcy estate, which essentially means any asset owned by your company. Similarly, an insolvency or bankruptcy of an SPC could impair cash flows.

"Bankruptcy remoteness" refers to the goal of keeping the SPC itself out of bankruptcy proceedings. The structural mechanisms used to minimize the risk that the SPC itself will be the subject of voluntary or involuntary bankruptcy proceedings include limiting the SPC's activities so as to minimize the number of potential creditors,[4] requiring others participating in the ABS offering to agree not to put the

---

[3] In third-party enhanced structures, ABS investors will not be relying solely on the collectibility of the receivables, but will instead look also to the third-party credit enhancement for recovery. However, that does not mean you are off the hook. The investors will still be looking to the receivables for the primary source of repayment, and will therefore be interested in these issues.

[4] Although the SPC will not be permitted to have any voluntary creditors and should not have any tort creditors, it could still have other creditors. For example, statutory creditors such as the Internal Revenue Service and the Pension Benefit Guaranty Corporation could, under certain circumstances, assert a claim against an SPC that would be senior to any claim on the equity of the SPC.

SPC into bankruptcy and making it more difficult for the SPC to elect bankruptcy voluntarily through the use of independent directors as described below.

The true sale and substantive consolidation analyses are intended to keep the SPC out of the bankruptcy proceedings of your company, the SPC's parent. By effecting a "true sale" of the receivables to the SPC, your company will no longer have an ownership interest in the receivables. If a given transfer of receivables is not a "true sale," then it is by definition said to be a "disguised loan" (*i.e.*, a secured transaction). If the transfer is merely a secured transaction, the legal significance is that the receivables are still owned by your company, which will merely have created a security interest in favor of such SPC. By establishing an SPC as a separate subsidiary, your company will attempt to eliminate the risk that the SPC would be substantively consolidated with your company in a bankruptcy proceeding of your company or that it would voluntarily join in a bankruptcy filing for your company. (A substantive consolidation would have the effect of combining an SPC's assets and liabilities with those of your company, which would negate the benefit of the true sale.)

Here is not the place to expound on the intricacies of the true sale and non-consolidation concepts. Suffice it to say that the key consideration in a true sale is the degree of "recourse" that a purchaser of receivables has to the seller for losses due to uncollectibility on the portfolio of receivables transferred; the greater the recourse, the less likely the transaction is to qualify as a true sale. While lawyers' and courts' opinions vary significantly, a widely used rule of thumb established by the rating agencies is that recourse that is equal to or less than historical losses on the portfolio is indicative of a true sale, whereas recourse in excess of that level is indicative of a secured transaction.

Substantive consolidation is less easily reduced to a single analytic element. It is an equitable remedy and a number of factors may be considered in determining whether substantive consolidation is appropriate: creditor reliance, observation of corporate formalities, overlap of officers and directors, adequacy of capitalization, and degree of segregation of assets are among the factors. Two similar, although not identical, tests have evolved for use by courts in assessing the propriety of substantive consolidation in particular situations. Under the first test, substantive consolidation will be ordered by a bankruptcy court if "(i) creditors dealt with the entities as a single economic unit and did not rely on their separate identity in extending credit . . . or (ii) . . . the affairs of the debtors are so entangled that consolidation will benefit all creditors."[5] Under the second test, the essential analysis is whether "the economic prejudice of continued debtor separateness" outweighs "the economic prejudice of consolidation."[6]

Practical Application
These legal concepts directly shape the structure and implementation of your ABS offerings. Each transfer of receivables from your company to either SPC is

---

[5] *Union Savings Bank v. Augie/Restivo Banking Co.*, 860 F.2d 515, 518 (2d Cir. 1988).

[6] *Eastgroup Properties v. Southern Motel Assoc., Ltd.*, 935 F.2d 245, 249 (11th Cir. 1991).

intended to be a true sale, with no recourse for credit losses. Each SPC is intended to be bankruptcy remote and not susceptible of substantive consolidation, and a number of procedural safeguards will be put in place to maintain that status.

The rating agencies will insist that they receive an opinion of recognized outside counsel that concludes both that the sale of receivables from your company to the SPC is a true sale and that the SPC would not be consolidated with your company in the event of an insolvency by your company. These opinions are long, "reasoned" opinions, and they theoretically provide the rating agencies with the requisite comfort that allows them to disregard the possibility of a bankruptcy by your company when rating the securities that will be issued.

The documents for an ABS transaction and the organizational documents of the SPC will typically contain certain restrictive provisions intended to support the true sale characterization, to reduce the risk of substantive consolidation, and to assure the bankruptcy remoteness of the SPC. These safeguards may, in your view, be unnecessary incursions into your operating flexibility. In addition, there may be features that you would like to see in the deal that will undermine the true sale or the non-consolidation analysis and that will therefore be resisted by other participants (particularly the lawyers).

The amount of equity that your company will invest in each SPC is one example of a potential issue. Ordinarily, the originator (*i.e.*, your company) will contribute to the equity of an SPC an amount of cash equal to the portion of the receivables sold to the SPC at closing that represent the degree of overcollateralization (which amount, when added to the proceeds of the sale of the asset-backed securities, will provide such SPC with sufficient funds to purchase the receivables from your company) and, depending on the transaction, the cash necessary to make any initial deposit required in the reserve or similar account.

Minimizing the amount of equity in the SPC is important to some originators. For example, the originator's existing creditors may not want a lot of equity created in a subsidiary, because they are then going to become structurally subordinated to creditors of that subsidiary to a greater extent. Alternatively, state franchise taxes may be lower if the equity is lower. The standard financial policies of some originators also require that the equity in their subsidiaries be minimized.

For these or other reasons, your company may want to reduce the amount of equity invested in each SPC and substitute in its place a purchase money loan from your company to the applicable SPC.[7] The presence of this loan makes the "true sale" analysis more difficult, however, because such SPC's ability to repay the loan is contingent upon its generating income, which is in turn dependent in part upon the collectibility of the receivables. Thus, it is possible that the loan could be characterized as "recourse" on the receivables, which would undermine the true sale analysis. Stemming from its concerns about "true sale," Standard & Poor's generally requires that purchase money notes be of at least "investment

---

[7] Kirkland & Ellis pioneered the concept of using a purchase money loan in an ABS transaction in lieu of equity (a now standard practice).

grade" quality (*i.e.*, BBB– or better) and that the ABS documents include provisions to ensure that the credit quality of the note is maintained, such as imposing a limit on the aggregate amount of borrowings under the note that can be outstanding at any one point in time or requiring the issuer of the note to maintain a specified minimum level of net worth.

Another procedural safeguard that many issuers chafe under is the requirement that SPCs have one or more "independent" directors. The independent directors, who have no significant prior relationship with your company, are intended to supply the SPC with one of its critical indicia of bankruptcy remoteness. The consent of the independent directors is required for the filing of a voluntary petition in bankruptcy by the SPC. The theory behind this requirement is that the independent directors are more likely to heed the SPC's obligations to its creditors in the context of an insolvency of the SPC or your company and are less likely to act solely at the discretion of your company. For some law firms and rating agencies, the presence of an independent director also facilitates the issuance and acceptance of a non-consolidation opinion.

It is both expensive and somewhat cumbersome to deal with independent directors. They usually receive annual fees in the range of $2,500 to $5,000, in return for which, you will no doubt feel, they do not appear to do very much work. You will need to give them notice of, and allow them to participate in, directors' meetings, which will be slower than using a "captive" board, and you will probably need to spend more time bringing them up to speed than you would a board composed entirely of insiders, who are more likely to be otherwise involved in the process and informed on a more regular basis. Since the presence of independent directors is most important in the insolvency context, the rating agencies and other ABS players sometimes accept a "springing" independent director requirement, such that independent directors are required only if the rating of the originator is at or below agreed to levels. Thus, originators that maintain higher credit ratings can avoid the expense and inconvenience of independent directors while still satisfying the theoretical bankruptcy remote concerns.

Examining the Originator's Practices Through an Insolvency Filter

One of the things that you will quickly find is that people in ABS deals spend a lot of time talking about the possibility of bankruptcy. Although it is rather unseemly to spend a lot of time focussed on bankruptcy in the context of a financing for your company, you will ultimately come to understand that the fixation on bankruptcy is a necessary evil in ABS deals. The rating agencies will take a doomsday approach ("the maximum stress case" or "worst case scenario," to use their terminology) in analyzing the transaction, because their ratings are premised on the SPC being able to avoid any adverse consequences of a bankruptcy by your company.

The practical impact of this bankruptcy fixation is that you will be forced to re-examine all of your company's receivables origination and collection practices through an "insolvency filter." You will be asked questions the answer to which you will not know; the question may not even be answerable. Indeed, you may ultimately be asked to modify or discard certain business practices.

"Executory contracts" pose one type of bankruptcy-related risk: if receivables in an ABS program arise from agreements which are "executory" (*i.e.*, the originator's obligations under the agreement have yet to be fully performed), the Bankruptcy Code allows the originator, once it is in bankruptcy, to reject the underlying agreement, entitling the obligor to offset or withhold payments on receivables. This happens a lot in trade receivables transactions. For example, receivables arising out of "bill and hold" transactions (*i.e.*, transactions where an originator bills its customer for goods that are to be delivered at a later date) are thought to carry this risk: if an originator enters bankruptcy after it has invoiced a customer for a "bill and hold" transaction but before it has shipped the related goods, it may reject its obligation to ship, arguably entitling the customer to withhold payment on the receivable. As a result, receivables of this type are typically either excluded from the transaction or the program reserves are sized to take them into account.

Under some circumstances, a trade receivables originator's relationship with its customers may enable its customers to assert rights of "recoupment" or "offset" with respect to the receivables, even if the receivables do not arise from agreements which are executory. While these rights arise independent of the originator's bankruptcy, the likelihood that they will be exercised increases once the originator is insolvent. For example, originators will frequently allow their trade customers to offset against their receivable balances the amounts of "co-operative advertising" that the customers have done.[8] Participants in the ABS deal will want to know whether the customer has the legal right to offset its obligation to the originator by the amount of the current co-operative advertising cost. The reason, of course, is that if the originator were to go into a bankruptcy proceeding, the holders of the receivables would seek to collect the full amount due from the obligors, and they would want to avoid any offsets.[9]

Business Constraints

These ABS transactions may also impose some constraints on the operation of your company's business in ways that you have not anticipated. For example, the rating agencies and the monoline insurer will be very interested in changes that your company makes to its credit and collection policies, and they will seek to impose covenants that limit your company's ability to modify those policies materially.

---

[8] These co-operative advertising costs arise when, for example, a retailer prints an advertising circular that is included in local Sunday newspapers. The originator and the customer often have an understanding that they will split the allocated cost of space in the circular that is devoted to the originator's products.

[9] Concern will also be expressed about the possibility that an originator, during the last fateful days of its pre- supposed "slide into bankruptcy," will be feverishly granting imprudent discounts and offsets in a vain attempt to forestall the inevitable.

Another business constraint peculiar to ABS transactions is the possibility of a servicer termination. As you know, your company will continue to service the receivables, notwithstanding their sale to an SPC or a conduit. In that capacity, your company will send out monthly statements, take in collections, make adjustments for discounts and rebates, pursue delinquent obligors and perform its other usual servicing functions. The rating agencies and the banks will require, however, that certain "servicer termination events" be defined and that the banks be able to replace your company as servicer if any such event occurs.

The threat of being replaced as servicer in many industries is usually more apparent than real. For a manufacturer, for example, it is highly unlikely that a substitute servicer could adequately step in on short notice to service the trade receivables generated by the manufacturer's sales, given the idiosyncrasies of each manufacturer's receivables processes. On the other hand, for a more standardized type of asset origination, servicer replacement is more feasible. For example, there have been a number of bankruptcies among auto lenders (mostly subprime, admittedly) over the last few years, and monoline insurers, banks and investors have more than once had to replace the servicer in the middle of a transaction.

Strategies for Improving Efficiency and Managing Legal Fees

You should be concerned that the legal fees not "get out of hand" in this transaction and turn an advantageous financing into an uneconomic proposition. There are plenty of horror stories from corporate treasurers and general counsels about legal fees run amok in ABS deals. Toward that end, below we suggest various ways in which the legal fees might be minimized.

When the topic of managing legal fees is raised, many people think of alternative fee arrangements. The considerations involved for both the law firm and your company in connection with alternative fee arrangements are not particularly special in the context of an ABS offering as compared to other major corporate transactions. There are many different opinions on the merits and drawbacks of using fixed fees, capped fees, discounts, and other alternative fee arrangements. It should be stressed, however, that alternative fee arrangements are not the sole means of keeping legal fees down. Indeed, they may not even be the most effective way. It is crucial to manage the entire offering process effectively. Outside counsel is an important resource and one that should be employed well. Outside counsel is not the only player, however. A large number of people are involved in the typical ABS transaction and the transaction itself is complex in nature. Eliminating "structural" inefficiencies can create significant savings. Not only can the legal fees of outside counsel be reduced, but the legal fees of the counsel to the other parties (which typically must be paid by an originator) can also be reduced. A more well-managed, efficient process also lessens the wear and tear on the people working on the offering.

Our suggestions for managing the process include the following.

Start with a Term Sheet

It is essential to start the first transaction with a term sheet. Too many times, we have been engaged to handle transactions in which the business people were so impatient to start that they directed counsel to begin drafting definitive documents immediately. It is our strong belief that this practice is very costly to issuers, because it is much more expensive all around to revise a set of definitive documents than it is to revise a term sheet. The process of drafting and negotiating a term sheet can bring a number of critical issues to the forefront, where they can be resolved prior to the drafting of the definitive documents.

Set a Reasonable Timetable

The transaction timetable should be reasonable in light of the amount of work to be done. The fastest deal is not necessarily the cheapest deal. When counsel is pushed to complete a deal in a compressed time frame, there will be inefficiencies. For example, in an accelerated deal, counsel may be required to use more lawyers than would be needed otherwise, which will inevitably result in some duplication of effort and learning. Also, lawyers and others who are pushed to burn the midnight oil continuously will become fatigued, will have a harder time concentrating, and will be more likely to make mistakes. ABS documents are exceedingly complex and delicate; a tired drafter could miss a crucial subtlety or fail to see a simple way to resolve an issue. As well, late hours often result in charges for disbursements (e.g., secretarial overtime, late night courier services) that would not be incurred at such a high level on a more relaxed schedule.

Minimize the Number of Drafts

A corollary to the preceding two considerations is to limit the number of drafts of documents that are circulated. Do not push counsel to circulate an early draft simply for the sake of providing participants with something to read or to reflect the comments of only one or two participants. Rather, allow counsel a meaningful amount of time to prepare the first draft and to raise issues that arise in the process of preparing that draft prior to the time that it is circulated. Once a draft is circulated, give others enough time to read the draft and to consider the issues it raises. Experience tells that an all-hands drafting session is appropriate and beneficial after the first draft has been reviewed. Often, there is pressure just to have a conference call and to set counsel immediately to the task of preparing the next draft. That approach is a mistake. It is much more efficient to meet, consider the issues and try to resolve them. The difficulty with a constant churning of drafts is that unresolved issues tend to stay unresolved and participants tend not to read each draft carefully.

A related problem is "leapfrogging" drafts, which occurs when the drafter dribbles out one or two different documents every few days or tries to incorporate selected comments. Reviewers are then expected to read each document as it arrives and provide comments on a continuous basis. The difficulty with this situation is that there is not a consistently prepared set of documents for reviewers to read, because each newly revised document reflects the changes resulting from comments on the previously distributed documents. ABS documents are carefully interwoven and cannot be read effectively in isolation; the leapfrogging problem makes it difficult to review the documents thoroughly.

The result of all this extra work, of course, is a greater expenditure of lawyers' time, and hence, greater expense to the issuer. In a sense, this problem is a compounding one, since the issuer usually pays legal fees for the monoline insurer and the banks (and perhaps even the underwriter) in addition to the issuer's own outside counsel, and the time required from each set of lawyers, not only from issuer's counsel who is principally doing the drafting, will increase.

There are also costs and expenses involved in actually making the distribution of the documents. In addition to attorney time, the out-of-pocket costs for photocopying and shipping packages to a large working group can be substantial. Lately, it has become possible to distribute documents to many members in a working group via Internet transmission, and this can be a real cost savings (although the system is far from perfect, and transmission and printing difficulties are much too common).

Gather Internal Information Early

Outside counsel, the investment bankers, the monoline insurer, the banks and the rating agencies all will rely on the company to provide a great deal of information about the company's origination and collection policies, as well as the terms of the receivables, in order to effect and properly document the securitization. The company can facilitate this process by gathering as much information as possible early on and providing it to the lawyers and investment bankers. If a major issue regarding the company's practices or the terms of the receivables surfaces after the parties are well into the process, the resulting "fire drill" that is required to resolve the issue and restructure the documents can be very expensive.

ACTIVITIES TO BE PERFORMED BY COMPANY COUNSEL

We now turn to the topic of the activities to be performed by company counsel in the ABS offering. In this context, "company counsel" refers both to inside counsel and outside counsel, as it is certainly not the case that outside counsel needs to do all of the work. Consistent with your goal of holding down legal fees, part of managing the process effectively is to properly allocate work between inside and outside counsel.

The work outlined below covers a wide range of matters, all of which are pertinent to the securitization process. In essence, these tasks taken together constitute most of the necessary "due diligence" that counsel must undertake in connection with a securities offering. The reduced importance of your company's financial condition as a primary determinant of the creditworthiness of the offering reduces the level of inquiry into that topic, and it limits sharply the need to inquire into other areas of your company's business. (We should note, though, that warehouse lenders will be much less likely than the rating agencies to ignore your company's financial conditions; at heart, the warehouse lenders are still banks.) In any event, this reduced level of inquiry does not eliminate the need for some general financial and legal due diligence. Outside counsel will still need to be comfortable that your company is capable of meeting its obligations and is not close to insolvency. Outside counsel also will have a more detailed interest in your company's ability to perform its servicing functions than it would in a regular corporate finance transaction, because of the importance of servicing to this transaction.

Identifying Impediments to the Securitization

An initial objective must be to determine whether your company has any contractual or other restrictions that will prohibit it from effecting a securitization of any of its receivables.

Contractual Restrictions

Among the types of contractual restrictions that could cause problems are as follows.

Negative Pledge Clauses Indentures, note purchase agreements, loan agreements and revolving credit agreements often prohibit the placement of liens upon the company's assets (or require the equal and ratable securing of the debtholders under the indenture in the event a lien is placed on assets). First, we must determine whether the loans are the type of assets that are subject to the clause.[10] If they are, the next step is to determine whether there is an applicable exception to the negative pledge clause. The best exception would be a carve out for "liens incurred in connection with any transfer of an interest in accounts or notes receivable that qualified, at the time of transfer, as a sale under generally accepted accounting principles." Unfortunately, relatively few credit documents have such useful exceptions.

If there is no applicable exception, then outside counsel must determine whether the negative pledge applies only to your company's assets, or to those of your company *and its subsidiaries.* If the negative pledge clause applies only to your company, then the true sale of the receivables to an SPC should be sufficient to remove the assets from the scope of the negative pledge. If, however, the negative pledge clause applies to an SPC as well, then counsel will need to analyze

---

[10] For a number of manufacturing companies, the typical negative pledge clause in an indenture for a public debt offering will apply only to liens on "principal manufacturing properties." If that is the case, then there is no problem with the transfer of the receivables. However, some indentures and virtually all note purchase agreements, loan agreements and bank credit agreements contain restrictions which apply to a broader range of assets. (For purposes of our discussion, we have used the term "financing agreements" in this section to speak generally about a number of different kinds of agreements, each of which could, in accordance with established custom for that type of financing, have covenants that are more or less restrictive than (or different in kind from) the covenants described below. As noted below, each such agreement will, of course, have to be evaluated on its own terms.)

whether the SPC's subsequent transfer of an interest in the receivables to the master trust runs afoul of the clause. In that regard, it should be noted that opinions differ among lawyers and firms as to whether a transfer of receivables which qualifies as a sale under generally accepted accounting principles, but which would not generally be enough of a sale for a law firm to write a "true sale" opinion, should be outside of the scope of the negative pledge clause.

Limitations on Sales of Assets Financing agreements typically impose restrictions on the ability of a borrower and its subsidiaries to sell, lease or otherwise dispose of their assets. Such a covenant may be limited to assets of a certain value or to transactions having a certain effect (either individually or cumulatively) and may provide exceptions for certain types of sales (for example, sales of inventory in the ordinary course of business). A sale of all of the originator's accounts receivable will sometimes be subject to such a covenant, which might prohibit the sale or require that the proceeds of such sale be used in a manner that is inconsistent with the originator's intentions. As discussed above, it is important to analyze each covenant (including the asset sale limitations) as it applies to both your company and to SPC.

Limitations on Debt Incurrence Financing agreements will often limit a company's and its subsidiaries' ability to incur additional indebtedness (including, generally, guarantees of indebtedness). Depending on the scope of the covenant, it may cover not only the asset-backed securities issued in the ABS program, but also "purchase money" debt incurred by the SPC in purchasing receivables from originators, indemnification obligations, reimbursement obligations to swap counterparties or credit enhancement or liquidity providers and other ABS program obligations.

Limitations on Investment in Subsidiaries Covenants that govern investments in subsidiaries may affect the originator's (or its affiliates') ability to capitalize the SPC or to make purchase money loans to the SPC in connection with purchases of receivables.

Limitations on Certain Payments Financing agreements often include provisions which restrict the contracting party from making certain payments (or prepayments) in respect of its other debt or equity securities. Certain of these limitations could restrict the SPC's ability to pay dividends to its parent corporation or to pay or prepay program indebtedness (including purchase money loans from the originator and the asset-backed securities issued by the program).

Limitations on Transactions with Affiliates By their nature, ABS transactions involve a number of transactions between affiliates, including the purchase, sale and servicing of receivables. Restrictions in financing agreements on transactions among affiliates may prohibit or place unworkable restrictions on some or all aspects of the proposed ABS transaction.

Other Restrictions Financing agreements can contain a number of other restrictions that could cause problems with a proposed securitization, including limitations on lines of business, transactions outside the ordinary course of business and the like. It is important to keep in mind that while there are elements common to all, no two financing agreements (or ABS transactions, for that matter) are exactly alike, and each will frequently raise its own unique set of issues.

Outside counsel will also need to review the financial covenants in your company's financing agreements to determine whether securitization will cause any problems. If any of the financing documents distinguish between "restricted subsidiaries" and "unrestricted subsidiaries" (as is typical of note purchase agreements with insurance companies, for example), then you will need to decide whether to treat each SPC as restricted or unrestricted and calculate what the impact of the chosen treatment will be on financial covenants.

The financial terms and covenants that can be affected by a securitization include the following:

- consolidated tangible net worth
- indebtedness
- tangible assets
- unencumbered assets
- amount of gain or loss (if any) recognized on sale of receivables, which can affect:
  - EBIT
  - fixed charge coverage
- net quick assets

Consents In the event that any of the proposed securitizations violate any restriction in a financing agreement, you will need to obtain the consent of the relevant lender(s) prior to closing, or else restructure the transaction in a fashion that complies with the financing agreement. Obtaining the consent of public debtholders under an indenture is rarely attempted because it is a time-consuming and expensive process. Obtaining the consent of bank and insurance company lenders is much more commonly done, however, so restrictions in note purchase agreements, loan agreements and credit agreements are less problematic, unless you are dealing with a large syndicate or some quarrelsome participants.

The parties negotiating such an exemption will, as always, have competing concerns. The company will wish to preserve its flexibility in effecting a securitization and therefore should seek carve-outs that are broad enough to cover unanticipated issues. The debtholder's representative, obviously, will wish to preserve the effectiveness of the covenant and thus will be reluctant to except more than is absolutely necessary to the implementation of the ABS program. Moreover, such representative will want the covenant to remain strict enough to prevent securitizations that will jeopardize the interests of the debtholders in any manner.

Finally, it is important to keep these issues in mind when entering into new financing agreements, even if there are no present plans to effect an ABS transaction, particularly in cases where the new agreements will be difficult to amend (for example, a public debt indenture). Because you won't then know the structure of the ABS transaction that you ultimately consummate, you should negotiate for provisions that allow for the maximum possible amount of structural flexibility. General concepts of "Permitted Securitizations" are becoming more common in all types of financing agreements.

Statutory and Other Restrictions In addition to contractual restrictions, there can be other factors that impact an originator of receivables that is attempting to securitize those receivables. Entities like banks have a number of restrictions imposed by regulators, but those are beyond the scope of this chapter.

Accounting Issues You will want to consult with your accountants in structuring the transaction to obtain the accounting treatment you desire. FAS No. 140 ("Accounting for Transfers and Servicing of Financial Assets and Extinguishment of Liabilities") sets forth the criteria for determining whether a transaction purporting to be a sale of receivables is, in fact, a sale of such receivables for accounting purposes. As of this writing, FAS 140 is brand new, although it is replacing a standard (FAS 125) that was only about three and a half years old, but which had quickly become one of the more complicated accounting standards to apply.

It used to be the case that virtually all securitizers wanted to obtain sale treatment for their securitization transactions, in order to remove the assets from the balance sheet. In general, FAS 140 is fairly easy to apply to the ordinary type of liquidating pool transaction. However, more difficult issues will arise if, for example, you want to try to set up a warehouse facility on an off-balance sheet fashion.

A particular issue for specialty finance companies over the last couple of years has been "gain-on-sale accounting." A number of finance companies believe that the stock market is "punishing" finance companies that take gains on the sales of assets in securitizations, and these clients are now taking steps to avoid that accounting impact. This is a developing area that you will want to explore with your auditors.

Understanding the Receivables

Another activity to which company counsel will need to devote significant time and effort in the course of this transaction is in developing a thorough understanding of your company's various types of receivables. In this respect, company counsel will be in the same position as the investment bankers, the rating agencies, the banks, the monoline insurer and — yes — even the company. In every first time securitization in which we have participated (even when the originator was a seasoned securitizer that was securitizing a new asset class for the first time), the company financial officers have learned things about their company's receivables that those officers had not previously known. We have even heard listed as one of the advantages of securitization the ability of the originator to "learn more about its portfolio of assets."

Understanding the Servicing Procedures

All of the participants will also have great interest in your company's servicing procedures. Therefore, all of us should quickly gain an understanding of these procedures, so that we can anticipate and resolve issues before they become problems. Topics that outside counsel reviews include:

- existence of written credit and collection policies
- compliance of receivables with state laws
- frequency of payments
- collection policies on overdue accounts
- practices regarding rewriting/extending delinquent receivables
- number and location of lock-boxes for collections
- presence of unrelated corporate funds in the lock-boxes
- systems capability to track periodic data and relevant historic data
- collateral documentation for secured receivables
- ability to segregate collections from unrelated corporate funds

Drafting the Necessary Agreements

Ideally, we will complete — or at least get well underway in — the processes identified above before we begin the task of actually drafting the operative documents for each ABS offering. By developing our understanding of your company and each deal before we begin drafting for that deal, we hope to avoid setting off down blind alleys that turn out to be dead ends. However, this ideal is rarely achieved, and we expect that we will need to start drafting the documents shortly.

All of the documents will need to work well together, which brings us to one of our key recommendations for the drafting phase of each transaction: *Try to centralize all of the drafting in one law firm, preferably your own outside counsel.* There are several reasons for this recommendation. First, it is always preferable for one's own counsel to control the drafting. The drafter almost always has a better understanding of the documents than the reviewer: he or she knows "where the skeletons are," so to speak. Second, ABS documents are particularly full of nuances and interrelationships, and it is best to have one set of drafters for purposes of conforming all of the documents and maintaining all of the interrelationships. This practice does not guarantee perfect or mistake-free documents, but it does help. Third, you will almost certainly have a stronger relationship with — and a greater ability to motivate — your outside counsel than another firm, which will help maintain the timetable you have established. Fourth, while ABS transactions are relatively free of the Sturm und Drang that typically accompanies a negotiated bank financing (although the warehouse facility will probably have its share), the participants will find that they do have differing interests on a number of issues. These differences will include the scope of permitted modifications to an originator's credit and collection policies and procedures, the level of investor consent (if any) required for various types of amendments to the program documents, the procedures for adding originators to (or removing them from) the program, the level of subordination of any purchase money notes issued by an SPC to an originator, the scope of the SPC's permitted activities, the types of restrictions imposed on the SPC to minimize substantive consolidation risk, and the like. Under circumstances where such differences in interest between the issuer and the other participants can arise, it is almost always in the issuer's interest to have its counsel draft the documents.

This brings us to a second rule of drafting: *Do not slavishly copy precedent.* It is nearly universal practice in the securitization field, as in other areas of corporate finance, to take the last similar deal that you did (or, failing that, the last one that someone else did) and use it as the basis for the next deal. That practice can be very tricky, however.

The complexity of ABS deals and the disproportionate impact that a given company's origination and servicing practices can have on the deal documents guarantees that any one deal's documents will have some provisions that are appropriate only for that originator. Deal documents do not come with a "user's manual," so a counsel that is not intimately familiar with the documents (and often even one who is — or should be) may not recognize a custom provision when he or she sees it. Thus, if possible, it is useful to start with a generic set of documents that can be customized as appropriate. Such an approach will also assure the company that it is not inadvertently accepting negotiated or compromise provisions that the originator in the previous deal had reluctantly or unwisely accepted in the heat of negotiating those documents.

The third rule of drafting is a corollary of the second: *Avoid "mixing and matching" of documents; do not combine precedent from different deals, if possible.* ABS transactions are complex enough without trying to pair an "apple" Pooling and Servicing Agreement with an "orange" Receivables Purchase Agreement, for example. The interrelatedness of the documents makes it extremely likely that something will slip through the cracks (or be covered in contradictory ways) if documents from different deals are combined in your deal. Indeed, there are enough difficulties with using an "integrated" set of precedent documents to occupy the participants fully without compounding the problems.

Negotiating the Transaction

There are also some important considerations in negotiating the terms of these offerings. The most significant difference in these transactions from any other financing you have previously negotiated is undoubtedly the prominent role of the rating agencies. Their presence substantially alters the tone and content of the negotiating process, in a variety of ways:

- *The rating agencies have significant leverage and little incentive to compromise.* As mentioned earlier, the rating agencies can be difficult to deal with at times. As a practical matter, an ABS offering cannot be completed without their ratings. Once you have selected the agencies with whom you intend to work, it can be very difficult (although not impossible) to drop them, so we will generally have to accommodate their preferences. We do not wish to imply that they are not willing to listen to reason, because they are. However, if there is an issue on which they can build a plausible scenario that a problem could arise, then even if the problem is remote they will often insist on remedying the situation.
- *The rating agencies do not necessarily agree with each other on certain matters.* There is no requirement that the rating agencies agree with each other on various issues. It is possible that the rating agencies might have a fundamental disagreement that would prevent an offering from proceeding at all. We have not seen that situation, but we have been involved in situations in which different rating agencies had opposing views regarding certain actions that the issuer wished to take, which prohibited the issuer from investing in certain types of securities. It is also common for the rating agencies to have different views of necessary credit enhancement levels at different points in the lifecycle of a securitization, resulting in some odd-looking hybrid provisions.
- *The rating agencies and the banks or the monoline insurer generally do not defer to each other, so your company could be "whipsawed" by the two groups.* The monoline insurer in the term offering, even though it is in large measure a creature of (and dependent on) the rating agencies, will analyze the transaction quite independently of the rating agencies. It will make its own judgments about the merits of the documents and the deal structure. It will rarely be swayed by the argument that it should not bother with an issue on the basis that the rating agencies are not concerned about it. The same is true of the banks, who are not dependent on the rating agencies to nearly the degree that the monoline insurer is.

Thus, there is a significant potential for issues that you thought were resolved in your favor with one party being re-opened by another party. There is little you can do about this situation, unfortunately, other than recognize that you are engaged in a "multi-lateral" negotiation that "ain't over 'til it's over." It will also be hard to concede an issue in, say, the term deal, without also having to concede the same issue in the warehouse facility.

Identifying Opinion Issues

Another important task for company counsel is to identify early on any problematic legal opinion issues and to find a way to resolve those issues. We have already discussed the most significant opinions: the bankruptcy non-consolidation and true sale opinions.

Another significant opinion that the rating agencies and the investors will expect is the so-called "non-contravention" or "no conflict" opinion to the effect that the execution, delivery and performance by your company and an SPC of the deal documents will not contravene any agreement, decree or law to which either is subject. This opinion relates directly to the preceding discussion about impediments to the securitization. We have occasionally found that the rating agencies, insurers and banks will accept inside counsel's opinion covering these matters. An obvious advantage of inside counsel delivering this opinion is the savings in legal fees that will result from outside counsel avoiding the due diligence (*i.e.*, document review) that would be required for it to deliver such an opinion. Inside counsel is generally much more familiar with the full range of contracts, decrees and laws to which the company is subject than is outside counsel.

CONCLUSION

In this chapter we have described the process of completing an ABS offering and outlined the key legal activities to be performed by counsel to an ABS offering. An ABS offering is a complicated process. However, we believe you will be better prepared by understanding the critical issues before you start transactions.

Chapter 6

To Securitize or Not?

Shane A. Johnson, Ph.D.
Charles Clifford Cameron Endowed Distinguished Professor of Finance
E. J. Ourso College of Business Administration
Louisiana State University

INTRODUCTION

There are a few decisions in a managing a financial institution that can be considered no-brainers. How much effort and resources should be devoted to securitization is not one of them. Of course, unless one has been a coma for a number of years, it is obvious that many financial institutions have employed securitization strategies, even focused almost solely on them, with great success. But the success of these institutions does not mean that all other institutions should jump on the bandwagon, and pour their limited resources into setting up and implementing securitization strategies.

Very large banks seem to be continuing their shift to "transaction banking" where products and services are treated and priced as commodities. They can often exploit substantial economies of scale and their capital market reputations to pursue aggressive securitization strategies as part of an overall strategy. Regional and some large community banks often still focus on "relationship banking" where they acquire special information over time about their clients that they can then use in providing future products. These banks sometimes employ securitization strategies on an "as-needed" basis rather than as part of an overall strategy. Still smaller institutions may find that acquiring the expertise and other resources need for a successful securitization strategy is too costly. As usual, there are exceptions to these generalizations, and institutions need to ensure they make the "right" securitization decisions.

Following recent trends in the financial services industry, the importance of making the "right" securitization decision has increased. The continued consolidation of the industry via mergers and acquisitions, the entry of banks into non-traditional areas (e.g., insurance and mutual funds), and the continued entry of non-banks into areas traditionally served by commercial banks and thrifts have dramatically increased competition. These competitive pressures, combined with a relatively flat-yield curve environment, have put downward pressures on profit margins, and increased the importance of allocating an institution's limited resources to the most profitable areas. The purpose of this chapter is to describe carefully the benefits and costs of securitization, and to offer some guidance on how to think carefully about whether securitization is for your institution.

63

To set up the discussion, consider the following example that illustrates the steps involved in securitizing a package of loans. First, the financial institution originates a loan to a borrower, and then uses funds to disburse cash to the borrower. (What types of loans these are is discussed later in more detail because this turns out to be a very important factor in evaluating the attractiveness of securitization). Next, the institution pools a number of these loans together and sells the claims to their repayments as a traded security like a bond to investors. This can be a security issued directly by the institution or through an agency like GNMA or FNMA that provides a guaranty to the investors who buy the security. (Assume here that the loans are sold without recourse — that is, if the loan defaults, it is the investors' or the guaranteeing agency's problem. Selling loans with recourse is considered later). Because the institution sells the loans, it is able to replace the funds it originally disbursed to the borrowers well before the loans are actually repaid. Moreover, sometimes an institution can sell the loans for more than their book values, and thus make a gain on the sale.

The institution will often continue to service the loan by collecting payments from the borrower, and pass along these payments to the investors holding the securities. The institution gets a "servicing fee" for this, which adds to its revenues. Indeed, many institutions originate loans with the primary intent of building up a "servicing portfolio" of loans that will generate future fee income for them. If an agency like GNMA or FNMA is involved, then the agency will also need to be compensated for its efforts and insurance. The part of the payment remaining after the financial institution and the agency get paid flows to the investor. If all goes well, the servicing continues until the loan is fully repaid, and everyone receives the payoffs they expected.

BENEFITS OF SECURITIZATION

With the basic description above, one can understand when and how securitization creates benefits for financial institutions.

Diversification

First, note that the institution in the example shifted the credit risk of the loans it securitized to the guaranteeing agency or investors that bought the securities. When would this be especially beneficial? Suppose that a small to medium-sized institution's loan portfolio has a relatively high geographic concentration. Securitizing some of the loans and replacing them with securities backed by a pool of loans from a different geographic region allows the institution to diversify geographically, which would reduce its loan portfolio risk. Besides geographic concentrations in the loan portfolio, an institution may have a high concentration in a particular type of loan. If this particular type of loan is securitizable, then it should be clear that selling off some of these loans via securitization and replacing them with other types of loans could also result in needed diversification.

It is probably obvious why diversification is desirable, but it might be useful to reflect for a moment on the plight of financial institutions in Louisiana, Texas, and Oklahoma during the oil-bust. Likewise, financial institutions on the east and west coasts experienced large losses when those areas had their respective real-estate busts. A more timely example may be financial institutions in Texas with heavy farm loan concentrations in the middle of a record heat-wave. While everyone knows the value of diversification, some institutions still under-diversify because their asset size or markets make diversification within their loan portfolios difficult. Securitization helps get around these constraints. Thus, the first main point is that financial institutions that have high loan portfolio risk concentrations can benefit greatly from a securitization strategy.

Note that loans that are securitized with recourse present a different situation. When a loan is sold without recourse, the credit risk shifts to the investor holding the securities. Thus, the institution does not sustain any future default losses on loans sold without recourse. This is the primary reason that securitization facilitates diversification. In contrast, loans sold with recourse still present risk to the institution, and thus do not result in diversification.

Enhanced Income

Second, note that the institution in the example keeps earning the servicing fees even though the assets have moved off its balance sheet. Servicing a large number of loans efficiently requires investments in some physical assets, but notably does not require the financial assets (i.e., the loans) to stay on the balance sheet. With the financial assets off the balance sheet, capital requirements are reduced because they are partly determined by the dollar amount of assets on the balance sheet. Assuming the institution can service loans in a cost-effective manner, the servicing fees generate additional net income, but in general do not require substantial increases in assets or equity. Increasing net income without increasing assets or equity increases both return on assets (ROA) and return on equity (ROE). Thus, the second main point is that an institution that uses securitization to build a servicing portfolio can significantly enhance its ROA and ROE without changing its asset size or equity capital base.

Although potentially very attractive, it is well to keep in mind a potential problem with earnings derived from servicing rights. Many institutions capitalize these servicing fees and report the full amount on their income statement. This can overstate earnings and require negative future revisions if mortgage prepayments come faster than expected so that the servicing life is shorter than expected. This risk is most pronounced in environments where interest rates could fall unexpectedly and lead to refinancings that cause much higher prepayments than expected.

Overcoming Capital Constraints

Third, and related to the second point, note that the institution in the example moved the loans off its balance sheet. Recall that most financial institutions are subject to some sort of risk-based capital requirements, in which loans typically have higher equity capital requirements than cash or securities.[1] Getting the loans off its balance sheet means that the institution's required (equity) capital is lower than it would be had it not sold the loans.

To see why this is beneficial, consider an institution that has just enough capital given its asset size and structure. "Just enough" might mean the regulatory minimum or a self-imposed minimum above the regulatory minimum. Suppose this institution securitizes $100 million in mortgage loans, and then immediately uses the resulting funds to buy $100 million in GNMA securities. This institution's asset size has not changed, and if the yield on the GNMA securities is close to the yield on the mortgage loans it just sold, the institution's interest income has also not changed.

So what has changed? Because the GNMA securities are in a lower risk class for risk-based capital purposes, the institution's risk-adjusted assets fell, and thus its required capital fell. Now, the institution has more capital than its minimum, so it can increase asset size without having to raise new equity capital or wait for it to accumulate through retained earnings. Alternatively, the institution can reduce its capital by paying a larger dividend to shareholders, repurchasing some of its stock outstanding, or retaining less earnings over time.

How do these "capital factors" affect the institution's performance? Consider the following true story. At a banker's convention in 1989, I spoke to a large group of bank presidents and directors about the then-new risk-based capital regulations. One of the main goals was to get them to think about the financial implications of moving to risk-based capital requirements from the old capital requirements that were primarily a function of asset size, independent of risk. Given my corporate finance training, I analyzed every different scenario and every different implication in the context of its effect on return on equity (ROE), instead of the return on assets (ROA) that bankers frequently focus on. At the end of two hours when I thought I was successful in keeping everyone on the same wavelength as I, one of the bankers said "Well Shane, this is all fine and dandy, but we focus on ROA not ROE!" I screamed and pulled all of my hair out.

Okay, so maybe I didn't really pull all of my hair out, but the rest of the story is true and helps to illustrate an important point. In the capital-constrained institution above, securitization reduced the amount of required capital even when the institution immediately purchased GNMA securities equal in dollar value to the mortgage loans they sold. This is because the mortgage loans are in a higher risk class for capital requirements than the GNMAs are. As discussed above, the

---

[1] Risk-based capital requirements mandate that an institution hold equity capital equal to a specified percentage of the amount of risk-adjusted assets they have. For purposes of calculating risk-adjusted assets, assets fall into one of four categories: (1) a 0% class for assets with zero or low credit risk (e.g., cash, U.S. government securities); (2) a 20% class for assets with slightly higher credit risk (e.g., some municipal securities); (3) a 50% class for assets with slightly higher credit risk (e.g., 1-4 family residential mortgages); and (4) a 100% class for assets with still higher credit risk (e.g., most consumer and commercial loans). Assets in each class are multiplied by the percentage weight for its class. Because an asset in a higher risk class (e.g., the 100% class) is counted at a higher percentage, it requires more equity capital be held against it.

institution could purchase even more GNMA securities because its capital could support a higher level of assets in this lower risk class. What happens if the institution does this? Assuming a positive spread on the GNMAs, net interest income and total assets both rise. ROA would likely change very little. But here's the punchline: Since the amount of equity capital did not change, ROE increases!

To see exactly why, recall that ROE equals ROA times the assets-to-equity ratio. The institution held the same amount of equity, but increased its asset size (by $100 million), and thus increased the assets-to-equity ratio. For example, suppose that the institution previously had $500 million in assets, $50 million in equity (which it considered just enough), and an ROA of 1.25%. This produces an ROE of 12.5%, which is 1.25% times $500 million (assets) divided by $50 million equity. After the sale of the $100 million in loans, and the replacement of them with $100 million in GNMAs, the asset size is still $500 million. But due to risk-based capital requirements and the fact that the GNMAs are more liquid and represent superior diversification, the institution now has "too much" capital. Suppose that it can grow assets by another $100 million to $600 million, and still meet capital requirements while feeling comfortable with the cushion that the capital represents. This, of course, would require raising a like amount of new deposits or other liabilities. If the ROA remains at 1.25% (meaning the new assets earn what the existing assets did), then the ROE increases to 15%, which is 1.25% times $600 million (assets) divided by $50 million (equity).

Before risk-based capital requirements, the assets-to-equity ratio was independent of the type of assets an institution held, so maximizing ROA also typically maximized ROE. This explains why bankers in the past frequently focused on ROA. The example above showed that now an institution can increase ROE without changing ROA. Of ROE and ROA, which is more important? Well, it should not be too difficult to figure out — equityholders own the institution! If that is not sufficient motivation, consider the fact that shareholders are much more likely to sell out to an acquirer if they are earning a low return on their investments, a fact especially important in the current merger and acquisition climate of the industry.

Thus, the third main point is that financial institutions that are capital-constrained can benefit greatly from a securitization strategy. Small and medium-sized institutions, in particular, often find it difficult to raise new equity capital at low cost. Thus, they can be especially good candidates for securitization strategies.

As above, note that loans that are securitized with recourse present a different situation. When a loan is sold without recourse, the credit risk shifts to the investor holding the securities. Thus, the institution does not sustain any future default losses on loans sold without recourse. This is the primary reason that regulators allow an institution that sells loans without recourse to remove them from the calculation for risk-based capital purposes. In contrast, loans sold with recourse still present risk to the institution, and as a result remain in the risk-based capital calculations. Thus, it is clear that the above discussion about how securitization helps to avoid capital constraints does not apply to loans sold with recourse.

Overcoming Liquidity Constraints

Fourth, suppose that an institution is "loaned up" and cannot raise new deposits so that it does not have the funds (i.e., liquidity) to make new loans until other loans are repaid. Without securitization, the institution has two options: (1) it can use short-term borrowings like federal funds to fund new loans, or (2) it can simply turn away new loans and forego earnings growth. Recalling the problems that Continental Illinois had in the 1980s when it could not rollover its short-term borrowings, it is easy to see why the first option is typically not a good idea. An institution that wants to grow and increase earnings obviously also finds the second option unattractive.

With securitization, note that the institution in the example gets back the funds it had disbursed to the borrower well before the loan was repaid. This provides needed liquidity to a loaned-up institution so that it can then make new loans. The institution can retain these new loans in its portfolio, or securitize them and then perhaps repeat the process. This is especially important for small and medium-sized financial institutions that may lack the size and credit reputation needed to purchase liquidity easily in the money markets. Securitization allows these institutions to operate beyond their liquidity constraints by transforming their formerly illiquid loans into liquid securities, and then cash. Thus, the fourth main point is that financial institutions that are liquidity-constrained can benefit greatly from a securitization strategy.

COSTS OF SECURITIZATION

As with most things in life, where there are benefits there are also costs, and one should not do something if the costs exceed the benefits. Thus, in deciding whether to securitize or not, an institution needs to weigh the costs of securitization against its benefits. The benefits described above pointed to fairly specific characteristics of an institution that can benefit from a securitization strategy. Thus, it is seemingly easy to see when an institution would not find securitization especially beneficial — when they are not liquidity-constrained or capital-constrained, and do not have significant loan portfolio risks from concentration. Of course, an institution with these characteristics could still focus on securitization strategies, but there are costs that may outweigh the benefits.

To understand the costs, one needs to delve further into the types of loans that are securitizable. In reviewing the steps in the securitization process described above, some readers may have noticed the absence of what many regard as a fundamental and important step in the lending process — monitoring the borrower after the funds have been disbursed. For example, loan officers frequently conduct site visits and regular interviews of small and medium-sized commercial borrowers. With most securitized loans, however, neither the originator, nor the guarantor, nor the investors in the securities monitor the borrowers.

Why is no one monitoring the borrower with a securitized loan, and why does no one seem to care? All of the parties involved in the securitization process find this acceptable only because the types of loans that are securitized are typically highly standardized.[2] For example, mortgage loans sold to GNMA or FNMA have certain limitations with respect to loan-to-value ratios, borrowers' debt-to-income ratios, and the characteristics of the collateral properties. Standardized loans present less risk to the guarantors and the investors because it is easier to evaluate pools of loans that have very similar characteristics. Moreover, in the specific case of securitized mortgage loans, the characteristics of acceptable collateral are well-specified so that losses following a default are less of an issue.

In general, products or services that are highly standardized can be considered "commodities." Wheat, crude oil, and pork bellies are all commodities, as are highly standardized loans made by financial institutions. Why is it important to realize that the types of loans that are typically securitized are commodities? If one thinks about the competition and pricing in commodity markets, it is easy to see that profit margins are usually not very high on commodities. Consider the likely success of a crude oil producer who decided to set its selling price for oil very far above the prevailing market price. Because the crude oil from this particular producer does not differ significantly from other, cheaper crude oil, no one would purchase this producer's crude oil until it lowered its price, or until shortages drove the market price up to this producer's higher price.

Now consider a producer that could provide highly specialized (as opposed to highly standardized) crude oil that required much less refining to be usable. Could this producer charge a selling price above the market price of crude oil? Probably so, and if the additional production cost of the highly specialized crude oil was less than the increase in selling price, this producer would have a higher profit margin. For this producer, the "cost" of choosing to produce the commodity product is an "opportunity cost" of foregone profits. Thus, the main cost of securitization is an opportunity cost of foregone profits on nonstandardized loans.

So how does the commodity story apply to financial institutions? To set the stage, consider the following vignette:

> A young, married man had made up his mind to be a farmer, but did not have the money to purchase a plot of land and the necessary equipment. Approaching a banker whom he knew reasonably well, he asked for a loan. "No," the banker replied, "I'm sorry, but I cannot in good conscience make you that loan." "Why not?" the young man asked, puzzled that his banker did

---

[2] While most loans that are securitizable are highly standardized, there are some asset-backed securities that pool loans that can be considered non-standardized. Markets for these asset-backed securities tend to be less liquid and competition to provide these loans less intense. Thus, they share characteristics of loans that some institutions keep in their portfolios. Thus, much of the discussion later in the chapter of the costs of securitization applies to these loans.

not want to help out a new farmer. "I know your wife and I know that she doesn't want a passel of kids. Without a passel of kids, you can't be a successful farmer," the banker explained to the young man. The young man eventually went on to borrow money to open up an automobile dealership, and made more money than he had ever dreamed he would. After several years in the car business, he remarked that he sure was glad that he did not become a farmer. Oh, and by the way, the young man and his wife had only one child.[3]

What does this vignette illustrate? It illustrates that in certain lending situations the financial institution has special information that is not easily observable by, and not easily transferable to, other parties. What this means in practice is that often a borrower has characteristics that disqualify it from a securitized loan, even though the institution knows that the borrower is creditworthy enough to warrant the granting of a loan. Alternatively, there are circumstances when a loan cannot be structured to simultaneously meet the requirements of securitization and meet the borrower's special needs. In more general terms, sometimes the characteristics of the loan or the borrower are highly non-standardized, which is precisely the opposite of what is typically required for successful securitization.

Like the price of the highly specialized crude oil discussed above, the interest rates on highly specialized loans can typically be higher than on commodity-type loans. These types of loans are somewhat akin to custom-made suits. Some stores sell off-the-rack suits that are less expensive and generate smaller profit margins, but sell more of them. Other stores sell custom-made suits that are more expensive and generate higher profit margins. Naturally, they sell fewer of these suits than the off-the-rack store, but can still produce the same level of profits. A store decides which type to sell based on profits, not on selling price. With higher interest rates, specialized loans can generate higher profit margins assuming that the financial institution can produce those loans at low enough cost.

Despite the potential differences in the profit margins on securitizable versus non-securitizable loans, many institutions adopt securitization strategies and then refuse to make loans that do not meet the requirements for them to be securitizable. To be sure, most institutions do make both securitizable and non-securitizable loans, but for a given loan type many institutions will not make both. For example, many institutions that securitize mortgage loans will not make mortgage loans that they will have to portfolio because they are nonstandardized.

This has resulted in certain segments of loan markets not being adequately served. A small number of institutions have recognized this void, and essentially specialize in serving these markets. Like the custom-suit maker above, these institutions often do less in volume, but make it up with higher profit margins. Borrowers with specialized needs, after being turned away by a number of

---

[3] I thank Steve Wyatt for sharing this story with me.

institutions, are often happy when the specialty institutions agree to the loan and are even willing to pay higher prices.

In more general terms, these institutions are deciding to operate in markets where the demand is less elastic. In a market with a very elastic demand, customers are very price sensitive. Trying to raise prices slightly to increase profits can result in a total flight of the institution's customers to competitors with lower prices. Conversely, in markets where demand elasticity is lower (i.e., demand is inelastic), customers are less price sensitive. Prices can be slightly higher than competitor's prices without driving customers away. Think about what the Baby Bells could have charged for telephone service in the absence of any regulations. This is primarily because there was not significant competition in their markets and because most people would not be willing to go without telephone service.

Given the competitive and other pressures on profit margins discussed in the introduction, a useful strategy for many institutions is to try to operate in markets where they have some degree of monopoly power. Regulators typically frown on an institution being the only one in a geographic market area, but even if an institution has numerous "competitors" in its market area, many of these competitors may choose not to serve certain segments of certain loan markets. These markets represent exploitable opportunities for a non-securitizing institution to increase its profits.

CONCLUSION

So, should your institution adopt a securitization strategy or be the specialty lender that portfolios nonstandardized loans? Yes. People often hate having a question answered that way, but frequently that answer makes a good point. The point here is that both strategies can be employed successfully, and one is not clearly superior to the other in all situations. It should be clear that to be the specialty lender and portfolio loans requires that an institution have adequate liquidity, capital, and portfolio risk concentration levels. Thus, institutions that find these constraints binding should clearly lean towards a securitization strategy. Institutions that can portfolio loans, however, need to think more carefully about the opportunity costs of deciding to devote their efforts to the types of loans that are securitizable, but that frequently generate low profit margins.

In principle, there is nothing to prevent an institution from securitizing some loans and keeping others of the same general type in its portfolio. It is typically much easier and lower cost, however, to set up policies and procedures to either securitize or portfolio a particular type of loan, but not do both. In fact, many institutions find it difficult to set up and maintain different policies and procedures to deal with both possibilities, and thus choose to focus on only one possibility. There is nothing wrong with this as long as it results from a careful analysis of both the benefits and the costs of securitization.

Chapter 7

Strategies for Community Bankers

Joseph F. Sinkey Jr., Ph.D.
Edward W. Hiles Professor of Financial Institutions
Terry College of Business
The University of Georgia

INTRODUCTION

The ongoing structural change in the financial-services industry (FSI) can be viewed as a form of institutional metamorphosis. The process can be described as the "... equivalent of a laboratory photograph catching a caterpillar halfway through its transition to a butterfly."[1] With the traditional brick-and-mortar bank building representing the cocoon, visualize the modern financial-services firms (FSFs) bursting out of its shell with legs, antennae, cords, and control devices that serve to wire it into the electronic age of e-money, e-banking, and e-commerce. Less visible, but just as important, transformations are taking place within the brick-and-mortar facade of FSFs as various technologies change internal production processes, product lines, and organizational structure.

Community bankers are especially challenged by this dynamic process of change. Moreover, some analysts see their continued existence as fragile as the vulnerable butterfly. In this difficult environment, bankers must answer three critical strategic questions about their companies:

1. Where is the bank today?
2. Where is the bank going?
3. How is the bank going to get there?

---

[1] Edward J. Kane, "Metamorphosis in Financial-Services Delivery and Production," in *Strategic Planning for Economic and Technological Change in the Financial-Services Industry* (San Francisco: Federal Home Loan Bank, 1983), pp. 49-64.

Parts of this chapter draw on themes from the fifth edition of my book, *Commercial Bank Financial Management* (Upper Saddle River, NJ: Prentice-Hall, 1998). I thank Matej Blasko for his research assistance and detailed comments, and Zack Fulmer, Stephen Jamison, Andy McGhee, and Joanne Sinkey for comments and suggestions. The usual disclaimer applies.

In the face of unprecedented change, successfully addressing these questions has never been more important for FSFs. Furthermore, the need for strategic clarity has been intensified as the traditional role of banks as portfolio lenders has been challenged by the increasing use of the techniques of asset securitization and structured finance. This chapter focuses on how FSFs, particularly community banks, can use these techniques to enhance their performance in the 21st century.

THE "IZATION" OF THE FINANCIAL-SERVICES INDUSTRY AND THE INNOVATIONS OF SECURITIZATION, STRUCTURED FINANCE, AND DERIVATIVES

The financial-services industry is in a state of flux in which the only constant is change. The phenomena of computer*ization* (technology), global*ization*, institutional*ization*, privat*ization*, and securit*ization* capture the dynamic innovations occurring in the FSI and suggest the "*ization*" of the industry. Of course, these events are not independent; they react to and feed back on each other. Arguably, securitization, structured finance, and derivatives have been among the most important financial innovations affecting banks over the past quarter century.

Competitive disintermediation, on both sides of bank balance sheets, and industry consolidation are reshaping the financial landscape. Although the traditional role of banks as intermediaries that fund loans with deposits is still important, banks are looking ahead to their future roles as information processors and financial specialists. These new functions involve creating new products, such as securitized assets, structured finance, and derivatives, that make financial markets more complete. These innovative products respond to investors' preferences about the size, timing, and riskiness of cash flows and take into account the ability of different investors to bear different types of risk.

Although the Group of Thirty makes the following important observation about derivatives, it also can be applied to securitization and structured finance:[2]

> What makes derivatives so important is not so much the size of the activity, as the role it plays in fostering new ways to understand, measure, and manage financial risk. Through derivatives, the complex risks that are bound together in traditional instruments can be teased apart and managed independently, and often more efficiently.

In this regard, securitization, structured finance, and derivatives have fundamentally changed financial management and have made risk management and the selling of risk-management services prominent fixtures of corporate

---

[2] Group of Thirty, *Derivatives: Practices and Principles* (Washington, D.C.: Global Derivatives Study Group, 1993), p. 2.

banking and finance. Merton claims that risk management is "perhaps the central topic for the management of financial institutions in the 1990s."[3] Furthermore, in *The Economist*'s international banking survey, Freeman contends: "To survive in a consolidating industry, banks must become better at defining, managing and pricing risk. The best are already trying."[4]

DEFINITIONS OF SECURITIZATION, STRUCTURED FINANCE, AND DERIVATIVES

This section briefly defines the three most important terms used in this chapter.

Securitization

Asset or loan securitization is the process of removing loans from a bank's balance sheet by selling them to a third party, which then pools and packages them as securities sold to investors in capital markets. Loans subject to this process are referred to as "securitized assets" and popularly known by the acronyms ABS (asset-backed securities) and MBS (mortgage-backed securities). The principal and interest payments of the underlying loans generate the cash flows received by ultimate investors. Because of credit enhancements, default on a public ABS has been a rare occurrence. Prepayment risk and interest-rate risk, however, are the relevant dangers that ABS investors face. Residential mortgages, automobile loans, and credit-card receivables are the most commonly securitized assets. For example, a collateralized mortgage obligation (CMO) is an MBS with multiple bond classes or tranches that is backed by the underlying cash flows of the pooled mortgages. Because some observers regard a CMO as a "structured" MBS, the distinction between securitization and structured finance, defined next, can become blurred.

Structured Finance

Almost parallel to the development of securitization has been the phenomenon of structured finance. On the street, whether it be Wall Street or Main Street, USA, structured finance has a literal interpretation: It simply means a deal, contract, or product that is designed, customized, or engineered ("structured" if you will) to meet a client's specific financial or investment objectives. Because commercial-and-industrial (C&I) loans have always been tailored to meet the needs of business customers, bankers have been doing structured deals for centuries. The new twist in structured finance has been the addition of "derivatives" (i.e., futures, forwards, swaps, and options) that transform a financial asset into one with a different (nonstandard) set of cash flows and risk-return characteristics.

---

[3] Robert C. Merton, "Influence of Mathematical Models in Finance Practice: Past, Present, and Future," *Financial Practice and Education* (Spring/Summer 1995), p. 12.

[4] *The Economist*, "Survey of International Banking" (April 10, 1993), p. 2.

Braddock describes the business activities related to the creation, marketing, and valuation of structured products as "financial engineering,"[5] which is a broader definition than the academic interpretation of financial engineering as the repackaging of cash flows in nonstandard ways. This narrower view of financial engineering is expressed by Smith and Smithson, who describe it in terms of fundamental building blocks whereby more complex products are constructed from basic financial components.[6] To illustrate, a swap contract can be viewed as a portfolio of forward contracts. Moreover, because the basic credit-extension building blocks of fixed-rate, floating-rate, zero-coupon, and amortized obligations provide the foundation for all debt contracts, an interest-rate swap also can be viewed as a package of cash-market instruments (i.e., a combination of a fixed-rate debt contract plus a floating-rate debt contract).

Derivatives

A derivative asset or security obtains its value and cash flows from another asset known as the "underlying asset." The most common derivative contracts are futures, forwards, options, and swaps; they derive their values from underlying assets whose values are tied to interest rates, foreign currencies, commodity prices, or market indices. Because these underlying assets are off-balance-sheet items, derivative contracts are classified as off-balance-sheet activities (OBSAs). Given this definition, a securitized asset can be viewed as a derivative, but traditional structured finance in the form of a customized C&I loan cannot. Modern structured finance deals, however, can be arranged to create a synthetic derivative or a portfolio that replicates a derivative contract. For the purposes of this chapter, structured finance refers to the modern version; that is, we equate it with transactions that are derivatives-based or that include derivatives as part of the deal.

INCREASED MARKET EFFICIENCY VERSUS STRATEGIC THREAT TO BANKS

According to John Reed, former Citigroup and Citicorp chairman, "Securitization is the substitution of more efficient public capital markets for less efficient, higher cost financial intermediaries in the funding of debt instruments."[7] A financial system's major function is resource allocation. The efficiency of this process is judged by three criteria: (1) moving scarce funds to investment projects with the highest returns (allocative efficiency), (2) moving those funds as cheaply as

---

[5] John C. Braddock, *Derivatives Demystified: Using Structured Financial Products* (New York: John Wiley and Sons, Inc., 1997).

[6] Clifford W. Smith, Jr. and Charles W. Smithson. *The Handbook of Financial Engineering: New Financial Product Innovations, Applications, and Analyses.* (New York: Harper Business, 1990).

[7] In a speech at the Kellogg Graduate School of Management as reported by Kendall in Leon T. Kendall and Michael J. Fishman (eds), *A Primer on Securitization* (Cambridge, MA: The MIT Press, 1996), p. 2.

possible (cost or operational efficiency), and (3) moving those funds to provide as much information to investors as possible (informational or price efficiency).

Securitization leads to improved cost and informational efficiencies by reducing intermediation expenses (e.g., transaction costs) and increasing the transparency of previously opaque assets (i.e, by making information about them more readily accessible). On balance, securitization makes financial markets more efficient and more complete. Less obviously, as discussed later in this chapter, securitization presents a major strategic danger to banks because it threatens their existence. To highlight these benefits and costs, it is useful to compare direct finance, indirect finance, and pass-through finance.

Direct finance exists when lenders and borrowers get together directly, usually in financial markets, and exchange claims or contracts against each other. These contracts are referred to as public debt.

Indirect finance exists when an intermediary, such as a bank, plays a role in this process. The contracts associated with this process are referred to as private debt.

Pass-through finance exists when intermediaries pool their assets (e.g., loans funded by deposits), package them as securities, and sell them to investors. These securitized assets are referred to as hybrid contracts between private and public debt. Equivalently, pass-through finance can be viewed as an amalgam or hybrid of direct and indirect finance.

At the beginning of 2000, the market for securitized assets was estimated at over $3 trillion with the bulk ($2.3 trillion) dominated by Ginnie Mae, Fannie Mae, and Freddie Mac (Government National Mortgage Association, Federal National Mortgage Association, and Federal Home Loan Mortgage Association). These agencies support housing finance and account for almost $9 out of every $10 in the MBS market. The other major components of the ABS market include commercial mortgages, credit-card and home-equity loans, and automobile loans. Recently, the subprime, home-equity segment of the ABS market has been the fastest growing and the riskiest, partially due to an overextension of credit and the lack of historical data on the performance of subprime borrowers needed to estimate future cash flows.[8]

Two views dominate explanations about why securitization exists. One theory emphasizes the process as being driven by changes in and the interaction between taxes and regulations (implicit taxation). These explicit and implicit taxes raise banks' cost of funds relative to their competitors (see, for example, John Reed's statement above). The other view emphasizes the importance of technological change in reducing the costs of processing information associated with selling assets and informational asymmetries between borrowers and lenders (i.e., transparency). An eclectic approach includes the roles of taxation, regulation, and technology as driving the process of securitization, structured finance, and derivatives.

---

[8] Information in this paragraph is from "Special Report: Corporate Finance." *Business Week* (October 26, 1998), pp. 123-140 and the *Federal Reserve Bulletin* (May 2000), Table 1.54, p. A35.

THE DUAL ROLES OF MODERN BANKERS

The dual roles of modern bankers reflect the financial innovations that are driving new financial products and services. Because the combination of structured finance and securitization permits them to be major players, the most innovative bankers have calling cards with "Structured Lender" on one side and "Securitized Lender" on the other.

The Structured Lender

The structured lender works on the right-hand side of client balance sheets by providing them with a complete menu of financing alternatives, including derivatives. The assets generated by structured lenders can be traditional ones that are held on the banks' balance sheet, securitized ones that evolve into marketable securities, or hybrid ones in the form of syndicated loans.

The modern techniques of structured finance are asset-based lending and leveraged cash-flow lending. The former is based on hard asset values such as inventory and account receivables, while the latter is based on the present value of firms' future cash flows. While banks have always made working capital loans, asset-based lending is seen as requiring a higher level of due diligence and monitoring. Since leveraged cash-flow lending has a higher degree of uncertainty, some of which borders on "junk" financing, the deal must be done right with respect to such features as monitoring, credit lines, and spreads. These types of transactions blossomed in the 1980s under the names of leveraged buyouts (LBOs) and highly levered transactions (HLTs).

While structured lenders may want to do everything on the right-hand side of client balance sheets, they may not want to hold as assets all the deals they do for their customers. Securitization, syndicated loans, and credit derivatives (guarantees) provide techniques for managing these unwanted risks and permit banks to evolve into commodity, senior-debt lenders. Although risk-based capital requirements and the explicit and implicit costs of the federal safety net (i.e., Federal Deposit Insurance Corporation (FDIC) insurance and the Federal Reserve (Fed) discount window) force insured depositories to be more prudent lenders than other types of intermediaries, they still want to be in the game.

The Securitized Lender

The card of the securitized-lending specialist reads: "Have Loans, Will Securitize." The securitized lender works mainly on the left-hand side of its own balance sheet, funding implications notwithstanding, so that loans are securitized or asset securitization takes place. This technique began in the mortgage market and has been extended to other assets such as consumer installment contracts, leases, receivables, and other relatively illiquid assets. The common denominators in these "structures" (as some analysts regard the term "structured finance" as being synonymous with securitization) are assets with similar features that are packaged or pooled into interest-bearing securities with the characteristics of marketable investments. "Pass-through finance" has a literal interpretation to the securitized lender. The original borrower makes principal and interest payments to the original lender or a subsequent loan servicer, who in turn passes through the payments, minus fees for itself and any third-party enhancers, to the ultimate investor or holder of the security.[9]

Strategic Benefits from Securitization
In a nutshell, asset securitization transforms private debt in the form of bank loans into marketable securities or public debt. In the process, it generates liquidity for intermediaries and increases the transparency of previously opaque loans. More specifically, four important benefits accrue to banks from securitization:

1. Increased liquidity from the ability to sell assets
2. Enhanced revenue/profits from asset sales
3. Increased servicing income
4. Conservation of capital

All other things being equal, because these specific benefits permit banks to improve their liquidity, profitability, and capital adequacy, they represent strategic uses of securitization. In addition, securitization offers community banks something they cannot buy in their local loan markets: the chance to diversify their loan portfolios. With hindsight, portfolio diversification gained through the proper use of securitization could have reduced the savings and loan (S&L) crisis and the concentrations of credit in failed energy and farm banks. With foresight, any bank that does not take advantage of the potential diversification benefits of securitization suffers from failed risk management.

The primary motivation for MBS development was avoidance of interest-rate risk by lenders. Neither thrift institutions (e.g., S&Ls) nor their customers wanted to bear that risk. In contrast, banks have been motivated to securitize assets by explicit and implicit taxes on bank capital, competitive pressures on bank profits, and the desire to exploit their comparative advantage as originators of credit. Although the concept of pass-throughs has been extended to various kinds of bank loans, automobile loans and credit-card receivables have been the most popular. Although various kinds of loans and other financial assets have been securitized, the most successful ones share the following characteristics:[10]

---

[9] A structure called "pay-through finance" also exists. The main financial difference between it and a pass-through deal is that pay-throughs allow for active cash management (i.e., reinvesting balances extends the average life of a pay-through structure). Paul W. Feeney, *Securitization: Redefining the Bank* (New York: St. Martin's Press, 1995).

[10] See Kendall, *A Primer on Securitization,* for a description of the assets that have been successfully securitized and the characteristics of the underlying assets.

- Standardized assets (e.g., 8%, fixed-rate mortgages) generate standardized contracts
- Rating of risk through underwriting
- Reliable and reputable credit enhancers
- Standardized framework of applicable laws
- Standardized servicing quality
- Technical capability for handling complex securities analysis
- Data base of historical statistics

The securitization process for nonmortgage loans closely follows the one for mortgages. Specifically, the loan originator (or sponsor/servicer) usually handles the task of servicing the loan by collecting the principal and interest payments and passing them through to the ultimate investor. Given the resources for originating loans (e.g., loan officers, customer relationships, computer facilities, capital (dollar and reputational), the marginal cost of producing additional loans for sale can be quite low (i.e., due to economies of scale). All of this presents securitization in a positive light; drawbacks, however, also exist.

Strategic Threats Posed by Securitization

John Reed's words, "less efficient, higher cost financial intermediaries," capture the major strategic threat to banks, namely, their survival. The role of banks diminishes in a world of securitized assets. The distinction between traditional bank lending and securitized lending clarifies this situation.

Traditional bank lending has four functions:

1. Originating (making the loan),
2. Funding (holding the loan on the balance sheet),
3. Servicing (collecting the payments of interest and principal), and
4. Monitoring (conducting periodic surveillance to ensure that the borrower has maintained the financial ability to service the loan).

Securitized lending introduces the possibility of selling assets on a bigger scale and eliminating the need for funding and monitoring. The securitized lending function has only three steps: originate, sell, and service. This change from a four-step to a three-step process has been described as the fragmentation or separation of traditional lending. In addition, when servicing rights are sold, securitized lending can be reduced to a two-step routine: originate and sell.

If a bank has the expertise and reputation as an originator, but lacks the liquidity, capital, or cost structures to fund loans, it can specialize as a securitized lender. In the case of large banks, the effective constraints tend to be equity capital (especially prior to the mid-1990s) and cost considerations. Because large banks usually can buy all the liquidity they need in the marketplace, provided they maintain their creditworthiness, liquidity is less of a constraint. In contrast, smaller banks with higher capital ratios, less recognition, and slack loan demand usually have the capacity to provide funding.

The process of securitization involves five basic parties:[11]

1. The loan originator or broker (bank or financial intermediary)
2. The loan purchaser (an affiliated trust, also called a special-purpose vehicle or SPV)
3. The loan packager (underwriter of the securities)
4. A guarantor (insurance company)
5. Investors that buy the securities (mainly institutions such as banks, insurance companies, and pension funds).

The threat to banks from securitization arises because they are not major players in the process outside of being originators of the underlying assets that are securitized. For this reason, large banks want to make further inroads into underwriting securities and providing insurance, which they have done. The benefits to investment bankers from securitization include new product lines, increased flows of originations and fees, increased trading volume and profits, and the potential for innovation and market expansion.

Because commercial bankers want some of these benefits, they have been dismantling the wall that separates commercial and investment banking in the United States. The acquisition of Citicorp by Travelers Group and the creation of Citigroup, approved by the Fed in September 1998, was perhaps the final nail in Glass-Steagall's coffin. The Gramm-Leach-Bliley or Financial-Modernization Act of 1999 effectively repealed the product restrictions imposed on FSFs by the Banking Act of 1933 (Glass-Steagall).

Because securitization, like any other business, runs in cycles, the expansion of the process to "subprime" or higher risk borrowers during the early-to-mid 1990s led to a shakeout in the late 1990s. The underlying assets in these deals were home equity lines of credit and automobile loans. The originators in these deals included traditional lenders such as banks and S&Ls but also hotshot new public companies operating in the specialty finance sector. One analyst likened the rapid growth of the specialty firms to a kind of Ponzi scheme because they lacked reliable information on which to estimate future cash flows.[12] As a result, accounting earnings and values based on multiples of these earnings were illusory. Rising spreads, collateral underperformance, and ratings downgrades captured the downturn in the subprime sector of the ABS market.

To recap, securitization differs from traditional lending in three basic ways:

1. Underlying illiquid loans are packaged as marketable securities.

---

[11] This section draws on Sylvester Johnson and Ameilia E. Murphy. "Going Off the Balance Sheet," *Economic Review,* Federal Reserve Bank of Atlanta (September-October 1987), pp. 23-25.

[12] Kendall, *A Primer on Securitization*, p. 13.

2. Because loans are sold, the risks that accompany them are removed from the lender's portfolio, assuming no recourse.
3. As a form of asset disintermediation, the traditional risk-bearing role of the bank portfolio is bypassed in favor of securities that are sliced and diced in ways that meet the risk preferences of ultimate investors.

SECURITIZATION AS A RISK-MANAGEMENT TOOL

Securitization is more than the market phenomenon known as pass-through finance. It is an important risk-management tool for banks that primarily works through risk removal but also permits banks to acquire securitized assets with potential diversification benefits. When assets are removed from a bank's balance sheet, without recourse, all the risks associated with the asset are eliminated, save for prepayment risk,[13] assuming the originator continues to service the loan. Credit risk and interest-rate risk are the key uncertainties that concern domestic lenders. By passing on these risks to investors or to third parties when credit enhancements are involved, FSFs are better able to manage their risk exposures.

If securitized loans or straight loan sales have been transacted with recourse, which means that the bank remains exposed to some risk associated with the underlying asset, securitization is referred to as an off-balance-sheet activity (OBSA).[14] For example, because residential mortgages securitized through one of the federal housing agencies are done without recourse, they are not an off-balance-sheet item. In contrast, credit-card securitizations are usually structured with a "material adverse change" clause that requires the originating bank to repurchase the outstanding receivables if the repayment performance of the underlying accounts deteriorates. In this case, the securitization is an OBSA. In general, recourse stipulations make securitization less effective as a risk-management tool.

Other Motives for Securitization

In addition to risk management, managers' concerns about profitability and capital adequacy drive them to remove assets from their balance sheets. These concerns are captured and illustrated by the return-on-equity (ROE) model:

$$ROE = ROA \times EM$$

---

[13] Prepayment or "contraction risk" refers to the shortening of a debt contract because the borrower pays off the obligation before its due date or maturity. In contrast, when prepayments slow down, as they do when interest rates rise, "extension risk" exists.

[14] To dramatize the substantial changes occurring in commercial banking, John Kareken notes that the business of banking is "very much the business of making contingent promises or commitments; and even just a decade ago it was not." John H. Kareken, "The Emergence and Regulation of Contingent-Commitment Banking," *Journal of Banking and Finance* (September 1987), p. 359. These contingent commitments capture the essence of off-balance-sheet banking.

where ROE is return on equity, ROA is return on assets, and EM is equity multiplier. In this framework, ROA equals net income divided by total (or average) assets, and EM equals total (or average) assets divided by total (or average) equity capital. (The inverse of EM is the ratio of equity capital to assets.) Thus, when FSFs engage in asset securitization,[15] they restrain asset growth and increase fee income. These effects increase ROA and lower EM, all other things being equal.[16]

Given that the marketplace and regulators want improved profitability and stronger capital positions, asset securitization can serve both of these masters. The ROE framework can also be used to explain why banks want to do structured deals and sell risk-management services (e.g., derivatives) to their clients: they generate fees, conserve capital, and reduce the underlying risk exposure of client balance sheets.

The Traditional Approach for Removing Risk: Loan Participations and Syndicated Loans

A loan participation is an arrangement by a group of banks to share a loan that is too large for one bank to make. The constraint can be the bank's legal lending limit or a more stringent rule imposed by its prudent risk-management policy. Loan participations, also known as participation financing, are arranged through correspondent banking networks in which smaller banks buy part of an overall financing package. Thus, another reason for the existence of participations is relationship banking, whereby correspondent banks (larger banks) sell or "downstream" portions of loans to respondent banks (smaller banks). Participations also permit smaller banks to make loans that they otherwise could not make because of their legal lending limits. By "upstreaming" loans to correspondents, community bankers earn fee income by servicing loans and are better able to serve their loan customers and maintain relationships. In addition, because community bankers know their local markets better, they can exploit this comparative advantage.

A syndicated loan, which is a lending arrangement supported by a number of banks, can be viewed as a hybrid of private and public debt. Large syndications may involve more than 100 banks sharing millions of dollars of loans. Credits of $50 million or more are regarded as syndicated loans.[17] During 1996

---

[15] An important distinction exists between assets that are sold without recourse and those that are sold with recourse (i.e., the ability of a person or entity owning a negotiable instrument to compel payment). With securitized assets, usually no recourse exists; in the case of certain loan sales, however, recourse may exist. In the case of transactions with recourse clauses, the risks of the underlying asset have not been removed from the balance sheet.

[16] It is assumed that the transaction does not otherwise affect net income except for the increase in fee income net of any operating and servicing costs. Also, in terms of the balance-sheet constraint: Assets (A) = Liabilities (L) + Net Worth NW), when A declines, L declines (reduced funding) and the ratio of NW/A (the capital ratio) increases.

[17] Data and quotes in this paragraph are from a 1996 speech by the Comptroller of the Currency as reported in the *American Banker* (December 11, 1996), pp. 1-2. For an interesting analysis of the market for syndicated loans, see also Steven A. Dennis and Donald Mullineaux, "Syndicated Loans," paper presented at the European Finance Association Meetings, INSEAD, France (1998).

and 1997, these loans totaled more than $1 trillion in each year with corporate mergers driving the volume. The less developed countries' debt crisis of the 1980s and the commercial real estate crisis of the late 1980s and early 1990s prompted many large banks to avoid concentrations of credit greater than $20 million. As a result, syndicated lending has been growing at well over 20% per annum in the 1990s. This growth has been facilitated by the birth of the market for syndicated loans circa the mid-1980s, and more recently by the afterbirth of the segment devoted to leveraged loans. The result has been increased liquidity and efficiency. Moreover, interest by institutional investors has spurred the development of more objective risk measures based on such techniques of modern finance as portfolio theory and risk-based pricing.

Regulatory Concerns About Syndicated Loans

According to the Comptroller of the Currency, the rapid growth of syndicated lending has been fueled by underwriting standards that "continue to erode and have eroded to the point where there is not much farther they can go and remain prudent." The Comptroller was particularly concerned about "downstream participants" who were buying "thin" loans. Regarding the risks, the Comptroller's view was: "There's lots of money chasing deals, and people who are making decisions are running the risk of making bad decisions."

In a survey of syndicated lending by 82 national banks that covered the 12 months ending May 1996, the Office of the Comptroller of the Currency (OCC) found that 30% of the largest institutions had eased their lending standards. And, since then, examiners uncovered further reductions in underwriting standards. However, according to the OCC, its risk-based exams enabled it to be on top of the potential problem before any serious losses resulted. Nevertheless, the severity of the financial crises in Asia, Russia, and South America in 1998 indicate that neither lenders nor their regulators were on top of all the potential problems. Even more disturbing, however, was the lack of monitoring by lenders in the collapse and subsequent $3.5 billion bailout of Long-Term Capital Management LP, a hedge fund founded in 1993 and rescued in September 1998. Only ten days before the Fed-orchestrated bailout, Fed Chairman Alan Greenspan stated at a congressional hearing: "Hedge funds are strongly regulated by those who lend the money. They are not technically regulated in the sense that banks are, but they are under [a] fairly significant degree of surveillance."

The Comptroller of the Currency recommends several steps that bankers should take to avoid unnecessary risks posed by syndicated loans:

- Senior management should ensure that systems are in place to monitor exceptions to the bank's underwriting standards.
- Downstream participants (buyers) should conduct independent credit analysis of the deals and these judgments should dictate whether or not the bank participates in the loan.

- Banks should have strategies for backing out of participations.
- Buyers should not be pressured into participating to ensure they have enough time to do due-diligence analysis.
- Banks should stress test their portfolios against alternative economic scenarios to gauge their downside vulnerability. This focus highlights the economic "conditions" factor in the five Cs of credit analysis. The four other Cs are character, capacity (cash flow), capital (net worth), and collateral.

BARRIERS TO SECURITIZATION

Three barriers that can restrict lenders, especially community banks, from securitizing assets are size, recourse, and risk.

Size Considerations

To cost justify a private placement of securitized assets, a minimum pool of $50 million provides a realistic benchmark; for a public offering, about twice that size is required. Legal and investment banking fees are the major issuance costs. Because the U.S. banking system has thousands of banks whose total assets do not exceed $250 million, these banks are not capable, on an individual basis, of delivering such large pools of assets for sale. However, on a collective basis, via syndication or some other pooling method, community banks can combine resources to enter the securitization business.

Recourse

A second barrier to securitization focuses on the issue of recourse, which means that if any of the securitized assets defaults, the buyer then has a claim on the originator. If recourse is provided, an asset's risk is not effectively removed from the lender's balance sheet (i.e., it still must be backed by capital). Under current banking laws, assets sold with recourse are treated for the purpose of capital requirements as if they had not been sold. In addition, in the case of loan participations, buybacks are not permitted by banking laws. Thus, they are without recourse to the originator (seller). However, through standby letters of credit or other guarantees, the buyer may attempt to arrange legally to have indirect recourse to the originator.[18] Through the same process, securitized assets may establish contingent claims on the originating bank.

Risk Exposure

Is securitization all gain without any potential pain? From an investor's perspective (e.g., a community bank), securitized assets, as pools of loans, are safer than

---

[18] Christopher James shows that loan sales and loans backed by standby letters of credit have payoff characteristics similar to secured debt. As a result, banks can sell a portion of their cash flows associated with future growth options. Christopher James, "Off-Balance Sheet Activities and the Underinvestment Problem in Banking," *Journal of Accounting, Auditing, & Finance* (Spring 1989), pp. 111–24.

traditional loan sales or participations because they are diversified. Specifically, the pooled assets represent a number of borrowers rather than the one (or perhaps two) found in traditional loan sales. Statistically, pooling causes both the overall risk to be lower and the default rate to be more predictable than individual loans.

The adverse side of pooling is the inability of the buyer to assess the quality of the underlying credits. Rather than having one borrower to analyze, the buyer may have hundreds of credits in the package. Moreover, if the buyer does not have the time and expertise to analyze the credits, obtaining the documentation would be costly and defeat the purpose of engaging in securitization in the first place. Nevertheless, the buyer must watch out for "lemons." In this regard, market discipline is probably the buyer's best defense. Specifically, if an originator or packager of securitized assets gets a reputation for selling "lemons" (i.e., bad credits), its credibility in the marketplace will be tarnished. In the credit game, being a "scorned" player can be fatal because a bank's lifeblood, its liquidity, can dry up.

On the other side of the issue of reputation, an originator's quest for maintaining its own quality standing in credit markets may lead it to drain the best credits from its portfolio, leaving only weaker ones behind. If originators choose the former, buyers do not have to worry about loan quality; however, if they choose the latter, buyers must beware and conduct due diligence. Obviously, neither of these extremes would prevail in an efficient market. Specifically, a bank that sells bad credits will be discovered and not be able to sell its assets. Of course, if the loans are marketed as "junk securities," then no deception is involved. In this case, however, regulators probably would not permit community banks and thrifts to buy such high-risk securities. In contrast, a bank that keeps too many riskier credits will find the relative quality of its loan portfolio souring and its credit rating declining.

The solution to the originator's dilemma is to maintain a balance between the quality of its securitized assets and the quality of its own loan portfolio. In an efficient market, extreme behavior in either direction is likely to prove costly and to bring on greater regulatory intervention.

To summarize, consider the words of Henry Kaufman:[19] "There are hidden risks in securitization that from time to time result in very substantial losses. Securitization gives the illusion of unlimited liquidity and marketability." All markets have cycles, and the ABS market is not exempt from such fluctuations. Players in the securitization process must be aware of and prepare for unexpected changes in these underlying ("hidden") risks.

REGULATORY CONCERNS ABOUT STRUCTURED FINANCE

The Comptroller of the Currency has also expressed concerns about derivatives and structured finance and urged bankers to be prudent with such activities. For example, 1993 OCC Guidelines warn bankers: "In derivatives, the slicing, dicing,

---

[19] "Special Report: Corporate Finance," p. 136 (insert mine).

and recombining of risk elements of products makes it harder to see the risk. Banks need to be prepared to expect the unexpected...." To illustrate, Eugene A. Ludwig, former Comptroller of the Currency, described the kind of structured finance that concerned him: A bank with less than $200 million in assets that had a structured note in its investment portfolio where the interest rate was tied to the performance of the Deutsche mark and the Spanish peseta versus the dollar. He said: "We are not convinced that they have this instrument for legitimate hedging purposes or that they understand it." The initial rate on the note was 9%, but it subsequently paid no interest — and it lost 20% of its market value. While the popular press and Congress have emphasized the riskiness of derivatives, hedge funds, and other financial innovations, the Group of Thirty concluded that derivatives by their nature do not introduce risks of a fundamentally different kind or of a greater scale than those that already exist in the financial markets. Hence, systemic risks are not appreciably aggravated, and supervisory concerns can be addressed within present regulatory structures and approaches.

Given the hedge fund problem of 1998, it appears, however, that systemic risks were appreciably aggravated such that the Fed felt compelled to use its moral suasion to arrange a private bailout of Long-Term Capital Management (LTCM).

On the other hand, as Nobel Prize winner Merton Miller asks:[20] Since derivatives are zero-sum games, should we be concerned about these wealth transfers? Although LTCM racked up huge losses, we didn't hear about the huge gains booked by its counterparties. On balance, the hand wringing and cries for regulation of zero sum activities can be viewed as too much ado about nothing.

HOW STRATEGIC VALUE IS ADDED THROUGH SECURITIZATION AND STRUCTURED FINANCE

To see the value added through securitization and who receives that value, we need to consider the characteristics of the underlying assets before and after they are securitized. Exhibit 1 summarizes this information. In a nutshell, the process of securitization takes loans that are essentially illiquid and lacking transparency and makes them marketable securities that provide benefits to various parties.

As capital markets become more complete, financial intermediaries become less important as contact points between borrowers and savers. They become more important, however, as specialists that can perform the following functions:

- Complete markets by providing new products and services
- Transfer and distribute various risks via structured deals
- Use their reputation as delegated monitors to distinguish between high- and low-quality borrowers by providing third-party certifications of creditworthiness

---

[20] Merton H. Miller, *Merton Miller on Derivatives* (New York: John Wiley & Sons, Inc.).

Exhibit 1: The Bottom Line: Strategic Value Added Through Securitization

Characteristic of		Benefit to
Underlying asset (loan)	Securitized asset	
Illiquid	Liquid	Banks, investors, borrowers
Valuation lacks continuity and precision	Market values more efficient	Investors, banks
Credit analysis and monitoring by lender	Third parties assess risk	Banks, investors, third parties
High operating expenses	Lower operating costs	Banks, borrowers
Limited rates and terms offered to borrowers	Wider range of rates and terms	Borrowers, banks
Local market for investors	National and global investor markets	Investors, banks, third parties

Source: Adapted and expanded from Leon T. Kendall and Michael J. Fishman (eds.) *A Primer on Securitization* (Cambridge, MA: The MIT Press, 1996), Table 1.1, p. 5.

These changes represent a shift away from the administrative structures of traditional lending to market-oriented structures for allocating money and capital. More practically, these innovations capture attempts by banks to provide all the financing opportunities that existing and would-be customers need. Beyond providing structured products to survive, banks must do only value-creating deals for their shareholders. Value-destroying cannot be maintained over the long run. Nevertheless, bankers must analyze the overall profitability of customer relationships. Thus, while some structured products may not be profitable on a stand-alone basis, they may be necessary to maintain customer relationships. This discussion raises the important issue of products versus relationships. To illustrate, critics contend that Bankers Trust's focus on global wholesale and derivatives, in particular, led it to neglect developing long-term customer relationships. Following its derivatives' debacles of 1994, Bankers Trust focused on rebuilding relationships and even established a high-level committee devoted to building these relationships.

Although banking appears to be in transition from a relationship business to a commodity-driven product business, the ability to balance these two opposing forces may very well determine who survives in the FSI of the next millennium. Securitization and structured finance are important innovations driving this transition. Moreover, as the complexity of these processes increases, the effort and skills needed for successful management of these techniques also increase. Prior to the 1980s, banks were fairly content with the traditional lending function, including loan participations and syndicated lending. Today, however, banks, especially the larger ones, are increasingly originating loans with the idea of selling them or arranging loan syndications and buying the servicing rights of other securitized lenders. In addition, they are looking to do more complex structured deals and creating synthetic contracts (e.g., synthetic leases).

CAN COMMUNITY BANKS PLAY THE SECURITIZATION AND STRUCTURED FINANCE GAME?

Although the possibility of engaging in securitization and participations as originators is open to all banks, small banks in reality lack the size and reputation to be effective players in these activities. Moreover, since the 1982 failure of Penn Square Bank (Oklahoma City), bankers (and regulators) are much more cautious about who originates loan participations. Accordingly, the traditional lending function is separating along the lines of big banks as originators and little banks (but mainly securities investors) as suppliers of funds. In addition, foreign banks have been purchasing loans from large U.S. banks. Nevertheless, since community banks are literally and figuratively closer to their customers, they have an information advantage over large banks. However, as spreads on making loans funded by deposits are squeezed, community banks, like all other banks, must increase their fee income. Moreover, it is myopic to think that increasing fee income simply means nickel-and-diming retail customers to death.

Community banks must look for innovative ways to increase fee income. Securitization and structured finance offer two potential directions that community banks may pursue. One bank consultant offers yet another avenue:[21]

> Probably the most important fee business (for community banks) will be consumer-investment sales and trust management. What I'm saying to community banks is, if you don't offer the products, at least facilitate the transactions. Keep your customer relationship, maintain the point of sale, and generate fees.

Because the most important customers for community banks are retail and small business clients, community bankers need to structure deals to keep these relationships.

According to *The Economist*, "From cinema tickets to parking fines, almost everything is being securitized."[22] Although a bit of hyperbole, community bankers would settle for the opportunity to securitize small business loans. Enter Lori Mae, the Loan Origination Management and Exchange Corporation, a private company that securitizes small business loans originated by community banks.[23]

Lori Mae, which was established in 1997, helps community banks originate small business loans using software that facilitates standardization of processes and documents for credit applications, analyses, and closings. Armed with loans written to a uniform set of pricing and underwriting guidelines, Lori Mae stands ready to buy the loans and securitize them. The originating community banks retain all servicing rights, customer contact, and some portion of ownership.

---

[21] Federal Home Loan Bank of Boston, "Community Banks: How to Thrive in Our Rapidly Consolidating Industry" (1997). See "Success Stories" at www.fhlbboston.com.

[22] *The Economist* (May 9, 1998), p. 71.

[23] For information about Lori Mae, see *America's Community Banker* (May 7, 1997) and Matt Chapman, "Using Securitization to Maintain Small Business Market Share," *US Banker* (September 1997), p. 68.

Credit scoring represents another technological innovation that has made inroads into small business lending. This technique develops a statistical relationship between a borrower's financial characteristics and its probability of loan repayment. Each borrower's credit score provides an objective criterion to be used in conjunction with other information to judge the borrower's creditworthiness. Lenders at large banks view credit-scoring models applied to small business loans as one way of competing with the information advantage of community bankers. A Pittsburgh banker who uses credit scoring puts it this way:[24] "If we are going to grow at the rate we want to, we have to go outside our geographic market. When we go to Kansas, we will have the lowest costs and go after the highest credit quality."

Because community bankers presumably have the time, personnel, and local knowledge to conduct detailed reviews of loan applications, they don't use credit-scoring techniques. Nevertheless, the shift to credit scoring by out-of-area lenders could have important implications for the market share of small business loans held by community banks. From this perspective, community bankers need to consider whether credit scoring can be used to reduce their lending costs without compromising their reputations for service. Without human input, however, blind use of a credit-scoring model is a disaster waiting to happen.

Credit scoring and securitization take community banks further down the road toward a product-driven business and further away from a relationship-driven trade. Although such a path may seem anathema to community bankers who pride themselves as service providers, it may be inevitable for their survival.

THE NEXT MILLENNIUM IN THE FINANCIAL-SERVICES INDUSTRY

The pressures for generating fee income, providing liquidity, and meeting capital requirements have led all FSFs, but especially large commercial banks, to securitize assets, syndicate loans, and engage in structured finance. Although banks have been doing loan syndications for years, securitization and structured finance with derivatives are more recent phenomena. Some observers see them as the financial innovations for the next millennium.

As financial markets become more complete, the continued existence of banks and other financial intermediaries is challenged. As securitization and structured finance are two innovations that present both opportunities and risks for banks, FSF managers must think about the strategic uses and threats associated with these innovations. Because the raising of debt through commercial paper and corporate bonds in financial markets is not new and because these secu-

---

[24] As reported by Ron Feldman, "Small Business Loans, Small Banks and a Big Change in Technology Called Credit Scoring," *Economic Review*, Federal Reserve Bank of Minneapolis (September 1997).

rities are substitutes for bank loans (i.e., asset disintermediation), structured or hybrid finance can be viewed as part of the continuum between direct and indirect finance, albeit one that has more bells and whistles than plain-vanilla financing.

Securitization and structured finance represent two trends in the FSI and modern banking. The forces of change associated with technology, taxes, regulation, and competition help explain why banks are undertaking nontraditional activities and nonbanks are undertaking banking activities. Within the context of the ROE model (in which ROE = ROA × EM), the downward pressures on both ROA and EM reflect these forces of change in ways that get managers' attention, thus explaining why they want to move assets off their balance sheets and attempt to service all the financing needs, including risk management services, of existing and would-be customers. Moreover, the important role that noninterest or fee income has played in improving bank profitability can be traced, in part, to securitization and structured finance, especially among the largest commercial banks. These structural shifts permit FSFs, all other things being equal, to (1) increase ROA through the generation of fee income, (2) generate liquidity, and (3) remove assets from their balance sheets, easing the increasing pressure imposed by higher capital requirements.

Nevertheless, when FSFs have easier access to alternative markets (e.g., bank equity markets) as they have recently, they feel less pressure to get assets off their balance sheets. It is helpful to think of these two points in terms of the equity multiplier (where EM = assets/equity — the leverage factor in banking). That is, securitization removes assets from bank balance sheets, while easier access to equity markets provides external sources of capital. Thus, market and regulatory pressures for adequate capital can be met by either method or a combination of the two.

While syndicated lending has been a traditional technique for spreading risk, it competes with securitization, structured finance, and other synthetic securities in the dynamic markets of the FSI. The bottom line is that banks are doing nonbank things and vice versa. In the process, banking moves more and more toward becoming a commodity-driven product business and away from its traditional lending function tied to customer relationships. The recent development of the subprime market for home equity and automobile loans illustrates this phenomenon.

The FSI can be viewed as undergoing a metamorphosis much like that of a caterpillar into a butterfly. The slow moving caterpillar reflects traditional banking, while the dramatic and dynamic changes taking place in the modern FSI are the forces pushing the butterfly out of its protective cocoon. In a less-protected environment, failures, as shown by the U.S. S&L and banking crises of the 1980s and early 1990s, and extensive consolidation within (e.g., the combination of NationsBank and Bank of America) and among industries (e.g., Citigroup) are not unexpected. Although the modern FSI butterfly is still evolving, it is too late to reverse the process and return to the caterpillar days of traditional banking. In a globalized world, the butterfly also is vulnerable, as witnessed by the international financial crises and hedge-funds problems of the late 1990s. The changing FSI and the advent of structured finance are symptoms of the shift from traditional lending structures to market structures for allocating money and capital — the ultimate function of a financial system.

Chapter 8

The Structure, Economics, and Risk of Conduits

Peter J. Elmer
Senior Economist
Division of Research and Statistics
FDIC

INTRODUCTION

One of the most important financial developments of the past two decades has been the growth of asset securitization. Given that securitization requires a complex combination of many financial intermediaries, the growth of securitization has spawned new types of intermediaries that specialize in understanding and developing the opportunities posed by securitization. Those new to securitization are often confused by the purpose of the new intermediaries, as they contain elements of traditional banking- and securities-related activities, but incorporate new and unique activities as well.

Among the most confusing securitization-related institutions are a group of intermediaries called "conduits."[1] These institutions are financial organizations whose business purpose is buying loans or other financial assets with the goal of earning a profit by repackaging and selling the assets as securities. That is, a conduit is a business that specializes in buying loans and other types of financial assets, then securitizing those assets and selling the securities in the capital markets.

At first blush, the business of buying loans at one price, then selling the loans through securitization at a higher price, appears to be a type of arbitrage.

---

[1] Adding to the confusion is the fact that the term conduit has been used to describe other entities. For example, the term has been used to describe bankruptcy-remote companies formed for the special purpose of issuing securities that are effectively collateralized by loans or other assets held by the company, such as asset-backed commercial paper. These conduits act more like trusts or financial vehicles for issuing securities than they do as independent organizations seeking a profit. The 1986 Tax Act used the term in a different context when it named a vehicle for structuring securities Real Estate Mortgage Investment Conduit (REMIC). These legal structures are best thought of as a special class of securities rather than as ongoing business enterprises.

This chapter is adapted from Peter J. Elmer, "Conduits: Their Structure and Risk," *FDIC Banking Review*, 12:3, 1999, pp. 27-40.

However, the substantial time, resources, and risk required to execute the strategy suggest that conduits are more appropriately viewed as performing a business than an arbitrage. Indeed, as we shall see, the host of problems encountered by conduits during the late 1990s suggest that their activities involve considerable risk, to the point that it may no longer be possible for conduits to exist as independent of organizations, but represent a viable function when incorporated into larger organizations with closely related activities.

CONDUIT STRUCTURE

Conduits began in the early 1980s by buying mortgages from originators, then securitizing the mortgages as mortgage-backed securities. Several government agencies, such as the Federal Home Loan Mortgage Corporation (Freddie Mac) and the Federal National Mortgage Association (Fannie Mae), had already proved that this could be done with government backing, so why not try it from a private base?

Conduits soon found that the business of buying and securitizing loans involves a remarkable array of activities and participants. As illustrated by Exhibit 1, "buy" side purchase programs must be set up with any of a variety of originators, such as banks, thrifts, and mortgage bankers. Loan servicers must be found to service the loans after sale, and "sell" side securities sales capabilities established with securities brokers and dealers.

However, even with the origination, servicing, and security-sale functions performed by other firms, a host of activities remain the responsibility of the conduit. For example, underwriting guidelines must be established, quality-control procedures implemented, funding secured, and interest-rate risk managed while the loans are held in portfolio. Long after the securities are sold, a variety of commitments may remain relating to representations (reps) and warranties, investor relations, and the maintenance of residual interests retained in the security.[2]

As a conduit grows, the need for internal support functions increases as well. Elements of risk management and quality control must to be set in place. As more investors hold the securities, investor-relations personnel must be added. The growth of internal staff implies a need for more sophisticated accounting and personnel functions. Thus, even a relatively simple conduit with a narrow product focus can quickly become a sizable operation.

Almost every activity shown in Exhibit 1 represents a merger opportunity for conduits. Since the lifeblood of a conduit is a steady supply of loans, expansion into the loan origination side of Exhibit 1 offers conduits the opportunity to control the flow of incoming loans. This control can be extended by either purchasing loan origination capabilities directly, or expanding into related functions, such as warehouse lending and real estate financing.

---

[2] For a discussion of reps and warranties, see Penelopy Moreland-Gunn, Peter J. Elmer, and Timothy J. Curry, "Reps and Warranties," *FDIC Banking Review*, 1995, 8:3, pp. 1-9.

Exhibit 1: Conduits and Securitization

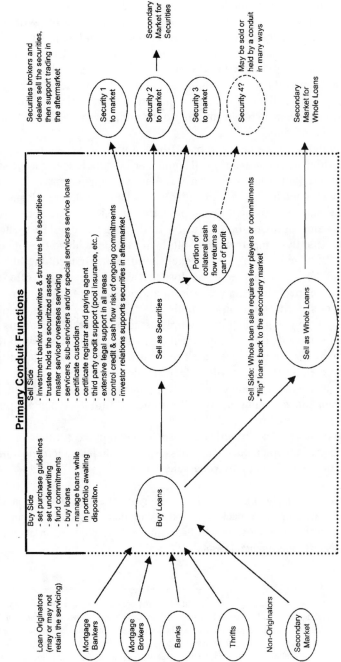

Primary Conduit Functions

Buy Side
- set purchase guidelines
- set underwriting
- fund commitments
- buy loans
- manage loans while in portfolio awaiting disposition.

Sell Side
- investment banker underwrites & structures the securities
- trustee holds the securitized assets
- master servicer oversees servicing
- servicers, sub-servicers and/or special servicers service loans
- certificate custodian
- certificate registrar and paying agent
- third party credit support (pool insurance, etc.)
- extensive legal support in all areas
- control credit & cash flow risk of ongoing commitments
- investor relations supports securities in aftermarket

Securities brokers and dealers sell the securities, then support trading in the aftermarket

Secondary Market for Securities

Security 1 to market

Security 2 to market

Security 3 to market

Security 4? — May be sold or held by a conduit in many ways

Sell as Securities

Portion of collateral cash flow returns as part of profit

Sell Side: Whole loan sale requires few players or commitments — "flip" loans back to the secondary market

Sell as Whole Loans

Secondary Market for Whole Loans

Buy Loans

Loan Originators (may or may not retain the servicing)

Mortgage Bankers

Mortgage Brokers

Banks

Thrifts

Non-Originators

Secondary Market

Servicing also represents a natural avenue for conduit expansion. Affiliating with a loan servicer enables conduits to purchase loans on either a servicing "released" or a servicing "retained" basis. That is, affiliating with a servicer allows a conduit to offer a premium for loans that are sold with their servicing, or pay a lower price and let the originator retain the servicing.[3] On the one hand, this flexibility appeals to sellers with little interest in servicing the loans after origination, such as loan brokers, while on the other hand it generates a flow of new servicing to servicer affiliates. Developing an extensive servicing network has other strategic advantages, such as providing opportunities to refinance loans and to cross-sell other products.

Conduits can also expand by affiliating with securities-related firms. As shown in Exhibit 1, conduits may sell some loans as whole loans at the same time they pool and sell other loans as securities. For example, loans with exceptionally high quality may fetch a higher price if sold as whole loans, while loans with very poor quality, such as those with legal problems or unique characteristics, may be preempted from inclusion in a security. In this regard, conduit securitization activities constantly compete with whole-loan sales to achieve the highest possible value ("best" execution) for any package of loans. Indeed, the link between conduits and the capital markets is so close that Wall Street dealers often maintain their own conduits, which may be run in an independent fashion or alongside whole-loan or securities trading functions.

Apart from expanding into complementary businesses, conduits throughout the 1990s expanded into complementary loan product lines. Given their start with mortgages, conduits were quick to securitize mortgage-related products, such as home equity loans and manufactured housing, as well as other types of consumer loans, such as credit cards and auto loans. From these roots in mortgage and consumer loans, conduits naturally branched into all types of commercial loans and receivables.

In summary, opportunities abound for conduits to affiliate and integrate with a variety of complementary businesses. Nevertheless, their most basic economic function is defined by two characteristics:

- they are engaged in the business of buying or accumulating financial assets for the purpose of packaging and selling them as securities, and
- they maintain close ties to the many players required in assembling and securitizing financial assets.

---

[3] The idea that servicing has value is confusing outside of the area of mortgage finance, because servicers incur significant expense in collecting and managing loan cash flows. However, buyers of loans often require the servicing fees paid to servicers to exceed the cost of servicing loans, as an incentive to maintain high quality servicing. When servicing fee income exceeds the cost incurred from servicing, the "right" to service loans has value. Selling loans on a servicing-released basis allows an originator to collect at least a portion of the value associated with servicing at the time the loan is sold.

These core activities generate two primary sources of income — the income deriving from holding performing loans in inventory and, especially, the income generated when loans are packaged and sold as securities. [4]

CONDUIT ECONOMICS: INVENTORY AND THE VALUE OF SPREAD

The starting point of the value created by conduit activities is the accumulation of inventory in anticipation of packaging and sale as a security. The most common approach involves linking to a source of newly originated loans or receivables, then waiting for the flow of loans purchased to build an inventory sufficient to issue a security. The flow of loans can come either from internal originators or from a variety of external sources, such as networks of correspondent originators, a limited network of wholesalers, or Wall Street. Most conduits cultivate networks of originators in an effort to ensure a steady flow of product. Buying loans from Wall Street dealers is problematic because the dealer markets are very competitive and the flow of loans is erratic. Moreover, Wall Street dealers often use their own conduits to securitize whole loans purchased through the capital markets, effectively limiting the ability of other buyers to profitably securitize loans purchased from the Wall Street dealers.

The level of loans in inventory traces a saw-tooth pattern: inventory builds, then drops at each securitization or whole-loan sale. At any point the inventory of loans may be substantial because not all loans may fit or work well in every securitization. The bulk of the loans are packaged in pools of at least $100 million to $200 million of relatively homogeneous loans. Unusual and heterogeneous loans are placed into securities with "miscellaneous" loans or are sold as whole loans. At the end of quarterly or yearly accounting cycles, a special effort may be made to reduce inventory by either securitizing or selling the excess loans.

Loans in inventory give rise to one source of conduit income, which is the interest-rate spread, or "carry," from loans held in portfolio. This income varies directly with the length of time the loans are held. Since most loans held by conduits are newly originated, there is little likelihood of default during the several months they may be held in the conduit's inventory "pipeline" awaiting securitization. During this period of low credit risk, conduits earn the difference between the interest income received from loans held in portfolio and the interest expense paid to fund those loans, net of hedge costs. That is,

$$\text{Carry} = \text{Interest Inc.} - \text{Interest Exp.} - \text{Hedge Cost} \tag{1}$$

---

[4] The two sources of income discussed in this chapter are the primary — but not necessarily the only — sources of income arising from conduit activities, especially for conduits that have branched into related activities. Conduits that originate loans earn income from origination fees, while those involved in warehouse lending, servicing, or other activities generate income from these endeavors. It is also possible for conduits to simplify their operations to the point that they earn income from only one source, for example, by not holding loans in portfolio before securitization.

Exhibit 2: Spreads from "Carrying" Commercial Mortgages

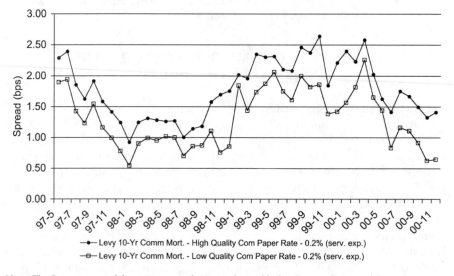

Note: The Levy commercial mortgage rate is reported monthly by *Barons*. Commercial paper rates are from Bloomberg Financial Markets. All yields are computed on a bond yield basis.

To further simplify, one can reasonably assume that the cost of hedging some types of risks, such as the risk of a general rise in interest rates, is relatively small, so these risks can be ignored for this analysis. Other risks that are difficult or expensive to hedge will be considered below in a discussion of conduit risks.

Exhibit 2 illustrates spreads earned during the 1997–2000 period by conduits carrying commercial mortgages. That is, the spreads reflect the difference between the interest income earned on long-term fixed-rate commercial mortgages and the interest expense paid on 3-month commercial paper, net of 20 basis points for servicing, hedging, or administrative expenses. The two series reflect the different net yields earned by conduits with relatively high versus low commercial paper funding costs.

The spreads in Exhibit 2 suggest that, during the late 1990s, the carry earned by commercial mortgage conduits with relatively low funding costs fell in the 1.0%–2.5% range, averaging about 1.80%. This translates to a value of about 60 basis points when the loan is carried for four months, or a value of 15 basis points if it is carried for only one month. The spreads were about 50 basis points lower for conduits that funded at the more expensive end of the commercial paper market. However, the 50 basis points of higher interest expense appear modest, given the fact that the total carry remained positive throughout the late 1990s and that the carry represents only one of two sources of conduit income. Moreover, funding expenses should not significantly limit competition, as hundreds of firms can fund within the high- and low-cost ends of the commercial paper market.

CONDUIT ECONOMICS: THE VALUE OF THE DEAL

The primary source of conduit income is the value of the "deals" created by packaging loans and selling them as securities. What often makes this value seem anomalous is that securitization represents simply a repackaging of cash flows. In fact, some securities, known as "passthroughs," are structured to have almost no effect on the cash flows of the underlying loans. Nevertheless, the additional liquidity and other advantages of securitized pools enhance value to the point that the value of the securities and other assets created from a pool exceeds the value of the corresponding loans; if it does not, the pool will be either held in portfolio or sold as whole loans.

Securitization deals have two basic structures. The most commonly used structure grants security investors an interest in the *specific assets* placed in a securitization trust, which is administered by the trustee. This structure is used for "closed-end" loans, such as mortgages or auto loans, because their maturities and payments are well defined. As the principal balance of the loans in the trust is paid down, so is the principal of the securities created by the trust. When the initial assets are paid off, the securities must also be paid off and the trust is dissolved. The second type of securitization structure grants investors an interest in a *pool of assets* without listing the specific assets that will be in the pool throughout its life. This structure is designed to hold loans with loosely defined maturates and/or highly variable characteristics, such as credit cards. This structure permits a "revolving asset" arrangement whereby paid off loans are replaced with new loans possessing similar characteristics. Generally speaking, the total balance of the loans is maintained even though the specific loans in the pool change. Since the payoff of the initial collateral bears no particular relation to the payoff of the securities, the principal balance of the corresponding securities remains relatively stable until the trust permits the payoff of principal.

Regardless of the differences between structures, the generation of value is relatively consistent. That is, in both structures the value created by securitization is the difference between the value of the securities ("classes," or "tranches") and other assets created by the deal, and the value of the loans or receivables placed in the deal, net of underwriting and sale-related costs. That is,

$$
\begin{aligned}
\text{Value of Securitization} = {} & \text{Value of Class A} + \text{Value of Class B} + \ldots \\
& + \text{Value of Excess Interest} + \text{Value of Excess Servicing} \\
& + \text{Value of the Residual (or Seller's Interest) Class} \\
& - \text{Cost of Assets} - \text{Underwriting/Sale Expenses} \quad (2)
\end{aligned}
$$

It is common for each deal to contain several or more classes of securities with different credit ratings, because doing so broadens the market for the securities, thereby enhancing the total value of the package. Unfortunately, however, all cash flows in a deal cannot be included into easily sold securities due to their higher risk. Therefore, the higher risk cash flows are used to produce several other types of assets, such as excess interest, excess servicing, and residuals. A deal makes economic sense when the total value of the securities and other assets created exceeds the cost of the assets by a minimum threshold required to compensate the conduit for its expenses, including equity.

Exhibit 3 depicts the creation of value that arises when the two primary components of a package of commercial-loan cash flows — principal and interest — are split.[5] The total principal balance of all loans in the pool is allocated to at least one class of bonds. Typically the principal is divided into one or more large pieces with AAA or AA credit ratings that are "senior" in priority to several smaller "subordinated" pieces with credit ratings below the AA range, which are often referred to as "mezzanine" classes. For example, Exhibit 3 shows a $75 AAA-rated senior security created by subordinating 25% of the principal among five mezzanine classes of securities with varying sizes and credit ratings. The residual, or "R," class claims bits and pieces of cash flows that are not claimed by any other class.

Exhibit 3: Sample Principal and Interest Distributions for Commercial Mortgage Senior/Subordinated Securitization

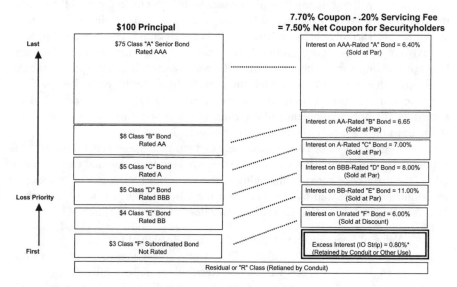

* Excess interest = net coupon (7.50%) less the combined interest expense of the bonds, $((0.75 \times 6.40) + (0.08 \times 6.65) + (0.05 \times 7.00) + (0.05 \times 8.00) + (0.04 \times 11.00) + (0.03 \times 6.0))$

---

[5] Exhibit 3 represents a security created from a specific pool of assets, such as mortgages or auto loans. However, securities created for revolving loan products, such as credit cards, tend to produce many of the same unusual assets, such as excess interest and excess servicing. One asset unique to a revolving loan deal, the "seller's interest," is similar to the residual in a specific asset structure.

Subordinated bonds have lower ratings than senior bonds because they stand ready to absorb default-related losses before those losses can be applied to bonds with senior priority. The subordinated bonds are often sliced into several classes with varying credit ratings that depend on the level of subordination supporting each bond. Bonds in the BBB and higher "investment grade" rating range are normally easier to price and sell. The bond with the lowest priority has the highest risk of loss and, if rated, has the lowest credit rating. However, the highest-risk bonds may not be rated because they are either retained by the issuer, an affiliate, or privately placed to sophisticated investors. Since only a limited number of buyers purchase the highest-risk bonds, selling these components of the securitization can be the pivotal factor in consummating a deal.

The level of credit support or subordination varies with the risk of the underlying loan collateral. Securitizing loans with higher levels of default risk, such as second mortgages, results in higher levels of subordination and therefore a smaller senior class of AAA rated securities. Similarly, loans with lower default risk, such as first mortgages with low loan-to-value ratios, require lower levels of subordination, leaving a larger senior class. Thus, the risk of the underlying loans is directly related to the level of subordination required to secure the AA-AAA rated senior class securities. In this regard, it is a mistake to interpret relatively high levels of subordination as suggesting a lower-risk security, as they actually indicate higher-risk loans in the underlying collateral.

Splitting the interest component of the cash flows is distinct from splitting the principal cash flows. While all principal is allocated to the bonds, all interest may not be. In essence, the coupon rate on the loan collateral, net of servicing fees, tends to exceed the weighted average interest rate required by the market on the securities backed by the loans, and this generates "excess interest." Excess interest can be lumped into servicing contracts to generate excess servicing, or it can be formally structured as an interest-only (IO) strip, or it can be used to cover losses, or it can be allocated in a variety of ways to the residual. Portions of the excess interest may be held by a conduit, in which case accounting and valuation issues arise. (This is discussed further below.)[6] Thus, excess interest is central to an understanding of the most problematic assets and issues associated with securitization.

Exhibit 3 illustrates the creation of excess interest in a deal that allocates the excess to a separate claim retained by the conduit. In the example, the AAA rated class pays a rate of only 6.40%, which represents an interest savings of 110 basis points vis-à-vis the 7.50% net coupon received from the loan collateral. The

---

[6] The IO strip adds significant complexity to a deal because it can be structured in many ways. For example, the IO strip may be formed into a separate security (as suggested by Exhibit 3), used as first-loss credit support, included as a portion of the residual, or made a part of excess servicing. The easiest way to use the strip is simply to sell it and collect its value up front. However, since the strip often has very high risk, especially before the underlying pool has established a payment history, its market value tends to be relatively low when the security is created. Issuers hold either all or a portion of the strip to avoid deep market discounts on value while generating cash flow and assuring investors that they have retained a financial interest in the deal.

AA rated class pays 6.65% for an interest savings of 85 basis points. Bond yields do not rise above the net loan coupon until the class "D" bond, rated BBB. This and other lower-rated bonds use up some, but not all, of the interest savings associated with the higher-rated bonds. The end result of receiving 7.50% net interest from the loan, then paying between 6% and 11% on the bonds, is an IO strip equaling 80 basis points or 0.8%.

As we have said, excess interest may be formally structured as an IO strip, in which case the value of the IO strip represents most of the profit available to compensate conduits for their efforts. For example, in Exhibit 3 the present value of the 0.8% IO strip is about 3.10–4.50 points, which is much larger than the 0.15–0.60 points estimated above as the value of the pipeline "carry" between one and four months, respectively.

We can now estimate the value that securitization creates. To simplify matters, assume that (1) the carry is used to cover sale expenses, (2) the rated classes ("A" through "E") are sold at par, and (3) the class with no rating (class "F") is sold at 50% of its face value. Given these assumptions, the value created by the securitization shown in Exhibit 3 falls in the range of 1.60%–3.00% of the original balance of the securitized loans.[7] This estimate suggests that the profit margin accruing to the securitization of mortgage-related assets is very "thin," implying that small changes in the economic environment can have a substantial impact on the economic viability of securitization. For example, if the mortgage rate fall 25 basis points below the 7.70% rate used in Exhibit 3, and all other rates remain unchanged, the value of our sample securitization falls from the 1.60-3.00 range to the 0.60-1.60 range, which is normally considered too small a profit to justify doing the deal. Thus, seemingly small fluctuations in market rates and spreads can have a dramatic impact on the profitability of securitization, and economic viability of conduit operations.

The tendency to hold, in one form or another, significant portions of excess interest adds considerable complexity to conduit operations. That is, conduits often become involved in the investment and management of unusual cash flows, residuals, and other remnants of the securitization process. During periods of stability these unusual arrangements can generate a rewarding flow of income that can be valued and accounted for in an acceptable fashion. During times of stress, however, cash flow, accounting, valuation, and other issues can quickly overwhelm conduits.

ELEMENTS OF RISK

Conduits enjoyed remarkable success during much of the 1990s. As shown in Exhibit 4, the value of publicly traded conduit equity increased much faster than

---

[7] This calculation values an 0.80% strip from a commercial mortgage with a 30-year amortization schedule, a balloon at the end of 15 years, a gross coupon of 7.70%, and a prepayment rate that begins at 0, then rises to 5% at the 30th and following months. For this scenario, the strip value equals 4.49 and 3.07 points at discount rates of 10% and 20%, respectively. Subtracting 1.50 points for the discount on class "F" results in an approximate range of 1.60–3.00 points.

the value of the stock market until early 1997. This conduit success was attributable to a robust economic environment, a relatively stable financial environment, and a broadening range of financial products securitized by conduits. During the mid-1990s conduits quickly carved niches for themselves by learning to securitize new loan products, such as commercial mortgages, manufactured housing loans, and home equity loans. As securitization brought new funds to well established loan products, some conduits ventured into riskier types of loans, thereby setting the stage for additional securitizations, but at the cost of additional risk.

The stock index in Exhibit 4 suggests that conduits began encountering problems in early 1997, followed by a nearly complete recovery. A second round of problems developed in the latter half of 1997, but this was followed by only a modest recovery. The industry has yet to recover from a third, disastrous drop in the second half of 1998. The problems encountered by conduits during the 1997–1998 period serve to illustrate nine elements of conduit risk.[8]

Exhibit 4: Value of Public Conduit Equity versus S&P 500

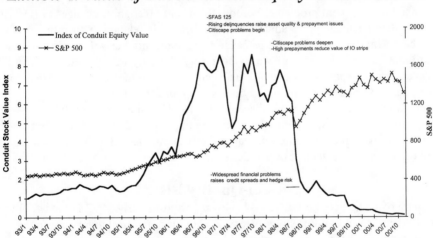

Note: The index of conduit equity, set with January 1993 = 1, is calculated by summing the value of public equity of six public conduits listed in the top 25 conduits by The Mortgage Market Statistical Annual for 1998: Firstplus Financial Group, Advanta Corp., Aames Financial Corporation, AMRESCO, Citiscape Financial Corporation, IMC Mortgage, and Southern Pacific. Two other public conduits in this listing, Greentree Financial Corp. and The Money Store, Inc. were omitted from the index because they were purchased by other institutions in 1998 prior to the decline in the stock market July 1998.

[8] Comments about the risk-related problems of individual financial institutions were gathered from news articles reported on Bloomberg Financial Markets. The elements of risk presented here provide an overview of the topic, with special emphasis on problems observed in the 1997–1998 period. Thus, the list of risks is not comprehensive.

Accounting Risk

At the start of 1997, conduits had to confront a fundamental change in their accounting practices because of a new accounting rule, Statement of Financial Accounting Standards No. 125 (SFAS 125). SFAS 125 requires that entities recognize, or "book," the value of financial and servicing assets and liabilities that remain under their control after a securitization. In particular, conduits are required to estimate and record as a gain-on-sale the value of excess servicing fees and related IO strips. IO strips are treated like marketable equity securities, so they must be carried at fair market value throughout their lives — a requirement that implies the possibility of adjusting entries in the event the value of the asset changes.

SFAS 125 affected conduit financial reporting in two ways. First, conduits began recognizing the value of IO strips as gains-on-sale. Although this reporting necessarily improves the transparency of conduit financial statements with respect to the types of assets held, it significantly raises reported earnings and equity at the issuance date of each securitization. In addition, the reported gains reflect projections of uncertain cash flows. The fact that the cash flows are often irregular and may not begin until several years after a securitization is completed gives rise to financial management problems. Second, the need to recognize changes in IO strip values often results in profit adjustments that bear little relation to operating performance during the same period. Because benchmark market values are often not available on IO strips and other related assets, the only way to determine an IO strip's value is to perform present-value calculations. But these estimates are notoriously sensitive to a variety of underlying assumptions (ranging from loan payoff and default rates to the present-value discount rate), and considerable discretion exists in the setting of these assumptions. Thus, interpreting reported values is difficult. Even modest changes in the assumptions can produce significant adjustments to earnings and capital, adjustments that bear little relation to current operating cash flows.

Asset-Quality Risk

A spate of unexpected credit card losses reported in early 1997 helped fuel the first downturn in conduit stock prices. Although portfolio lenders continued to more than cover their losses with the high interest rates received on loans, the asset-quality problems that had surfaced raised special issues for conduits. The IO strips, residuals, and other remnants of a securitization are often exposed to much higher levels of credit risk than are found in traditional portfolio structures. Conduits that elect to hold subordinated and other remnants used as credit support probably carry much more credit risk in a given level of assets than does a traditional lender holding a comparable level of loans. Moreover, the value of other remnants that ostensibly have no credit risk can also be adversely affected by credit problems. For example, a rise in delinquencies can squeeze the excess interest generated by a pool, thereby reducing the value of IO strips that might otherwise have no credit risk. Per SFAS 125, a drop in excess interest can force a downward adjustment of IO asset values and of a firm's capital.

Servicing Risk

In the spring of 1997 asset-quality problems highlighted another dimension of risk for Cityscape Financial Corp. (Cityscape). In April of that year Moody's downgraded Cityscape's bonds, citing asset-quality problems and the fear that Cityscape's servicing capabilities were not prepared to deal with higher levels of problem assets. As noted earlier, there are sound business reasons for conduits to integrate servicing into their internal operations.

Nevertheless, servicing is a distinct business function with its own risks and efficiencies. For example, significant economies of scale accrue to larger servicing operations, and the quality of the assets serviced plays an important role in the determination of servicing expenses. Delinquent and defaulted loans are much more expensive to service than performing loans, especially for smaller and inexperienced servicers in nontraditional loan products. High-cost servicing can directly reduce excess interest, and inefficient servicing can raise default rates. Conduits that service the loans in their securities risk higher expenses, and if delinquencies rise above the expected levels, these higher expenses will coincide with a drop in the value of IO strips and other assets.

Regulatory Risk

In mid-1997 Cityscape encountered a second round of problems, this time with a regulatory and political origin in the United Kingdom. Several years earlier Cityscape had grown its operations in the United Kingdom through loans to individuals with high credit risk (sub-prime loans). In addition to requiring high interest rates, these loans also imposed high penalties for delinquency. As delinquencies rose so did the penalties, along with political pressure in the United Kingdom for consumer relief. Cityscape finally acquiesced by reducing its penalties, but these reductions cut into Cityscape's anticipated income. In the end, uncertainty enveloped earnings from loans originated in the United Kingdom, forcing write-downs of IO strips and similar assets, per SFAS 125.

Cityscape's problems in the United Kingdom illustrate the influences that political and regulatory factors may have on the management and value of outstanding loans. Sovereign authorities always retain the ability to change or otherwise affect a variety of elements in the lending and loan-management environment, ranging from fair lending practices to bankruptcy laws. This intervention is especially likely in high-risk consumer lending, an activity embraced by many conduits in the 1990s but nevertheless a relatively new area for which regulatory concerns were uncharted.

Originator (Rep and Warranty) Risk

Fraud by originators is an especially sensitive issue for conduits because their core business involves purchasing loans originated by other entities. Association with inappropriate origination procedures not only reflects badly on a conduit's ability to control the quality of the loans it has securitized but also raises questions about the quality of loans in any of its securities. Of course, conduits rely on the reps and warranties made by originators before they make similar reps and warranties on the loans they place in securities, so they have recourse to originators if problems are detected. However, this recourse has little value if the originator is small or otherwise unable to repurchase problem loans. Moreover, smaller conduits may have little capacity either to deal with legal problems related to bad loans or to manage the bad loans themselves. SFAS 125 may enter the picture as well by requiring write-downs to IO strip and similar asset values.

Prepayment Risk

Falling interest rates during the second half of 1997 raised concerns about prepayment risk. The decline in interest rates inevitably raised prepayment rates for many types of consumer loans and, accordingly, raised the possibility of adjusting IO strip, excess servicing, and other related asset values, per SFAS 125. However, prepayment risk was especially uncertain for home equity, sub prime, and other types of consumer loans that had been originated in volume, and through conduit channels, for only a few years. The prepayment characteristics of borrowers found through direct mail, borrowers with credit problems, and borrowers having no ongoing relation with the originating lender could simply not be known until a cycle of prepayments had run its course. Complicating matters was the fact that after years of increasing competition for home equity and high-risk borrowers, market interest rates for these types of consumer loans fell, thereby increasing the potential savings to these borrowers from refinancing. In the end, several types of consumer loans securitized by conduits responded to falling rates with substantial refinancing activity, and this activity generated write-downs of IO strip-related assets, per SFAS 125.

Hedge Risk

Global financial stress and the stock market meltdown in mid-1998 marked the start of new problems for conduits. The financial problems of mid-1998 helped motivate a rise in the market cost of credit risk, causing spreads-to-Treasuries to rise, even as the general level of interest rates fell. This market anomaly exposed the true meaning of "hedge risk." For most changes in interest rates, standard hedging practices mitigate risk for a reasonable cost. However, when spreads-to-Treasuries widen, hedging activities often fail to mitigate interest-rate risk. In this case, holding substantial amounts of loans can result in losses many times greater than the modest "carry" that accrues from holding loans with lower-cost financing earns. For example, Exhibit 5 shows commercial mortgage spreads increasing over 100 basis points in the fall of 1998, an increase that could easily cause hedge losses to exceed the full benefit expected from a securitization. This problem of hedge losses was encountered by conduits with many types of loans, including products such as commercial loans that had largely escaped the consumer finance trials of 1997.

Exhibit 5: Spreads-to-Treasuries for Commercial Mortgages versus AAA and BBB Commercial Mortgage Securities

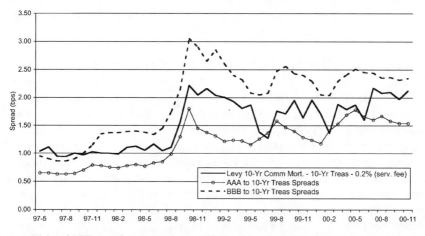

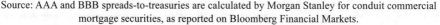

Source: AAA and BBB spreads-to-treasuries are calculated by Morgan Stanley for conduit commercial mortgage securities, as reported on Bloomberg Financial Markets.

Market Risk

Exhibit 5 also illustrates the less-favorable market conditions conduits confronted after the jump in spreads in October 1998. One can see this by comparing the mortgage versus AAA and BBB spreads in Exhibit 5. Before October 1998, commercial mortgage rates were always above the rates on securities created from loans in the AAA range, but after that date the difference between the rates was much wider. When this difference narrows, conduits find it harder to securitize loans profitably. The immediate effect is that conduits have more difficulty making the profit on each securitization needed to justify continued activity. Moreover, higher spreads for investment-grade securities are often associated with much higher spreads for non-investment-grade securities, as well as greater difficulty finding buyers for the non-investment-grade classes of each deal. In short, conduits' close proximity to the financial markets makes them susceptible to financial ebbs and flows, even apart from the hedge risk associated with an isolated spike in spreads.

New-Product Risk

Once a conduit has drawn together the many players needed to securitize assets, it can often apply its experience easily to other loan products. As conduits matured in the 1990s, established firms gained control over origination networks, and profit margins for established and lower-risk loan products thinned. Accordingly, many conduits began to securitize higher-risk loan products that had never been originated on a nationwide scale, such as "B/C" quality loans and mortgages with loan-to-value ratios as high as 125%. Even if the credit risk of these new products is ignored, the refinancing and other payoff characteristics of these products remain largely unknown. Because a significant portion of the value of securitization can be traced to the value of the excess interest and because this value is heavily influenced by loan payoff patterns, an additional level of risk arises for conduits in new loan products with unknown payoff characteristics.

Recent Organization Structures

The problems encountered in the late 1990s underscore many (not all) of the risks faced by conduits. These risks seem especially problematic for independent conduits because of the complex nature of the conduit business. Conduits that affiliate with larger institutions appear better suited to focus on the core "middleman" role they were initially intended to play. Affiliating with larger organizations also increases the possibility of synergies with affiliates, provides a steadier source of funding, and ensures a degree of insulation from the market during periods of stress. For these reasons it is not surprising that, as Exhibit 6 shows, large conduits affiliated with larger institutions have survived the stress of the late 1990s, whereas independent conduits have faired poorly.

Exhibit 6: Transformation of Affiliated versus Independent Mortgage Conduits

Name	Rank in 1997	Rank in 1999	Status in 2000
Top 5 Affiliated Conduits in 1997			
GMAC-RFC	1	1	Continuing operations.
Norwest Asset Securities Corp.	2	2	Continuing operations.
GE Capital Mortgage Services	4	3	Continuing operations.
Salomon Brothers	8	9	Continuing operations.
Countrywide Mortgage Securities	9	6	Continuing operations.
Top 5 Independent Public Conduits in 1997			
ContiMortgage	3	19	Filed for Chapter 11 bankruptcy in 5/00.
IMC Mortgage	5	Not Rated	Severe financial problems motivate 1999 merger with Greenwich Street Capital Partners. Prior to merger, stock price declined over 95% during previous year.
The Money Store	6	Not Rated	Purchased by First Union 6/98 (prior to market fallout). Prior to merger, stock price trading near the year's high.
Firstplus Financial	7	Not Rated	Portions placed in Chapter 11 in 3/99.
Advanta Corp.	11	12	Major revision of business strategy involving sale of credit card business in 2/99 and mortgage business in 10/00. Significant jump in stock price after both strategic moves.

Note: 1997 and 1999 conduit rankings are from *The Mortgage Market Statistical Annual* for 1999.

CONCLUSIONS

In many respects, conduits have been remarkably successful. They now function as a small industry, operating in a variety of forms ranging from independent to affiliated entities. Conduits have grown throughout the 1990s, to the point that their operations account for a large proportion of the private-label securitization market. Conduits led the way to securitizing commercial loans as well as many other loan products that lie outside the domain of Freddie Mac and Fannie Mae, and they have done so without federal intervention. Conduits enhanced the strategic options available to financial intermediaries by increasing their ability to specialize in any of the component activities associated with securitization.

Nevertheless, although conduits were very successful in the early and mid-1990s, and the benefits of securitization remain considerable, recent experience has illustrated many risks. In particular, the late 1990s exposed risks ranging from regulatory and accounting problems to prepayment and market issues. During this period almost every independent conduit had severe problems, as evidenced by stock prices languishing at small fractions of the values that had been observed only one and two years earlier. This experience suggests that conduits are more successful when they are affiliated with larger entities engaged in related activities, such as securities-brokerage or banking-related enterprises. In these institutional contexts conduits appear sufficiently viable that they can be counted on to play a central role in securitization well into the next century.

Chapter 9

FASIT Flexibility Applied to Subprime Securitizations

Phillip R. Pollock
Partner
Tobin & Tobin

Michael E. Shaff
Partner
Jeffers, Shaff & Falk, LLP

INTRODUCTION

The Financial Asset Securitization Investment Trust (FASIT) provides increased flexibility in structuring subprime asset securitizations. While the use of FASITs is not limited to subprime assets, the enhanced structuring possibilities created by FASITs can be important in maximizing the efficiency of subprime securitizations, from the issuer's standpoint. (Efficiency, for this purpose, can be measured by the relative amount of proceeds received by the issuer at closing from a given amount of collateral. The more efficient the transaction, relatively speaking, the more proceeds will be realized by the issuer and/or relatively lower levels of collateral will be required.)

Subprime assets generally possess two characteristics that limit the efficiency of securitizations. First, subprime assets by definition have higher risk of credit loss and, hence, require higher levels of credit support than prime-quality assets. Second, subprime assets have higher yields than prime assets, which creates "excess yield" that is usually required to be applied as additional credit support. FASITs can enhance the efficiency of subprime securitizations by reducing the required level of credit support in the form of initial overcollateralization and by reducing the amount of excess yield required to be applied to credit support by, among other things, permitting earlier release of collateral. These enhancements can result in the issuer receiving more proceeds, more quickly, compared with non-FASIT structures.

The purpose of this chapter is to identify a number of the structural advantages of FASITs compared to REMICs and other forms of securitization. These structural advantages can be applied by issuers in a variety of ways, based on their particular assets and objectives, to increase the efficiency of their

111

subprime securitizations. The chapter concludes with a summary of the securities registration issues that arise when employing FASIT securitization structures.

ALTERNATIVES AVAILABLE PRIOR TO FASITS

Before adoption of the FASIT legislation, the Small Business Job Protection Act of 1996 (effective September 1, 1997), there were essentially three structural categories available for securitizing subprime assets, all of which are still available. For certain subprime real estate mortgage loans, including subprime first-lien mortgages and home equity closed-end mortgages, there is the real estate mortgage investment conduit (REMIC) vehicle. For mortgage loans that do not qualify for REMICs — such as home equity lines of credit (HELOCs), high loan-to-value mortgage loans (125%) and progress installment construction loans — there are the grantor trust and "debt for tax" structures. Neither of these non-REMIC structures permits multiple maturity securities to be issued, due to the Taxable Mortgage Pool (TMP) rules. (The TMP rules effectively limit passthrough tax treatment for entities that issue tranched debt supported by real estate mortgage loans to REMICs and FASITs.) Finally, for non-mortgage subprime assets, there is the trust classified as a partnership structure coupled with issuance of debt securities. This structure permits issuance of multiple maturity securities, since the assets being securitized are not subject to the TMP rules.

In general, gain is recognized when the holder of the ownership interest transfers debt to a FASIT. The FASIT provisions of the Internal Revenue Code permit an entity that was in existence on August 31, 1997, and that was structured in a manner that would have permitted the entity to elect FASIT status (i.e., as a trust or partnership and whose underlying assets consist solely of debt, credit enhancements, and hedges) as a pre-effective-date FASIT. Gain is not recognized on the election of FASIT status by a pre-effective-date FASIT.

ADVANTAGES OF FASITS VERSUS TRUST AND DEBT FOR TAX STRUCTURES

At least 99% of the assets of the FASIT must consist of debt instruments. The general rules under the tax law for distinguishing debt from equity apply, with some notable exceptions, and clarifications furnished by recently proposed regulations. Those regulations add some minor clarifications that expressly permit fixed-rate, variable-rate, and inflation-indexed debt instruments, revolving credit card receivables, REMIC and FASIT regular interests, stripped bonds, and a beneficial interest in a pass-through certificate representing an ownership interest in a debt instrument. In most cases it will be fairly clear whether an instrument constitutes debt or equity for tax purposes. (In cases where that determination is not clear, for example convertible debt, the use of a FASIT as the securitization vehicle would not be permissible.) In cases where the assets are clearly classified as debt for tax purposes, the use of the FASIT vehicle provides predictable, if not always favorable, results.

A significant advantage is that, for the category of sub-prime mortgage loans that do not qualify for REMIC treatment, FASITs permit issuance of multiple maturity securities. This ability to have multiple tranches of senior-subordinated, fast pay/slow pay securities permits more efficient pricing and more attractive overcollateralization and collateral release terms compared with the grantor trust or debt-for-tax structures. It may also create more alternatives in the type of credit support used, such as tranching versus use of bond insurance.

Outside of the mortgage securitization context where the TMP rules limit multiple maturity tranching to REMICs and FASITs, the FASIT structure does not generally provide any structural advantages over a trust (taxed as a partnership) issuing debt securities. Since this structure is available for most nonmortgage financial assets, the FASIT structure may be less attractive to issuers of nonmortgage securitizations solely from the standpoint of maximizing efficiency. There may be other reasons, however, for such issuers to adopt the FASIT structure provided that the disadvantages of using it are not significantly greater than the trust issuing debt for tax structure.

The most significant disadvantages presented by use of FASITs versus the trust or debt for tax approach are the recognition of gain required upon formation of FASITs and the possible recognition of "phantom" income over time by the holder of the ownership interest. A discussion of these tax treatments appears below.

ADVANTAGES OF FASITS VERSUS REMICS

A major benefit of FASITs over REMICs is the ability to add or substitute assets to the structure after the startup period and to remove collateral from the structure. This flexibility permits use of mortgage assets in a trust or other entity that issues fixed-term maturities, similar to credit card or other receivable securitizations.

Prior to FASITs, such fixed-term securities would have to meet tests for classification as debt for tax purposes and would be subject to the restrictions of the TMP rules. Under the REMIC and TMP rules, the REMIC originally was designated to be the sole vehicle for issuing multiple-maturity mortgage-backed debt. In the nonmortgage context there are no such restrictions.

Another advantage of FASITs over REMICs is that FASITs can hold a combination of qualifying mortgages along with other types of debt instruments. REMICs permit only qualifying mortgages, plus cash, reserves and related assets. An issuer can combine a pool of mortgage loans with interest rate agreements such as rate caps or floors to mitigate risks to the investors in the securities issued by a FASIT. Among the permitted assets that may be transferred to the FASIT are an interest rate or foreign currency notional principal contract, letter of credit, insurance contract, guarantee against payment defaults, or other financial contract reasonably required to guarantee or hedge against the FASIT's risks associated with being the obligor on interests issued by the FASIT, contract rights to acquire debt instruments, any regular interest in another FASIT, and any regular interest in a REMIC.

ILLUSTRATIVE EXAMPLE OF TWO-STEP FASIT STRUCTURE

To facilitate analysis and discussion of the tax treatment and public offering status of potential subprime FASIT securitizations, it will be helpful to set forth a sample structure. The structure posited for this purpose is based on the structure recently used in the first publicly offered FASIT securitization issued by American Residential Eagle, Inc., in June 1998. This two-step structure can be particularly advantageous to subprime issuers for the following reasons.

In this structure, the originator/seller transfers (via a sale transaction) to a special purpose, bankruptcy-remote subsidiary a pool of HELOCs (or any other financial assets). The special-purpose subsidiary (SPS) then pledges the HELOCs to secure the issuance of a HELOC bond, treated as debt for tax purposes. This HELOC bond (and any subsequently issued HELOC bonds backed by future HELOC originations or future advances) is referred to herein as the "underlying security" or "underlying bond." The initial overcollaterization required by the rating agencies can be put in place at this stage, as security for the underlying bond.

As the second step, the SPS transfers the HELOC bond (and any subsequently issued HELOC bonds) to a FASIT trust or a Wall Street conduit depositor for deposit into a FASIT trust. The FASIT trust issues trust certificates representing FASIT regular interests and any high-yield interests to the SPS as payment for the HELOC bond, and the trust certificates are sold to investors. The ownership interest is issued to a third-party investor or retained by the Wall Street depositor. The FASIT trust certificates sold to investors can be multiple-maturity, fast-pay/slow-pay, tranched securities, or fixed-term securities followed by a liquidation period or bullet maturity. Additional transfers to the FASIT trust (in the form of additional HELOC bonds) can be used to support issuance of new classes of FASIT certificates or to support outstanding classes of certificates.

This two-step structure, which ultimately depends on the cash flow from the pool of loans or receivables backing the HELOC bond, is an attractive structure to maximize efficiency of subprime asset securitizations. It permits mortgage loan securitizations to realize the benefits of FASITs over the REMIC and debt for tax structures discussed above. It also permits any asset-backed FASIT securitization to mitigate the negative effects of the FASIT gain-on-sale provisions.

The two-step structure is a significant structural advantage of FASITs compared with REMICs and other forms of existing securitization structures. Because FASITs permit almost any instruments classified as debt for tax purposes as "permitted assets," it is possible to have an underlying bond or other underlying security as the permitted assets of a FASIT. This fact introduces the potential for the two-step and other creative structures which are not possible with REMICs, which permit only qualifying mortgages (and related items) as acceptable assets to back issuance of REMIC interests. The two-step structure has many potential applications in addition to the HELOC example described above, including the subprime mortgage loan FASIT offering completed by American Residential Eagle, Inc., in June 1998.

TAXATION OF SUBPRIME FASIT SECURITIZATIONS

Sponsor

As noted, the primary drawback of the FASIT structure is the requirement of gain (but not loss) recognition on the transfer of the debt obligations to the FASIT. When the sponsor transfers the HELOCs (or any other form of debt) to the trust that will elect FASIT status, gain is recognized. Under the proposed regulations, the gain is computed by discounting the projected cash flows of the transferred debt at 120% of the applicable federal rate (AFR) compounded semiannually, published monthly by the IRS. The December 2000 rate that would likely apply to calculate gain in most situations is 6.95% (120% of AFR for instruments with terms of more than three but not more than nine years).

In the two-step structure described above, the sponsor issues its own debt instrument. The sponsor generally will not have to recognize gain on the issuance of its own debt, but there will be tax implications for both the sponsor and the holder of the FASIT ownership interest.

Where the sponsor is a C corporation, it may retain the owner-ship interest in the FASIT. If the sponsor is a real estate investment trust (REIT), partnership, or other passthrough entity, it is ineligible to hold the ownership interest. The debt instruments that will be the assets of the FASIT are deemed sold to the entity that will hold the ownership interest.

Holders

Holders of regular FASIT interests are treated as holding debt. Regular interests yield no more than 5% above the AFR at the time of issuance. High-yield instruments (yielding more than 5% over the AFR, having a term longer than 30 years, or issued at a premium of more than 25% over the interest's stated principal) may be held only by a C corporation or by a dealer who acquires them for resale. The holder of a FASIT interest must use the accrual method for income from the FASIT interest. Where the holder is a REIT, the FASIT regular interest is a qualifying real estate asset where at least 95% of the FASIT's loans are mortgage loans secured by real estate. REITs and regulated investment companies (RICs) are not eligible to hold high yield FASIT interests. (The high-yield subordinated regular interests of a REMIC by contrast may be transferred to a REIT or RIC.) If the FASIT trust holds mortgages and not collateralized mortgage obligations (CMOs), the FASIT interests in one of the two highest rating categories should be "mortgage related securities" for depository institutions.

Owner

A FASIT is permitted to have only one ownership interest, which must be held by a C corporation. The FASIT's assets and liabilities, and items of income, gain, loss, deduction, or credit pass through to the holder of this ownership interest. All assets transferred to the FASIT are deemed sold to the holder of the ownership interest. The holder of the ownership interest includes in income all of the FASIT's income net of deductions for interest and original issue discount accruing on the regular interests. The owner may not offset the FASIT income by the holder's net operating loss.

IMPEDIMENTS UNDER CURRENT SEC RULES TO USE OF FASIT STRUCTURES IN PUBLIC OFFERINGS

Registration Form Problems

Right to Use Form

Form S-3 is available to certain types of issuers and securities that satisfy the criteria set forth in the form. Use of Form S-3 is important because it provides for incorporation by reference of certain information filed by the issuer pursuant to other public reporting provisions, and it permits "shelf" registration of securities to be issued from time to time up to two years following registration. The ability to use shelf registration is important to securitization issuers because the SEC does not review the shelf "takedowns" after its initial review of the registration upon filing. Hence, the timing of conducting a takedown offering is largely in the control of the issuer and is not subject to the uncertainties of timing that result from SEC review.

Form S-3 was revised in 1992 to permit use by issuers of asset-backed securities, provided certain criteria are met. If such criteria are not met, the only alternatives are (1) to file separately for each offering (with possible SEC review) or (2) if the assets being securitized are mortgage loans and satisfy the criteria for issuance of "mortgage related" securities (including first-lien status), shelf registration is available under Rule 415 for any classes of securities rated in the two highest rating categories. (Form S-3 permits classes that are "investment grade," which includes the four highest rating categories.)

Discrete Pool Requirement

To be eligible for Form S-3, the securities to be issued must be primarily serviced by the cashflows of a discrete pool of receivables or other financial assets, either fixed or revolving. The SEC release that accompanied the 1992 revisions to Form S-3 pointed out that the reference to "fixed or revolving" was added to make clear that revolving-balance financial assets, such as credit card receivables, were acceptable assets to be offered on Form S-3. The staff reached this conclusion while pointing out that, depending on the performance of the revolving assets included in a discrete pool, "the sponsor may be required to assign additional receivables from other accounts" to support the outstanding securities. The addition of other accounts in such circumstances apparently does not impair the original discrete-pool status.

The SEC staff now takes the position that the addition of assets to a FASIT pool, as well as the substitution or removal of assets from a pool, would violate the discrete pool requirement and hence the securities offered in such a FASIT structure would not qualify for Form S-3. This position requires FASIT issuers to forego the FASIT flexibility for adding and removing assets if Form S-3 is used.

Asset Concentration Requirement

Another requirement that must be met to be eligible for the "asset backed" security provisions of Form S-3 is that a pool of assets must be present so that the cashflows supporting the asset-backed security do not depend on a single or a limited number of sources but, rather, on a large number of obligors. Under the current SEC view, if the securities of a single obligor or group of related obligors comprise 45% or more of the pool, the asset-backed security provisions of Form S-3 are not available.

For purposes of this requirement, the SEC staff does not look through a security to the underlying source of payments due on the security. Hence, in the HELOC example or any other two-step structure, even though the underlying bond is wholly supported by and dependent solely on the underlying pool of HELOC mortgage loans, the structure is not eligible for Form S-3. This refusal to look through to the underlying source of payments supporting an asset-backed security is also a problem for single obligor commercial securitizations where the underlying source of payments comprises a pool of retail leases or other small obligations of unrelated obligors.

Convert into Cash Requirement

To qualify as an asset-backed security, the underlying assets must also "by their terms convert into cash within a finite time period." The SEC staff interprets this requirement as excluding any loans or receivables that are nonperforming (in foreclosure or nonaccrual status) and as permitting no more than 20% of a pool to be delinquent at the date of securities issuance. These limitations make Form S-3 unavailable to certain types of subprime securitizations, such as tax lien pools, real estate owned (REO) pools, and workout loan pools.

Multiple Core Prospectus Requirement

The SEC staff made clear in adopting the revisions to Form S-3 that the prospective disclosure in the core prospectus, reviewed by the staff, must be detailed and complete as to each type of asset to be securitized. "A registration statement may not merely identify several alternative types of assets that may be securitized."

This view of the staff is also applied without "looking through" to the ultimate source of payments. In the HELOC example, and any other two-step structure, the staff regards the underlying bond or other underlying security as a type of asset to be fully described in the core prospectus. Hence, a core prospectus that described HELOCs (as opposed to the underlying bond) would be unacceptable for purposes of offering the FASIT trust certificates in the HELOC example. This approach virtually precludes the use of Wall Street conduits to securitize an underlying bond or other security in a two-step structure because no conduit shelf will have anticipated such underlying securities as a type of asset to be described.

Furthermore, the SEC staff requires that separate core prospectuses be filed if the type of asset to be securitized is so different from other types covered by the core prospectus that a full description requires separate treatment (such as separate risk factors section, description of terms, etc.). This approach can lead to unwieldy multiple prospectuses that are more likely to discourage the reader than to inform, even in the age of "plain English."

Co-Issuer Problems

Single Obligor Requirement
Under present SEC staff interpretations, if the securities of a single obligor or group of related obligors comprise 45% or more of the pool, then such obligor or obligors may be deemed co-issuers required to file a registration statement covering such underlying securities, and to deliver a prospectus covering such underlying securities, along with the prospectus covering the securities being sold to investors. The only exceptions to this rule are (1) if the underlying securities have been registered and sold (in a valid secondary market sale) more than three months prior to the current securitization and (2) if the underlying securities were privately issued and sold more than two years prior to the current securitization (such that Rule 144(k) would apply). The underlying security in the HELOC example and other two-step structures will not fit within these exceptions and hence will be subject to compliance with the co-issuer rules.

Co-Issuer Form Problems
One major problem posed by the co-issuer interpretation is that the underlying security registration is subject to the same registration form requirements as the securities being sold to investors. Accordingly, even where using a Wall Street conduit that permits an underlying security of the type used in the HELOC or other two-step structure, since the underlying bond or the security will fail to satisfy one or more of the above Form S-3 criteria, each offering will fail the Form S-3 criteria and will have to be separately registered.

Multiple Core and/or Supplemental Prospectus Requirement
To satisfy the SEC staff interpretation that both the securities being sold to investors and the underlying security are being offered and sold in a two-step structure,

it may be necessary to have two separate core prospectuses and two separate prospectus supplements. The SEC staff is agreeable to combined core and/or supplemental prospectuses where one issuer can control the disclosure and describe fully in one document each security covered thereby. However, this flexibility is not present where, for example, a Wall Street shelf is being used to issue a separately registered security of an unaffiliated issuer. This situation can require multiple core and supplemental prospectuses that do not serve to inform investors in a meaningful way due to overlapping, duplicative disclosure and the sheer mass of the disclosure document itself.

Chapter 10

Strategic Choices in Asset Sales

Albert E. Avery, Ph.D.
Associate Professor of Finance
Towson University

INTRODUCTION

P ro forma statements are used to investigate the impact of whole loan sales or securitization on bank lending operations. With on-balance sheet funding of generated receivables, the capital ratio becomes the factor that limits growth for a healthy firm. As explained in this chapter, assets can be sold to move funding off the balance sheet while enhancing income and asset growth, while simultaneously improving return on assets and return on equity. The firm is positioned to enjoy the fastest rate of growth in generation of new receivables by selling some proportion of those assets to maintain the desired capital ratio. The asset/liability manager can also offload part of the funding and interest rate risk inherent in the receivables, while recession-resistant servicing income becomes a larger part of total income. The enhanced income stream and mitigated risk should be reflected in the value of the firm and stock price.

SETTING AND CONSIDERATIONS

As a banking institution generates receivables through lending operations, the factors limiting growth are the ability to generate additional, quality receivables and capital adequacy. One logically appealing solution to the capital adequacy problem involves packaging the receivables and selling them in the form of whole loan sales or through securitization. The funding of the receivables is therefore moved off the balance sheet. An additional benefit of asset sales is the ability to match fund the receivables by exporting the funding and interest rate risk to the asset investor.

Another aspect of strategic choice is risk mitigation. For community and regional institutions, there is a likelihood that generated receivables concentrate in particular industries, such as agriculture, real estate or consumer finance. If one or more of these industries weaken or decline, the impact on the health and profitability of the bank could be significant. While not a focus here, asset sales can be used to effectively increase the level of diversification of the remaining receivables portfolio or to provide the cash to acquire a broader pool of securitized assets.

Unless done carefully, with a clear strategic plan, selling assets can lead to inferior performance in terms of both dollars and return measures. Both simple logic and the simulations below reinforce this conclusion. When a bank with an asset portfolio sells it at a fair price, in part or in whole, the profitability of that portfolio is "shared" with another party. Future income may be moved into the current year or closer in time, but the long-term size of the income stream for the bank declines. If the difference is not "made up" by an increase in volume, dollar profitability falls. In addition, there are significant costs associated with asset sales, some specific to each transaction and some specific to the internal infrastructure needed to facilitate on-going asset sales. The net effect is that it is unwise to sell assets for the sole purpose of reducing debt when the objective is to maximize shareholders' wealth. Dollar and percentage profitability decrease in absence of a commensurate increase in receivables generation volume, as will be demonstrated below.

There can be distinct advantages to moving the receivables off of the balance sheet. When the ability to generate quality receivables is not the limiting factor, asset sales through whole loan sales and securitization can generate a superior income stream, be conducted on a smaller asset base, and be less dependent on short-term shifts in the health of the economy for income stability. The impact of asset sales on income stability is addressed below.

The desirability of securitization, as opposed to whole loan sales, is fundamentally determined by the nature of the receivables, the scale of operation and the goals of the firm, in interaction with operating realities. For example, many of the costs of securitization have a minimum threshold and cannot be aptly called variable in nature, making the minimum eligible portfolio volume $75 to $100 million.

Other aspects of the context of the bank also are important. For example, a bank may be limited in its ability to generate high-quality new receivables, due to its geographic region or competitive situation. If this is true, both whole loan sales and securitization may prove unattractive.

The goals of the firm would typically encompass the desirability of growth and willingness to accept risk to achieve an enhanced income stream. During normal economic times, income stream growth can be optimized through securitization because income generation is not strictly limited by the available capital resources. To the extent that profitability is negatively impacted by a flat yield curve and competition from major banks with lower cost structures, securitization may level the playing field. Many major banks are extensively involved with securitization.

BASE OF COMPARISON

The baseline for an investigation into limits of growth is shown in Exhibit 1. The pro forma income statements and balance sheets depict a hypothetical firm that has $20 million in stockholder equity and $500 million in newly generated receivables, leading to a 4% capital ratio in Year 1. Ratios for the statements appear below the statements. The on-balance sheet financing forecasts assume that no external equity capital infusion is available, so growth is limited by the capital ratio and the amount of income that is earned and reinvested. The data are shown in thousands of dollars and extend four years into the future. The data are also graphed, but extend eight years into the future to more clearly reveal strategic impacts.

Exhibit 1: On-Balance Sheet Financing with New Receivables Based on 4% Capital Ratio Maintenance (000 dollars)

Facts:	Year 1	Year 2	Year 3	Year 4
Gross Assets Sold	0	0	0	0
After-tax Gain on Sale	0	0	0	0
After-tax Operating Income	4,320	5,253	6,388	7,768
Cash Realized (Not used below)	4,320	5,253	6,388	7,768
New Receivables Created	500,000	113,200	137,651	167,384
Total Receivables Sold	0	0	0	0
Adjustment for Write-offs	0	0	0	0
Total Off-Balance Sheet	0	0	0	0
Income Statement:				
Interest Income	45,000	54,720	66,540	80,912
Interest Expense	27,600	33,562	40,811	49,626
Net Interest Income	17,400	21,158	25,729	31,286
Servicing Income	0	0	0	0
Total Income	17,400	21,158	25,729	31,286
Expenses and Charge-offs	10,200	12,403	15,082	18,340
Operating Income	7,200	8,755	10,646	12,946
Tax (40%)	2,880	3,502	4,259	5,178
After-tax Operating Income	4,320	5,253	6,388	7,768
Gain on Sale	0	0	0	0
Total After-tax Income	4,320	5,253	6,388	7,768
Assets:				
Excess Liquidity				
Receivables, Past - Adjusted	0	494,800	601,677	731,639
Receivables, New	500,000	108,880	132,398	160,996
Asset Reinvestment	0	4,320	5,253	6,388
Receivables Sold	0	0	0	0
Total Receivables	500,000	608,000	739,328	899,023
Total Assets	500,000	608,000	739,328	899,023
Liabilities and Equity:				
Liabilities	480,000	583,680	709,755	863,062
Stockholder Equity	20,000	24,320	29,573	35,961
Total Liabilities & Equity	500,000	608,000	739,328	899,023
Ratios:				
Capital Ratio	4.00%	4.00%	4.00%	4.00%
ROA	0.86%	0.86%	0.86%	0.86%
ROE	21.60%	21.60%	21.60%	21.60%

Exhibit 2: Performance Graphs
Pro Forma Results from Exhibits 1, 3, 4, and 5 with an 8-Year Forecasting Horizon

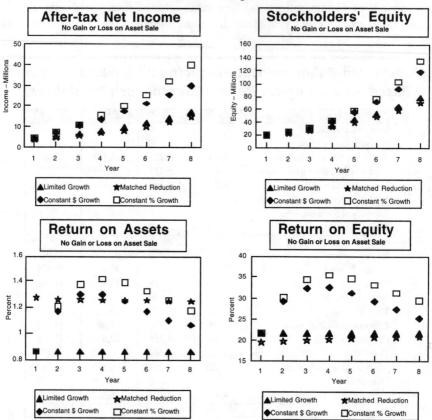

Legend and Sources of Data

Limited Growth – Exhibit 1 entitled "On-Balance Sheet Financing with New Receivables Based on Capital Ratio Maintenance"

Matched Reduction – Exhibit 3 entitled "Selling Receivables to Reduce Debt with New Receivables Generation as shown in Exhibit 1"

Constant $ Growth – Exhibit 4 entitled "Constant Dollar Receivables Generation and Receivables Sold to Maintain a 4% Capital Ratio"

Constant % Growth – Exhibit 5 entitled "Constant 10% Growth in Receivables Generation and Receivables Sold to Maintain a 4% Capital Ratio"

After-tax net income grows each year, from $4.32 million in Year 1 to $17.0 million in Year 8, while return on assets (ROA) is constant at 0.86% and return on equity (ROE) is constant at 21.6%. These values are shown graphically in Exhibit 2, with a legend of "Limited Growth." The data graphed are after-tax net income, stockholders' equity, ROA and ROE.

MATCHED REDUCTIONS IN ASSETS AND LIABILITIES

Exhibit 3 details the effect of selling 40% of generated receivables at no gain or loss, with the proceeds going to reduce debt during Year 1. The strategy of continuing to sell 40% of newly generated receivables is incorporated in the pro forma statements. This produces an increase in capital ratio from 4% to 6.51% and an increase in return on assets from 0.86% to 1.27% in Year 1. The apparent benefit, however logical, is illusionary and shows the fallacy of presuming that adjustments to a single set of statements portend the future.

Return on equity decreases from 21.6% to 19.58%, even in Year 1. The overall effect on stockholders' wealth can be judged by inspecting the pro forma statements. To make a fair comparison of this scenario with the on-balance sheet financing of the "Limited Growth" scenario, receivables generation ("sales") must be the same. The forecast results are graphically depicted in Exhibit 2, with a legend of "Matched Reduction," where debt is reduced by a constant percentage of asset sales.

Unless risk has been significantly reduced by off-balance sheet funding, using asset sales to reduce debt produces inferior performance. Looking to the Exhibit 2 performance graphs, the "Limited Growth" scenario produces higher income and higher stockholders' equity in each future year. If risk in the two scenarios is comparable, the "Limited Growth" scenario will produce the higher stock price at any point in time. The graph depicting return on assets shows that asset sales to reduce debt increases the ratio over the baseline case, but assets are being artificially reduced by design. However, return on equity is more important to stockholders. It is also difficult to argue with consistently higher dollar net income and dollar stockholders' equity, shown in the first two graphs in Exhibit 2. The baseline produces the best result. The inevitable conclusion is that asset sales done for the purpose of reducing debt constitute a poor strategy, and it is likely that stock price will be comparatively hurt.

STRATEGIES INVOLVING CONTINUED GROWTH

The scenario of selling receivables and using part of the proceeds to reduce debt ("Matched Reduction" scenario) does not take full advantage of available resources because the capital ratio was allowed to increase to 6.51% and remain high. Exhibit 4 has the same initial year, with $20 million in stockholders' equity and $500 million in newly generated receivables. The strategy employed is to sell assets as necessary at no gain or loss to maintain a 4% capital ratio, as in the Limited Growth scenario. Here, new receivables generation is not limited by circumstance. It is assumed that $500 million in receivables will be generated in each future year as well as during the first year. In the performance graphs of Exhibit 2, the legend is "Constant $ Growth."

Exhibit 3: Selling Receivables to Reduce Debt with New Receivables Generation as Shown in Exhibit 1

Facts:	Year 1	Year 2	Year 3	Year 4
Gross Assets Sold	200,000	45,079	54,801	66,631
After-tax Gain on Sale	0	0	0	0
After-tax Operating Income	3,818	4,605	5,581	6,768
Cash Realized	203,818	49,684	60,383	73,399
New Receivables Created	500,000	112,698	137,003	166,577
Total Receivables Sold	200,000	242,999	295,273	358,833
Adjustment for Write-offs	2,080	2,527	3,071	3,732
Total Off-Balance Sheet	197,920	240,472	292,202	355,101
Income Statement:				
Interest Income	27,000	32,805	39,862	48,443
Interest Expense	16,100	19,618	23,862	29,023
Net Interest Income	10,900	13,187	16,000	19,420
Servicing Income	1,583	1,924	2,338	2,841
Income Before Expenses	12,483	15,111	18,338	22,260
Expenses and Charge-offs	6,120	7,436	9,035	10,980
Operating Income	6,363	7,675	9,302	11,280
Tax (40%)	2,545	3,070	3,721	4,512
After-tax Operating Income	3,818	4,605	5,581	6,768
Gain on Sale	0	0	0	0
Total After-tax Income	3,818	4,605	5,581	6,768
Assets:				
Receivables, Past - Adjusted	0	296,880	360,708	438,304
Receivables, New	500,000	108,880	132,398	160,996
Asset Reinvestment	0	3,818	4,605	5,581
Less: Receivables Sold (40%)	200,000	45,079	54,801	66,631
Total Assets	300,000	364,499	442,910	538,250
Liabilities and Equity:				
Liabilities	280,000	341,183	414,989	504,748
Stockholder Equity	19,498	23,316	27,921	33,502
Total Liabilities & Equity	299,498	364,499	442,910	538,250
Ratios:				
Capital Ratio	6.51%	6.40%	6.30%	6.22%
ROA	1.27%	1.26%	1.26%	1.26%
ROE	19.58%	19.75%	19.99%	20.20%

As seen in the graphs, this scenario has distinctly improved net income growth and stockholders' equity growth. Return on assets and return on equity are also dramatically improved after Year 1, hitting peaks in Year 3 and Year 4, and then slowly trailing off. With recognition that asset sales have also match funded a large portion of receivables, there is no doubt that these results would significantly augment the value of the firm and stock price.

Exhibit 4: Constant Dollar Receivables Generation and Receivables Sold to Maintain a 4% Capital Ratio

Facts:	Year 1	Year 2	Year 3	Year 4
Gross Assets Sold	0	391,000	324,000	248,000
After-tax Gain on Sale	0	0	0	0
After-tax Operating Income	4,320	7,111	10,160	13,497
Cash Realized	4,320	398,111	334,160	261,497
New Receivables Created	500,000	504,320	507,111	510,160
Total Receivables Sold	0	391,000	710,934	951,540
Adjustment for Write-offs	0	4,066	7,394	9,896
Total Off-Balance Sheet	0	386,934	703,540	941,644
Income Statement:				
Interest Income	45,000	54,731	70,642	93,501
Interest Expense	27,600	33,569	43,325	57,345
Net Interest Income	17,400	21,162	27,317	36,156
Servicing Income	0	3,095	5,628	7,533
Income Before Expenses	17,400	24,258	32,945	43,689
Expenses and Charge-offs	10,200	12,406	16,012	21,194
Operating Income	7,200	11,852	16,933	22,495
Tax (40%)	2,880	4,741	6,773	8,998
After-tax Operating Income	4,320	7,111	10,160	13,497
Gain on Sale	0	0	0	0
Total After-tax Income	4,320	7,111	10,160	13,497
Assets:				
Receivables, Past - Adjusted	0	494,800	601,796	776,744
Receivables, New	500,000	500,000	500,000	500,000
Asset Reinvestment	0	4,320	7,111	10,160
Less: Receivables Sold	0	391,000	324,000	248,000
Total Assets	500,000	608,120	784,907	1,038,904
Liabilities and Equity:				
Liabilities	480,000	583,800	753,476	997,313
Stockholder Equity	20,000	24,320	31,431	41,591
Total Liabilities & Equity	500,000	608,120	784,907	1,038,904
Ratios:				
Capital Ratio	4.00%	4.00%	4.00%	4.00%
ROA	0.86%	1.17%	1.29%	1.30%
ROE	21.60%	29.24%	32.32%	32.45%

STRATEGIES INVOLVING CONSTANT PERCENTAGE OR ACCELERATED GROWTH

A constant percentage growth scenario is shown in Exhibit 5. The exhibit depicts the likely result for a bank committed to repeating the growth in a successful year with identical percentage performance in the following year. The legend in the performance graphs in Exhibit 2 corresponding to Exhibit 5 is "Constant % Growth."

Exhibit 5: Constant 10% Growth in Receivables Generation and Receivables Sold to Maintain a 4% Capital Ratio

Facts:	Year 1	Year 2	Year 3	Year 4
Gross Assets Sold	0	441,000	422,000	396,000
After-tax Gain on Sale	0	0	0	0
After-tax Operating Income	4,320	7,349	10,921	15,113
Cash Realized	4,320	448,349	432,921	411,113
New Receivables Created	500,000	554,320	612,349	676,421
Total Receivables Sold	0	441,000	858,414	1,245,486
Adjustment for Write-offs	0	4,586	8,928	12,953
Total Off-Balance Sheet	0	436,414	849,486	1,232,533
Income Statement:				
Interest Income	45,000	54,731	71,293	95,789
Interest Expense	27,600	33,569	43,727	58,750
Net Interest Income	17,400	21,162	27,566	37,040
Servicing Income	0	3,491	6,796	9,860
Income Before Expenses	17,400	24,654	34,362	46,900
Expenses and Charge-offs	10,200	12,406	16,160	21,712
Operating Income	7,200	12,248	18,202	25,188
Tax (40%)	2,880	4,899	7,281	10,075
After-tax Operating Income	4,320	7,349	10,921	15,113
Gain on Sale	0	0	0	0
Total After-tax Income	4,320	7,349	10,921	15,113
Assets:				
Receivables, Past - Adjusted	0	494,800	601,796	783,906
Receivables, New	500,000	550,000	605,000	665,500
Asset Reinvestment	0	4,320	7,349	10,921
Less: Receivables Sold	0	441,000	422,000	396,000
Total Assets	500,000	608,120	792,144	1,064,327
Liabilities and Equity:				
Liabilities	480,000	583,800	760,476	1,021,737
Stockholder Equity	20,000	24,320	31,669	42,590
Total Liabilities & Equity	500,000	608,120	792,144	1,064,327
Ratios:				
Capital Ratio	4.00%	4.00%	4.00%	4.00%
ROA	0.86%	1.21%	1.38%	1.42%
ROE	21.60%	30.22%	34.49%	35.48%

An important forecasting assumption in the previous example was that new receivables would be generated at a rate of $500 million per year. Since the firm is growing, a constant dollar amount of new receivables represents a decreasing percentage rate of growth as we move into the future. The constant percentage growth scenario corrects for this and incorporates a 10% rate of growth in receivables generation. Again, assets are sold at no gain or loss to maintain the 4% capital ratio.

The results are clearly superior to those for constant dollar growth. Across the 4-year horizon, after-tax net income grows from $4.3 million to $15.1 million, while the corresponding constant dollar growth forecast shows Year 4 income at $13.5 million. Stockholders' equity grows to $42.6 million instead of $41.6 million. In addition, return on assets and return on equity are also higher than in the constant dollar growth simulation. Exhibit 2 performance graphs show decidedly improved results, based on these ratios.

The not-too-surprising conclusion is that the faster the firm grows, the better it performs financially, in terms of both dollar and percentage measures. In the constant percentage growth case, the off-balance sheet assets exceed the on-balance sheet assets in Year 3, but they are, of course, still generating servicing income. It is apparent that there is some rate of growth that also maximizes return on assets and return on equity, but investigating this phenomenon is beyond the current scope of inquiry.

The most important result of the pro forma statements is that both the constant dollar growth scenario and the constant percentage growth scenario, with the embedded strategy of asset sales to maintain the capital ratio, removes the capital ratio as an effective limit to growth. The only significant limit to growth is the ability to generate new quality receivables that can be packaged and sold at a fair price. Since this strategy involves the partial sale of assets, the asset/liability manager also has the ability to determine which assets to move off the balance sheet and thereby match fund the assets.

ACCELERATING OR DEFERRING INCOME THROUGH A GAIN OR LOSS ON SALE OF ASSETS

Through securitization, there are methods to produce an immediate gain on sale, and circumstances may arise where the assets are intentionally or situationally sold at a loss. Due to market imperfections, assets sold through securitization may be particularly attractive to investors who would otherwise have no access to the assets. When replicated, the environment can easily lead to sales at a small percentage profit, but a significant dollar profit. Similarly, not all paper losses are undesirable. An example of a desirable loss would be a sale of receivables at a seemingly low price, as part of a package that results in particularly attractive servicing fees for the bank or off-loading assets that are detrimental to the overall asset portfolio composition of the bank.

Viewing the pro forma statements in Exhibits 6, 7, and 8, the impact of selling receivables at a 90 basis point gain is seen. The results are those that would be expected. All results improve in comparisons with the "On-Balance Sheet Financing with New Receivables Based on Capital Ratio Maintenance" pro forma statements shown in Exhibit 1. They also improve in comparison with Exhibits 3, 4, and 5.

Exhibit 6: Selling Receivables at a Gain to Reduce Debt with New Receivables Generation as Shown in Exhibit 1

Facts:	Year 1	Year 2	Year 3	Year 4
Gross Assets Sold	200,000	45,799	55,020	66,892
After-tax Gain on Sale	1,800	412	495	602
After-tax Operating Income	5,618	5,153	6,234	7,554
Cash Realized	207,418	51,364	61,750	75,048
New Receivables Created	500,000	114,498	137,551	167,230
Total Receivables Sold	200,000	243,719	296,205	360,016
Adjustment for Write-offs	2,080	2,535	3,081	3,744
Total Off-Balance Sheet	197,920	241,185	293,124	356,272
Income Statement:				
Interest Income	27,000	32,902	39,988	48,602
Interest Expense	16,100	19,473	23,704	28,849
Net Interest Income	10,900	13,429	16,284	19,753
Servicing Income	1,583	1,929	2,345	2,850
Income Before Expenses	12,483	15,358	18,629	22,603
Expenses and Charge-offs	6,120	7,458	9,064	11,017
Operating Income	6,363	7,901	9,565	11,587
Tax (40%)	2,545	3,160	3,826	4,635
After-tax Operating Income	3,818	4,740	5,739	6,952
Gain on Sale	1,800	412	495	602
Total After-tax Income	5,618	5,153	6,234	7,554
Assets:				
Receivables, Past - Adjusted	0	296,880	361,777	439,686
Receivables, New	500,000	108,880	132,398	160,996
Asset Reinvestment	0	5,618	5,153	6,234
Less: Receivables Sold (40%)	200,000	45,799	55,020	66,892
Total Assets	300,000	365,579	444,307	540,025
Liabilities and Equity:				
Liabilities	280,000	338,663	412,239	501,722
Stockholder Equity	21,298	26,916	32,069	38,303
Total Liabilities & Equity	301,298	365,579	444,307	540,025
Ratios:				
On-going Operations:				
Capital Ratio	7.07%	7.36%	7.22%	7.09%
ROA	1.27%	1.30%	1.29%	1.29%
ROE	17.93%	17.61%	17.90%	18.15%
Total, Including Gain on Sale:				
ROA	1.86%	1.41%	1.40%	1.40%
ROE	26.38%	19.14%	19.44%	19.72%

Exhibits 6, 7, and 8 are identical in forecasting assumptions to Exhibits 3, 4, and 5, except for the fact that the assets are being sold at a profit. The usual objective in structuring asset sales to produce a gain is to speed the arrival of profits. The arrival is evident in all measures of success as seen in the performance graphs in Exhibit 9. The 4-year results are summarized in Exhibit 10 for easy comparison. Since each forecasting scenario begins in the same situation, the results for shown for Year 4 reveal the overall significance of the forecasting assumptions. After-tax net income and stockholders' equity are higher in all cases. The total ROA and total ROE reported in Exhibit 10 include the gain on sale in addition to income from on-going operations. They are higher in all cases except for the matched reduction scenario, where assets are sold to reduce debt. The same pattern is evident in ROA and ROE calculated for on-going operations.

Exhibit 7: Constant Dollar Receivables Generation and Receivables Sold at a Gain to Maintain a 4% Capital Ratio

Facts:	Year 1	Year 2	Year 3	Year 4
Gross Assets Sold	0	391,000	238,000	187,000
After-tax Gain on Sale	0	3,519	2,142	1,683
After-tax Operating Income	4,320	10,630	12,665	15,798
Cash Realized	4,320	405,149	252,807	204,481
New Receivables Created	500,000	504,320	510,630	512,665
Total Receivables Sold	0	391,000	624,934	805,434
Adjustment for Write-offs	0	4,066	6,499	8,377
Total Off-Balance Sheet	0	386,934	618,434	797,058
Income Statement:				
Interest Income	45,000	54,731	78,698	107,190
Interest Expense	27,600	33,569	48,270	65,744
Net Interest Income	17,400	21,162	30,428	41,445
Servicing Income	0	3,095	4,947	6,376
Income Before Expenses	17,400	24,258	35,376	47,822
Expenses and Charge-offs	10,200	12,406	17,838	24,296
Operating Income	7,200	11,852	17,538	23,525
Tax (40%)	2,880	4,741	7,015	9,410
After-tax Operating Income	4,320	7,111	10,523	14,115
Gain on Sale	0	3,519	2,142	1,683
Total After-tax Income	4,320	10,630	12,665	15,798
Assets:				
Receivables, Past - Adjusted	0	494,800	601,796	865,332
Receivables, New	500,000	500,000	500,000	500,000
Asset Reinvestment	0	4,320	10,630	12,665
Less: Receivables Sold	0	391,000	238,000	187,000
Total Assets	500,000	608,120	874,426	1,190,996
Liabilities and Equity:				
Liabilities	480,000	583,800	839,476	1,143,382
Stockholder Equity	20,000	24,320	34,950	47,615
Total Liabilities & Equity	500,000	608,120	874,426	1,190,996
Ratios:				
On-going Operations:				
Capital Ratio	4.00%	4.00%	4.00%	4.00%
ROA	0.86%	1.17%	1.20%	1.19%
ROE	21.60%	29.24%	30.11%	29.64%
Total, Including Gain on Sale:				
ROA	0.86%	1.75%	1.45%	1.33%
ROE	21.60%	43.71%	36.24%	33.18%

Exhibit 8: Constant 10% Growth in Receivables Generation and Receivables Sold at a Gain to Maintain a 4% Capital Ratio

Facts:	Year 1	Year 2	Year 3	Year 4
Gross Assets Sold	0	441,000	328,000	312,000
After-tax Gain on Sale	0	3,969	2,952	2,808
After-tax Operating Income	4,320	11,318	14,275	18,670
Cash Realized	4,320	456,287	345,227	333,478
New Receivables Created	500,000	554,320	616,318	679,775
Total Receivables Sold	0	441,000	764,414	1,068,464
Adjustment for Write-offs	0	4,586	7,950	11,112
Total Off-Balance Sheet	0	436,414	756,464	1,057,352
Income Statement:				
Interest Income	45,000	54,731	80,110	112,377
Interest Expense	27,600	33,569	49,132	68,926
Net Interest Income	17,400	21,162	30,978	43,450
Servicing Income	0	3,491	6,052	8,459
Income Before Expenses	17,400	24,654	37,030	51,909
Expenses and Charge-offs	10,200	12,406	18,158	25,472
Operating Income	7,200	12,248	18,871	26,437
Tax (40%)	2,880	4,899	7,549	10,575
After-tax Operating Income	4,320	7,349	11,323	15,862
Gain on Sale	0	3,969	2,952	2,808
Total After-tax Income	4,320	11,318	14,275	18,670
Assets:				
Receivables, Past - Adjusted	0	494,800	601,796	880,856
Receivables, New	500,000	550,000	605,000	665,500
Asset Reinvestment	0	4,320	11,318	14,275
Less: Receivables Sold	0	441,000	328,000	312,000
Total Assets	500,000	608,120	890,113	1,248,631
Liabilities and Equity:				
Liabilities	480,000	583,800	854,476	1,198,718
Stockholder Equity	20,000	24,320	35,638	49,913
Total Liabilities & Equity	500,000	608,120	890,113	1,248,631
Ratios:				
On-going Operations:				
Capital Ratio	4.00%	4.00%	4.00%	4.00%
ROA	0.86%	1.21%	1.27%	1.27%
ROE	21.60%	30.22%	31.77%	31.78%
Total, Including Gain on Sale:				
ROA	0.86%	1.86%	1.60%	1.50%
ROE	21.60%	46.54%	40.06%	37.41%

Exhibit 9: Performance Graphs - Gain on Sale
Pro Forma Results from Exhibits 1, 6, 7 and 8 with an
8-Year Forecasting Horizon

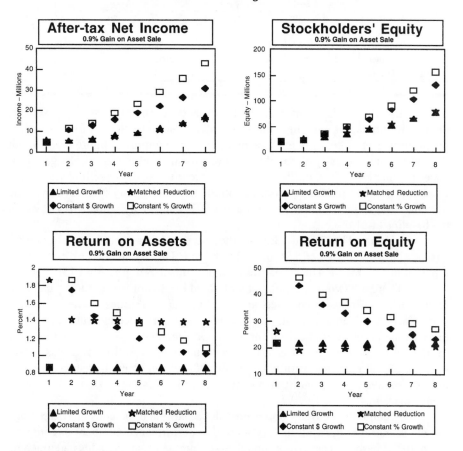

Legend and Sources of Data

Limited Growth – Exhibit 1 entitled "On-Balance Sheet Financing with New Receivables Based on Capital Ratio Maintenance"

Matched Reduction – Exhibit 6 entitled "Selling Receivables at a Gain to Reduce Debt with New Receivables Generation as shown in Exhibit 1"

Constant $ Growth – Exhibit 7 entitled "Constant Dollar Receivables Generation and Receivables Sold at a Gain to Maintain a 4% Capital Ratio"

Constant % Growth – Exhibit 8 entitled "Constant 10% Growth in Receivables Generation and Receivables Sold at a Gain to Maintain a 4% Capital Ratio"

Exhibit 10: Comparison of Forecast Results with a Gain on Asset Sales

Scenario	Net Income (M)		Equity (M)		Total ROA		Total ROE	
		No Gain	0.9% Gain	No Gain	0.9% Gain	No Gain	0.9% Gain	No Gain
Limited Growth	$7.8	N/A	$36.0	N/A	0.86%	N/A	21.6%	N/A
Matched Reduction	$6.8	$7.6	$33.5	$38.3	1.26%	1.40%	20.2%	19.7%
Constant $ Growth	$13.5	$15.8	$41.6	$47.6	1.30%	1.33%	32.5%	33.2%
Constant % Growth	$15.1	$18.7	$42.6	$49.9	1.42%	1.50%	35.5%	37.4%

Exhibit 10 also reinforces the previous conclusion that selling assets for the intent purpose of reducing debt is an inferior strategy that will not optimize the performance of the bank or stock price. The only improved figure is ROA, but the strategy intentionally elevated this ratio. Note that selling assets at a gain produces net income of $7.6 million, while the baseline case of not selling assets produces net income of $7.8 million. Stockholders' equity only increases over the baseline, if assets are sold at a profit, and ROE is decidedly worse at 19.7% than the baseline at 21.6%.

Exhibits 11, 12, and 13 show the outcome when assets are sold at a 90 basis-point loss instead of a 90 basis-point gain. The 8-year forecast results are reported in Exhibit 14. The 4-year results are summarized in Exhibit 15.

There are two major points highlighted by Exhibit 15. First, the matched reduction scenario in which assets are sold to reduce liabilities continues to be a particularly disadvantageous strategy. Again, all performance measures are below those of the baseline case except for ROA. One concludes that when assets have to be sold to reduce debt, it is very important to avoid selling at a loss. Also, drawing on the graphical results in Exhibit 10, selling assets to reduce debt not only postpones income, but it also postpones growth in the ROA and ROE efficiency measures.

Second, the constant dollar growth scenario and the constant percentage growth scenario both result in very attractive performance numbers in comparison with the baseline case. Even though assets are being sold at a loss, net income is either $9.6 million or $9.5 million in comparison with the $7.8 million baseline. Stockholders' equity does not fair as well with either $34.0 or $33.6 against a $36.0 baseline. ROA is improved to either 1.13% or 1.14% versus 0.86% in the baseline. ROE has markedly improved to either 28.2% or 28.4% in comparison with 21.6%.

While Exhibit 10 and Exhibit 15 clearly show it is better to sell at a gain or no gain than to sell at a loss, none of the potential benefits of selling at a planned loss, such as the production of an in-package superior servicing income, has been included in the pro format statements. Exhibit 15 also highlights the fact that unforeseen circumstances that produce an unplanned loss do not necessarily mean that a decision to engage in whole loan sales or securitization would appear to be wrong with 20-20 hindsight. Contingency plans can be developed to control this risk.

Exhibit 11: Selling Receivables at a Loss to Reduce Debt with New Receivables Generation as Shown in Exhibit 1

Facts:	Year 1	Year 2	Year 3	Year 4
Gross Assets Sold	200,000	44,359	54,587	66,372
After-tax Gain on Sale	−1,800	−399	−491	−597
After-tax Operating Income	2,018	4,070	4,933	5,987
Cash Realized	200,218	48,030	59,029	71,762
New Receivables Created	500,000	110,898	136,468	165,929
Total Receivables Sold	200,000	242,279	294,347	357,657
Adjustment for Write-offs	2,080	2,520	3,061	3,720
Total Off-Balance Sheet	197,920	239,760	291,286	353,938
Income Statement:				
Interest Income	27,000	32,708	39,737	48,284
Interest Expense	16,100	19,763	24,020	29,197
Net Interest Income	10,900	12,945	15,717	19,087
Servicing Income	1,583	1,918	2,330	2,832
Income Before Expenses	12,483	14,863	18,047	21,919
Expenses and Charge-offs	6,120	7,414	9,007	10,944
Operating Income	6,363	7,449	9,040	10,974
Tax (40%)	2,545	2,980	3,616	4,390
After-tax Operating Income	3,818	4,469	5,424	6,585
Gain on Sale	−1,800	−399	−491	−597
Total After-tax Income	2,018	4,070	4,933	5,987
Assets:				
Receivables, Past - Adjusted	0	296,880	359,639	436,928
Receivables, New	500,000	108,880	132,398	160,996
Asset Reinvestment	0	2,018	4,070	4,933
Less: Receivables Sold (40%)	200,000	44,359	54,587	66,372
Total Assets	300,000	363,419	441,520	536,486
Liabilities and Equity:				
Liabilities	280,000	343,703	417,734	507,767
Stockholder Equity	17,698	19,716	23,786	28,719
Total Liabilities & Equity	297,698	363,419	441,520	536,486
Ratios:				
On-going Operations:				
Capital Ratio	5.94%	5.43%	5.39%	5.35%
ROA	1.28%	1.23%	1.23%	1.23%
ROE	21.57%	22.67%	22.80%	22.93%
Total, Including Loss on Sale:				
ROA	0.68%	1.12%	1.12%	1.12%
ROE	11.40%	20.64%	20.74%	20.85%

Exhibit 12: Constant Dollar Receivables Generation with Receivables Sold at a Loss to Maintain a 4% Capital Ratio

Facts:	Year 1	Year 2	Year 3	Year 4
Gross Assets Sold	0	391,000	407,000	346,000
After-tax Gain on Sale	0	–3,519	–3,663	–3,114
After-tax Operating Income	4,320	3,592	6,142	9,617
Cash Realized	4,320	391,073	409,479	352,503
New Receivables Created	500,000	504,320	503,592	506,142
Total Receivables Sold	0	391,000	793,934	1,131,677
Adjustment for Write-offs	0	4,066	8,257	11,769
Total Off-Balance Sheet	0	386,934	785,677	1,119,907
Income Statement:				
Interest Income	45,000	54,731	62,855	76,614
Interest Expense	27,600	33,569	38,552	46,990
Net Interest Income	17,400	21,162	24,303	29,624
Servicing Income	0	3,095	6,285	8,959
Income Before Expenses	17,400	24,258	30,588	38,583
Expenses and Charge-offs	10,200	12,406	14,247	17,366
Operating Income	7,200	11,852	16,341	21,218
Tax (40%)	2,880	4,741	6,536	8,487
After-tax Operating Income	4,320	7,111	9,805	12,731
Gain on Sale	0	–3,519	–3,663	–3,114
Total After-tax Income	4,320	3,592	6,142	9,617
Assets:				
Receivables, Past - Adjusted	0	494,800	601,796	691,125
Receivables, New	500,000	500,000	500,000	500,000
Asset Reinvestment	0	4,320	3,592	6,142
Less: Receivables Sold	0	391,000	407,000	346,000
Total Assets	500,000	608,120	698,388	851,266
Liabilities and Equity:				
Liabilities	480,000	583,800	670,476	817,212
Stockholder Equity	20,000	24,320	27,912	34,054
Total Liabilities & Equity	500,000	608,120	698,388	851,266
Ratios:				
On-going Operations:				
Capital Ratio	4.00%	4.00%	4.00%	4.00%
ROA	0.86%	1.17%	1.40%	1.50%
ROE	21.60%	29.24%	35.13%	37.38%
Total, Including Loss on Sale:				
ROA	0.86%	0.59%	0.88%	1.13%
ROE	21.60%	14.77%	22.00%	28.24%

Exhibit 13: Constant 10% Growth in Receivables Generation with Receivables Sold at a Loss to Maintain a 4% Capital Ratio

Facts:	Year 1	Year 2	Year 3	Year 4
Gross Assets Sold	0	441,000	518,000	518,000
After-tax Gain on Sale	0	–3,969	–4,662	–4,662
After-tax Operating Income	4,320	3,380	5,852	9,529
Cash Realized	4,320	440,411	519,190	522,867
New Receivables Created	500,000	554,320	608,380	671,352
Total Receivables Sold	0	441,000	954,414	1,462,488
Adjustment for Write-offs	0	4,586	9,926	15,210
Total Off-Balance Sheet	0	436,414	944,488	1,447,278
Income Statement:				
Interest Income	45,000	54,731	62,296	75,450
Interest Expense	27,600	33,569	38,207	46,275
Net Interest Income	17,400	21,162	24,088	29,175
Servicing Income	0	3,491	7,556	11,578
Income Before Expenses	17,400	24,654	31,644	40,753
Expenses and Charge-offs	10,200	12,406	14,120	17,102
Operating Income	7,200	12,248	17,524	23,651
Tax (40%)	2,880	4,899	7,010	9,461
After-tax Operating Income	4,320	7,349	10,514	14,191
Gain on Sale	0	–3,969	–4,662	–4,662
Total After-tax Income	4,320	3,380	5,852	9,529
Assets:				
Receivables, Past - Adjusted	0	494,800	601,796	684,977
Receivables, New	500,000	550,000	605,000	665,500
Asset Reinvestment	0	4,320	3,380	5,852
Less: Receivables Sold	0	441,000	518,000	518,000
Total Assets	500,000	608,120	692,175	838,329
Liabilities and Equity:				
Liabilities	480,000	583,800	664,476	804,777
Stockholder Equity	20,000	24,320	27,700	33,552
Total Liabilities & Equity	500,000	608,120	692,175	838,329
Ratios:				
On-going Operations:				
Capital Ratio	4.00%	4.00%	4.00%	4.00%
ROA	0.86%	1.21%	1.52%	1.69%
ROE	21.60%	30.22%	37.96%	42.29%
Total, Including Loss on Sale:				
ROA	0.86%	0.56%	0.85%	1.14%
ROE	21.60%	13.90%	21.13%	28.40%

Exhibit 14: Performance Graphs - Loss on Sale
Pro Forma Results from Exhibits 1, 11, 12, and 13 with an 8-Year Forecasting Horizon

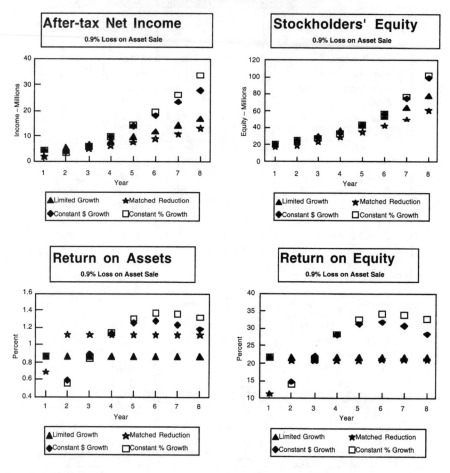

Legend and Sources of Data

Limited Growth – Exhibit 1 entitled "On-Balance Sheet Financing with New Receivables Based on Capital Ratio Maintenance"

Matched Reduction – Exhibit 11 entitled "Selling Receivables at a Loss to Reduce Debt with New Receivables Generation as shown in Exhibit 1"

Constant $ Growth – Exhibit 12 entitled "Constant Dollar Receivables Generation and Receivables Sold at a Loss to Maintain a 4% Capital Ratio"

Constant % Growth – Exhibit 13 entitled "Constant 10% Growth in Receivables Generation and Receivables Sold at a Loss to Maintain a 4% Capital Ratio"

Exhibit 15: Comparison of Forecast Results with a
Loss on Asset Sales

Scenario	Net Income (M)		Equity (M)		Total ROA		Total ROE	
	No Loss	0.9% Loss	No Loss	0.9% Loss	No Loss	0.9% Loss	No Loss	0.9% Loss	No Loss
Limited Growth	$7.8	N/A	$36.0	N/A	0.86%	N/A	21.6%	N/A
Matched Reduction	$6.8	$6.0	$33.5	$28.7	1.26%	1.12%	20.2%	20.9%
Constant $ Growth	$13.5	$9.6	$41.6	$34.0	1.30%	1.13%	32.5%	28.2%
Constant % Growth	$15.1	$9.5	$42.6	$33.6	1.42%	1.14%	35.5%	28.4%

IMPACT OF THE LEVEL OF ECONOMIC HEALTH

The above forecasts were conducted from the perspective of a healthy economy, where there were no external limits on the ability to generate new, quality receivables. Investigating the impact of changes in economic health or changes in competitive pressures in generating receivables is beyond the intended scope here. Nevertheless, two comments logically follow from the pro forma statements and other conclusions.

One of the linchpins to the superior overall results of the constant dollar growth or constant percentage growth scenario was that smaller profit on an individual receivable was offset by an increase in the volume of receivables generation and the profits were reinvested to expand the capital base. This provided for further growth. If a bank is following an asset sale strategy and new receivables cannot be produced at a rate to utilize income available to be reinvested, it would be unwise to begin a long-term strategy of retirement of debt with the excess funds. This would invoke the "matched reduction strategy" on a smaller scale, but have the same negative effects.

The second observation on possible effects of an economic downturn is that the asset sale strategy employed in forecasting assumed the retention of receivables servicing income. In the forecasts shown in Exhibit 5 where assets are sold at no gain and growth proceeds at a constant percentage, the Year 4 servicing income is $9.9 million out of $25.2 million pre-tax income. This is just under 40% of total pre-tax income. In the baseline case, with on-balance sheet funding, servicing income in Year 4 is $7.5 million, or 33% of $22.5 million pre-tax income. The servicing income is much more stable in times of economic distress or downturn than income from other sources. Since the constant percentage growth strategy has larger dollar servicing income and larger percentage servicing income, the income stream from lending operations is potentially less risky than on-balance sheet funding. When coupled with the asset-liability manager's ability to off-load and match fund less desirable receivables, whole loan sales and securitization as part of a larger strategy become quite attractive.

CONCLUSIONS

While the specific results above were based on selected forecasting parameters, the general conclusions are robust. With on-balance sheet funding of generated receivables, the capital ratio becomes the factor that limits growth for an otherwise healthy firm. Assets sales to reduce liabilities should only be done when it is required by circumstance, such as meeting regulatory requirements. Assets can be sold to enhance income and asset growth, while improving the standard measures of efficiency such as return on assets and return on equity. It is obvious to sell assets at a gain if possible.

The superior strategic approach involves positioning the firm to enjoy the fastest rate of growth in generation of new receivables and selling some proportion of those assets to maintain the desired capital ratio. This optimizes the rate of income growth in terms of both dollars and percentages. This scenario also provides the ability for the asset/liability manager to off-load part of the funding and interest rate risk inherent in the receivables. As discussed above, the income stream with whole loan sales or securitization can be more recession resistant. The enhanced income stream and mitigated risk should be reflected in the value of the firm and stock price.

Chapter 11

The Measurement of Prepayments and Defaults in ABS Markets

Anand K. Bhattacharya, Ph.D.
Executive Vice President
Countrywide Capital Markets Inc.

INTRODUCTION

W ith the growth of the asset-backed market and the increasing reliance of issuers on this market as a funding alternative, it is important for issuers to understand the general prepayment and default nomenclature used in these markets. Contrary to the other general class of prepayment sensitive assets, such as mortgage-backed securities, the ABS market is characterized by the usage of a variety of prepayment terms, some specific to certain asset classes, such as ABS, HEP, PPC, MHP, and MPR and default language such as CDR. In this chapter, the basic terms used to characterize asset-backed prepayments and losses are discussed within specific segments of the market. Note that our focus is on describing the terminology and nomenclature and our discussion does not focus on the determinants or the modelling of prepayments and defaults.

From the view point of the issuer, despite the variety of terms used in the ABS markets to define prepayments and defaults, understanding these terms and the underlying methodologies used to generate these metrics is important for the following reasons.

- Efficient risk based pricing at the origination level.
- Evaluation of the issuer's investment in the residual tranches, especially since such investments have an important effect on earnings and capital structure.
- Development of loss mitigation strategies.
- Aggregate risk and loss reserve management.

BASICS OF ASSET PREPAYMENTS

A major reason for the usage of various prepayment conventions in the ABS market is the diversity in the cash flow patterns of such assets, as the underlying cash flows can be categorized as amortizing or non-amortizing. For fixed-rate amortizing assets, such as fixed-rate mortgages, home-equity loans (HELs), and automobile loans, the monthly scheduled payment, consisting of scheduled principal and interest payments, is constant throughout the amortization term. If the borrower pays more than the monthly scheduled payment, the extra payment will be used to pay down the outstanding balance faster than the original amortization schedule. If the outstanding balance is paid off in full, the prepayment is a "complete prepayment;" if only a portion of the outstanding balance is prepaid, the prepayment is called a "partial prepayment," or curtailment. Prepayments can be the result of natural turnover, refinancings, defaults, partial paydowns, and credit-related events such as curing to a higher risk grade and hence, lower interest rate. In some of these assets, the evaluation of prepayments is further complicated by the fact that there is an interplay between defaults, which are effectively "credit-related" prepayments and interest rate related prepayments.

Prepayments and defaults can be analyzed on both the loan and pool level. Loan-level prepayment analysis, which requires detailed loan level information, is more accurate and computationally intensive than pool-level prepayment analysis. Additionally, this type of analysis allows the inclusion of specific obligor and property characteristics as determinants of prepayments and defaults. Loan-level analysis involves amortizing each loan individually, tracking defaults, and prepayments on an individual loan basis and combining these amount to calculate aggregated metrics. Due to the diversity of the characteristics of the underlying loans in most ABS deals, loan level analysis is generally more accurate and has greater predictive capabilities.

Non-amortizing assets (e.g. credit cards and home-equity lines of credit) do not have a fixed payment schedule. There is usually a minimum payment and the unpaid interest portion is added to the outstanding principal. Thus there is usually no "prepayment" for non-amortizing assets because there is no predetermined amortizing schedule; the borrower has a flexible repayment schedule. However, in the evaluation of these assets, the principal amount is heavily driven by the interaction between the paydown of the principal that occurs as part of the periodic payments and the draw down of additional credit as individuals incur additional charges on revolving lines of credit. In view of this observation, the net increase (or decrease) of the outstanding principal balance including finance charges adjusted for the amount of delinquent amounts is the relevant metric.

GENERAL PREPAYMENT NOMENCLATURE

While the expression of prepayments in the MBS markets is fairly standardized and comprises a combination of PSA curves and CPR calculations, a variety of descriptions are used to express the paydown behavior of different asset types in the ABS market comprising a virtual alphabet soup of terminology, ranging from ABS, HEP, MHP, MPR, and, more recently, PPC. Despite the diversity in terminology, most of the concepts used to indicate prepayments in the ABS markets use the CPR concept as the numeraire, which is a derivative of the monthly paydown rate, labelled as the SMM. Additionally, certain ABS methodologies, such as the MHP, HEP, and PPC curves use elements of the PSA ramping technology. In view of this consideration, we review the SMM, CPR, and PSA concepts as reference points prior to discussing terminology in the ABS markets.

Single Monthly Mortality (SMM)

The *single monthly mortality rate* (SMM) is the most fundamental measure of prepayment speeds; it is the unit upon which all other prepayment measures are based. SMM measures the monthly prepayment amount as a percentage of the previous month's outstanding balance minus the scheduled principal payment. Mathematically, the SMM is calculated as follows

$$\text{SMM} = \frac{\text{Total Payment, including prepayments} - \text{Scheduled Interest Payment} - \text{Scheduled Principal Payment}}{[\text{Unpaid Principal Balance} - \text{Scheduled Principal Payment}]}$$

For example, if the pool balance at month zero is \$10,000,000, assuming an interest rate of 12%, the scheduled principal and interest payments are \$2,920.45 and \$100,000 in month one, respectively. If the actual payment in month one is \$202,891.25, the SMM rate is 1%, calculated as:

$$\text{SMM} = \frac{(202{,}891.25 - 100{,}000 - 2{,}920.45)}{(10{,}000{,}000 - 2{,}920.45)} = 1\%$$

Therefore, if an asset prepaid at 1% SMM in a particular month, this means that 1% of that month's scheduled balance (last month's outstanding balance minus the scheduled principal payment) has been prepaid.

Conditional Prepayment Rate (CPR)

While the basic unit of expressing prepayments is the SMM, primarily due to the monthly nature of most ABS cash flows, it is usually expressed in terms of CPR (*conditional prepayment rate*), which is the annualized or compounded SMM. The formula to convert from SMM to CPR is similar to standard compounding formulations:

$$\text{CPR} = 1 - (1 - \text{SMM})^{12}$$

The annualized nature of the CPR metric is fairly intuitive — if an asset continues to prepay at a monthly SMM rate for one year, it is equivalent to the annualized CPR rate. For example, if an asset prepays at 1% SMM every month for one year, it is equivalent to 11.4% CPR, which means 11.4% of the asset will paydown in a year. Additionally, the CPR method of prepayments does not have a built in seasoning ramp, which makes it easy to understand and fairly easy to use for a variety of collateral types. As a point of reference, Exhibit 1 provides a table of SMM to CPR conversions.

PSA Curve

Any discussion of prepayment nomenclature would be incomplete without reference to the PSA (Public Securities Association) curve.[1] While the PSA curve is not directly applicable to the valuation of ABSs, it is the normal benchmark for expressing prepayments in the MBS markets, where history is rich with developments in measuring and evaluating prepayments. Additionally, due to the fact that the development of the PSA curve represented the first formal step towards the analytical standardization of prepayment nomenclature, elements of this technology, especially the ramping methodology have been used as the foundation for other concepts such as the HEP curve for home-equity loans and the MHP curve for manufactured housing loans. A prepayment rate of 100% PSA assumes a prepayment rate of 0.2% CPR in the first month of mortgage origination and an additional 0.2% CPR in each subsequent month until month 30, when speeds plateau at 6% CPR. Exhibit 2 displays the 100% and 200% PSA curves.[2]

Exhibit 1: SMM to CPR Conversion Table

Conversion Formula CPR (%) = $1 - (1 - SMM)^{12}$

SMM (%)	CPR (%)	SMM (%)	CPR (%)
1.0	11.4	14.0	83.6
2.0	21.5	15.0	85.8
3.0	30.6	16.0	87.7
4.0	38.7	17.0	89.3
5.0	46.0	18.0	90.8
6.0	52.4	19.0	92.0
7.0	58.1	20.0	93.1
8.0	63.2	21.0	94.1
9.0	67.8	22.0	94.9
10.0	71.8	23.0	95.7
11.0	75.3	24.0	96.3
12.0	78.4	25.0	96.8
13.0	81.2		

[1] Public Securities Association, which is the trade association for participants in the fixed-income securities markets, is now known as the Bond Market Association (BMA).

[2] The PSA curve is a relatively good measure of agency prepayment speeds in the absence of refinancings. The refinancing component, which does not exhibit an aging pattern, could significantly distort the PSA curve, which is a major reason that PSA is used mainly to measure discount and current-coupon prepayments, while CPR is used to measure premium-coupon prepayments.

Exhibit 2: PSA Curves

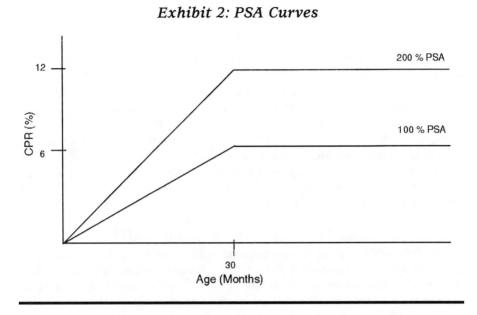

MEASUREMENT OF ABS PREPAYMENTS

Due to the heterogeneity of the types of asset cash flows that are labeled under the rubric of ABSs, there are two distinct types of prepayment methodologies employed in the evaluation of ABSs. For assets, such as credit cards and other types of revolving lines of credit, such as HELOCs, where the contractual payment is a minimum amount, the "prepayment" method involves adjusting the principal balance. For other assets, where there is a contractual paydown of principal as part of the amortization, the prepayment method is a modified form of paydown method similar to that involved in MBSs.

Monthly Payment Rate (MPR)

As noted, there are a variety of terms used in the ABS markets to describe prepayments for a different asset types. Perhaps, the earliest term used in the ABS markets is the *monthly payment rate* (MPR), which is used mainly for measuring credit card and, more recently, for home equity lines of credit payments. Since there is no amortization schedule associated with credit card and home equity borrowing, the concept of prepayments essentially does not apply to these asset classes. Each month, in a portfolio of revolving charge accounts such as credit cards, borrowers pay down a certain portion of the principal while others make additional draws on their lines of credit. At the same time cash flows of the portfolio are enhanced by finance charges and hampered by delinquent accounts.

In this regime of cash flows, MPR measures the monthly payment, including principal and interest payments, adjusted for delinquent accounts of a revolving accounts portfolio as a percentage of debt outstanding in the previous month. For example, out of a $100 million credit card portfolio, a 15% MPR rate means that the net payment for that month is $15 million, including all relevant finance charges. Since most credit card issues are under a master trust structure, the payment rate usually does not alter investment cash flow unless the MPR slows to extremely low levels, which might cause extension on principal payments. From the issuer's perspective, the MPR is also important because rating agencies require that revolving charge securitizations include a minimum MPR to avoid an early amortization trigger event. The rating agencies reason that, if the MPR were to drop to a very low level, there might not be enough cash flow to pay off all of the principal if an early amortization occurred for any reason.

Absolute Prepayment Speed (ABS)

While the MPR is the oldest concept used in the evaluation of non-amortizing ABSs, the *absolute prepayment speed* (ABS) measure is the earliest methodology used in evaluation of speeds for amortizing assets. In the early years of the development of the ABS market, where the majority of securitizations involved credit cards and autos, the ABS measure was primarily used to quantify prepayments on automobile loans and leases, truck loans, and RV loans. Other amortzing assets, such as home equity and manufactured housing loans use terms developed from the MBS markets using empirical validation specific to the asset class.

Contrary to the CPR measure, which measures prepayments as a percentage of the current loan balance, ABS measures prepayments as a percentage of the original loan balance. In general, short amortizing assets tend to exhibit increasing prepayment rates as the pool of loans seasons when measured on an SMM basis. This occurs due to the shorter amortization period of the asset and the inclusion of successively greater amounts of stated principal in fixed level payment. This is in sharp contrast to home mortgages where the amount of principal amortization is fairly small in the early years of the mortgage. However, when short dated assets are measured on an ABS basis, prepayment speeds exhibit greater stability.

Not surprisingly, the actual ABS computations are based upon the SMM concept. In particular, the ABS measure defines an increasing sequence of prepayment rates (SMMs) based upon the following conversion formula.

$$ABS = 100 \times SMM/[100 + SMM \times (M - 1)]$$

where M is the number of months after loan origination

Exhibit 3 shows a conversion table from ABS to SMM. For example, If an auto pool prepaid at 2% ABS at month 11 after loan origination, its corresponding SMM rate can be calculated using this table. As can be seen from the table, a constant ABS actually translates into increasingly faster SMM rates in order to account for the faster amortization of short dated assets.

Exhibit 3: Conversion Table from ABS (%) to SMM (%)

Loan Age (Months)	ABS (%)									
	0.50	0.75	1.00	1.25	1.50	1.75	2.00	2.25	2.50	2.75
	SMM (%)									
1	0.50	0.75	1.00	1.25	1.50	1.75	2.00	2.25	2.50	2.75
2	0.50	0.76	1.01	1.27	1.52	1.78	2.04	2.30	2.56	2.83
3	0.51	0.76	1.02	1.28	1.55	1.81	2.08	2.36	2.63	2.91
4	0.51	0.77	1.03	1.30	1.57	1.85	2.13	2.41	2.70	3.00
5	0.51	0.77	1.04	1.32	1.60	1.88	2.17	2.47	2.78	3.09
6	0.51	0.78	1.05	1.33	1.62	1.92	2.22	2.54	2.86	3.19
7	0.52	0.79	1.06	1.35	1.65	1.96	2.27	2.60	2.94	3.29
8	0.52	0.79	1.08	1.37	1.68	1.99	2.33	2.67	3.03	3.41
9	0.52	0.80	1.09	1.39	1.70	2.03	2.38	2.74	3.13	3.53
10	0.52	0.80	1.10	1.41	1.73	2.08	2.44	2.82	3.23	3.65
11	0.53	0.81	1.11	1.43	1.76	2.12	2.50	2.90	3.33	3.79
12	0.53	0.82	1.12	1.45	1.80	2.17	2.56	2.99	3.45	3.94
13	0.53	0.82	1.14	1.47	1.83	2.22	2.63	3.08	3.57	4.10
14	0.53	0.83	1.15	1.49	1.86	2.27	2.70	3.18	3.70	4.28
15	0.54	0.84	1.16	1.52	1.90	2.32	2.78	3.28	3.85	4.47
16	0.54	0.85	1.18	1.54	1.94	2.37	2.86	3.40	4.00	4.68
17	0.54	0.85	1.19	1.56	1.97	2.43	2.94	3.52	4.17	4.91
18	0.55	0.86	1.20	1.59	2.01	2.49	3.03	3.64	4.35	5.16
19	0.55	0.87	1.22	1.61	2.05	2.55	3.13	3.78	4.55	5.45
20	0.55	0.87	1.23	1.64	2.10	2.62	3.23	3.93	4.76	5.76
21	0.56	0.88	1.25	1.67	2.14	2.69	3.33	4.09	5.00	6.11
22	0.56	0.89	1.27	1.69	2.19	2.77	3.45	4.27	5.26	6.51
23	0.56	0.90	1.28	1.72	2.24	2.85	3.57	4.46	5.56	6.96
24	0.56	0.91	1.30	1.75	2.29	2.93	3.70	4.66	5.88	7.48
25	0.57	0.91	1.32	1.79	2.34	3.02	3.85	4.89	6.25	8.09
26	0.57	0.92	1.33	1.82	2.40	3.11	4.00	5.14	6.67	8.80
27	0.57	0.93	1.35	1.85	2.46	3.21	4.17	5.42	7.14	9.65
28	0.58	0.94	1.37	1.89	2.52	3.32	4.35	5.73	7.69	10.68
29	0.58	0.95	1.39	1.92	2.59	3.43	4.55	6.08	8.33	11.96
30	0.58	0.96	1.41	1.96	2.65	3.55	4.76	6.47	9.09	13.58
31	0.59	0.97	1.43	2.00	2.73	3.68	5.00	6.92	10.00	15.71
32	0.59	0.98	1.45	2.04	2.80	3.83	5.26	7.44	11.11	18.64
33	0.60	0.99	1.47	2.08	2.88	3.98	5.56	8.04	12.50	22.92
34	0.60	1.00	1.49	2.13	2.97	4.14	5.88	8.74	14.29	29.73
35	0.60	1.01	1.52	2.17	3.06	4.32	6.25	9.57	16.67	42.31
36	0.61	1.02	1.54	2.22	3.16	4.52	6.67	10.59	20.00	73.33

Manufactured Housing Prepayment (MHP) Curve

The *manufactured housing prepayment* (MHP) curve is a measure of prepayment behavior for manufactured housing, based on the Green Tree manufactured housing prepayment experience. MHP is similar to the PSA curve, except that the seasoning ramp is slightly different to account for the specific behavior of manufactured loans. 100% MHP is equivalent to 3.6% CPR at month zero and increases 0.1% CPR every month until month 24, when it plateaus at 6% CPR. Exhibit 4 shows the prepayment speeds at 50% MHP, 100% MHP, and 200% MHP.

Home Equity Prepayment (HEP) Curve

In the ABS markets, home equity loans are defined as first lien loans to sub-prime credits. In the ABS market, home equity lines of credit (HELOCs) are typically floating rate second lien loans made to prime borrowers. In the early stages of the development of the securitized market for home equity loans, the majority of the loans were fixed-rate closed-end loans. Over the years, the balance has slowly shifted in favor of adjustable-rate loans. The earliest definition of prepayment speeds in the home equity market was the *home equity prepayment* (HEP) *curve*.[3] The primary motivation for using a different prepayment methodology for home equity loans was to capture the faster seasoning ramp observed for prepayments. Typically, home equity loans season faster than traditional single family loans, making the PSA ramp an inappropriate description of the behavior of prepayments.

The HEP curve reflects the observed behavior in historic HEL data — it has a ramp of 10 months and a variable long-term CPR to reflect individual issuer speeds. A faster long-term speed means faster CPRs on the ramp because the ramp is fixed at 10 months regardless of the long-term speed. For example, a 20% HEP projection would mean a 10-month ramp going to 20% in the tenth month from 2% in the first month and a constant 20% thereafter. Exhibit 5 shows several HEP curves at 20% HEP and 24% HEP, where month 1 speeds of 2.4% CPR increase over 10 months to 24% CPR.

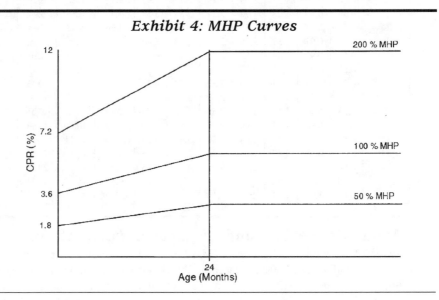

Exhibit 4: MHP Curves

[3] The HEP curve was developed by Prudential Securities based on the prepayment experience of $10 billion home-equity loan deals.

Exhibit 5: HEP Curves

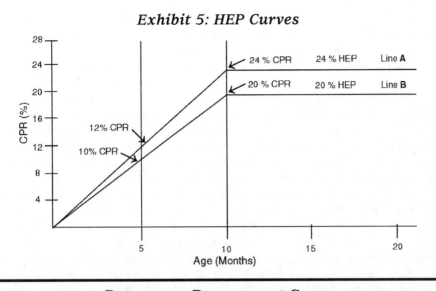

Prospectus Prepayment Curve

A recent addition to the HEL prepayment terminology is the *prospectus prepayment* (or *pricing*) *curve* (PPC). In the early stages of the development of the home equity markets, while the HEP curve was used as the prepayment standard, there was disagreement regarding the actual length of the seasoning ramp. Additionally, at the same time, the onset of securitization of mortgage loans originated using expanded criteria, such as "Alt-A" loans which did not meet the standard classification of agency or jumbo loans, created the need for prepayment vectors based on the specific paydown and seasoning characteristics of the collateral. As a result, PPCs are issue specific and differ from the HEP mostly in the seasoning ramp, with the designation of 100% PPC defined as the base-case assumption. However, there is no industry standardization for the usage of this terminology, as the specification is issue dependent. As a result, while the PPC may be used at pricing, the relative value evaluation usually defaults to the usage of PPC implied CPR vectors as an *ad-hoc* method of standardization. For example, for one particular issue, 100% PPC may be defined as prepayment speeds starting at 5% CPR at month zero, increasing 1.5% CPR a month until month 11 and then plateauing at 21.5% CPR. For another issue, however, 100% PPC may be defined with different starting points and with a different seasoning ramp. As a result, investors should carefully investigate how 100% PPC is defined for each particular issue.

DEFAULT AND LOSS TERMINOLOGY

Since all ABS structures rely on some form of credit enhancement which takes the form of some combination of subordination or insurance wrap, overcollateralization, cash deposit, and reserve fund, the measurement of defaults and losses is very important. The importance of these measurements stems from the fact that in addition to the relevance of these measures to assess the relative value of lower rated tranches, the issuer typically retains the unrated and residual components of securitized deals. Therefore, any differences in the actual loss and default experience from expectations at pricing may lead to significant writedowns and adversely affect firm valuation. Despite the importance of delinquencies, losses and defaults in the ABS markets, the terminology is not standardized.[4] For instance, static pool losses may be reported on a monthly or annualized basis as a percentage of either current or original balance with the metric based upon current balance being the preferred method to ensure consistency with prepayment reporting.

Before we discuss the measurement of defaults and losses, it is instructive to briefly review the various outcomes of the loan when the obligor defaults. Typically, when all collection efforts have failed while the loan is in delinquent status and it is eventually declared to be in default, the issuer (or the servicer) has several options. In unsecured loans, such as credit cards, there is an immediate charge-off. In secured loans, there may either be a short sale, where the borrower sells the asset in a negotiated transaction subject to approval by the servicer or the asset may go into the foreclosure or repossession process and be eventually sold by the servicer. Therefore, the process chain is delinquency to default to foreclosure or repossession to liquidation, at which time the severity of loss will be assessed.

In view of this process, there are several measures that are relevant from the perspective of both issuers and investors of ABS securities. With respect to a pool of loans,

$$\text{Cumulative Defaults} = \frac{\text{Unpaid Principal Balance of Defaulted Loans}}{\text{Pool Original Principal Balance}}$$

and

$$\text{Annual Default Frequency} = \frac{\text{Unpaid Principal Balance of Defaulted Loans}}{\text{Average Pool Balance}}$$

where *default* is generically defined as the event when a loan no longer makes contractual payments and remains in this status till liquidation.

In the parlance of asset-backed securities, this term is also referred to as the *cumulative default rate* (CDR), which may be measured either monthly or over a longer period of time. Note that the CDR metric measures only the amount of defaults and not the amount of losses because the actual amount of losses will depend upon the amounts that can be recovered on loans in default adjusted for the costs of collection and servicer advances, if applicable. In the extreme case, if there is full recovery of the unpaid principal balance of the defaulted loans, the

---

[4] The only standardized description of default behavior exists with respect to MBS. This methodology, labelled as the Standard Default Analysis (SDA) curve, was designed to be used with amortizing mortgages with an original term longer than 15 years and does not apply to other mortgage assets, such as commercial, home equity and balloon loans and all non-mortgage assets.

losses will be zero with the exception of the costs of recovery. However, depending upon the timing of the recovery of the defaulted loan balances, the cash flows to certain bondholders may be interrupted.

With respect to losses,

$$\text{Loss} = \text{Original Pool Balance}$$
$$- \text{Recoveries on Unpaid Principal Balance of Defaulted Loans}$$

$$\text{Loss Severity} = \frac{\text{Losses}}{\text{Unpaid Principal Balance of Defaulted Loans}}$$

$$\text{Estimated Annualized Losses} = \text{Annual Default Frequency} \times \text{Loss Severity}$$

From the viewpoint of issuers, the default and loss assumptions used to capitalize these investments are critical for assessing firm value as any deterioration of value in the retained tranches emanating from overly aggressive assumptions can have a material impact on the corporate valuation. As of this writing, there were several regulatory proposals that would require financial institutions to reserve dollar-for-dollar capital on residuals and limit concentrations of residuals to 25% of Tier I capital. Additionally, a new accounting standard, Financial Accounting Standards Board 140, would require increased disclosure on residual interests with respect to key assumptions, such as discount rates and prepayment rates, along with delinquency rates and credit losses on the total pools of securitized assets. Additionally, the performance of residual assets under stress test scenarios, as well as changes in key assumptions, would have to be reported at year end.

Chapter 12

Understanding MBS/ABS Loss Terminology

Thomas Zimmerman
Senior Vice President
Mortgage Strategy Group
PaineWebber

INTRODUCTION

As the MBS and ABS markets continue to grow, more issuers and investors are grappling with the sometimes convoluted and inconsistent terminology used to describe "losses" in these markets. Also, as investors have become more sophisticated, the timely and accurate reporting of credit performance data has taken on greater importance. This is especially true in the real estate-related ABS sectors which have experienced a sharp increase in delinquencies and losses in recent years. In fact, to function as a top tier issuer today it is almost mandatory that a firm provide investors with historical credit information.

With that in mind, it is important that issuers understand the various ways in which loss data can be presented and how it can be used to present a clear picture of their credit performance. In this chapter I will discuss the most common terms describing losses, and will try to put them into some kind of logical order. This is not a new problem. In a meeting several years ago with two Ph.D. statisticians, we were discussing a model to project losses in the sub-prime home equity market. During the first ten minutes of the meeting there was a contentious debate about the level of losses projected by the model. It took a while to realize that Statistician #1 (the prepayment specialist) was looking at the world through "CPR/CDR" glasses, while Statistician #2 (the structuring specialist) was viewing it through "cumulative loss" lenses. Once we defined our terms, life proceeded much more smoothly.

DEFAULTS VERSUS LOSSES

A good place to start is with the difference between defaults and losses. A *default* is essentially a loan that does not get paid back. A loan may go into the 90-day delinquent category or even into foreclosure, and still be made current again. So only those loans that are ultimately liquidated for non-payment are classified as defaulted loans.

153

Losses refer to the dollar amounts lost on defaulted loans. Often sale proceeds are not sufficient to cover the remaining balance on the loan as well as associated fees and costs. The difference is the loss amount.

Losses differ from defaults in amount and timing. Once a loan goes into foreclosure it can take months to complete the foreclosure and liquidation process. So there is often a lag between when a loan first goes into default and when any loss is incurred. Also, the amount of loss can vary greatly, depending on the LTV and the state of the property market. The loan can be a total loss, or if the LTV is low enough or the property market strong enough, there may be a default with no loss. That is, *loss severity* can range from 0% to 100%.

DEFAULT AND LOSS CURVES

In projecting losses for any particular pool of loans, it is common to first project a *default curve*, then a *loss curve*. To construct the second from the former, two additional pieces of information are needed — an estimate of average time between default and liquidation, and an estimate of loss severity. In the home equity sector it is common to assume a one-year lag between default and loss, and 35%-50% loss severity. Another example is the hi-LTV market. There, the convention is to write off 100% of a loan after 180 days of delinquency. The assumption is that since the loan is an unsecured second lien, there will be little or no recovery (i.e., 100% loss severity).

In hi-LTVs, there is very little difference between a default curve and a loss curve, but in all other sectors there is a big difference. However in practice, the terms "default rate" and "loss rate" are often used interchangeably, which muddies the waters. Many people write the term "default" when they are referring to "losses." If it is not clear in a report or article what is meant by the term "default rate," it is better to ask for clarification. If the term "default rate" truly means defaults, then an estimate of the time to liquidation and of loss severity is needed before losses can be projected.

SOURCE OF CONFUSION

There is a clear distinction between defaults and losses, but some of that is lost when analysts try to determine the impact of defaults and losses on structured securities. A loss does not occur until the property is liquidated. At that time, the loan is removed from the pool and liquidated. From a speed perspective, the entire loan amount is treated as a prepayment. From a loss perspective, only the net loss is treated as a loss. The timing of defaults calculated in this manner are exactly the same as the timing of losses. In reality, though, the loans went into default well before the losses were recorded.

Unfortunately, both loss-driven prepayments and losses are reported in terms of *conditional default rates* (CDRs). The involuntary prepayment CDRs are additive to a pool's voluntary CPRs to arrive at a total prepayment speed. The loss

CDRs are not additive to prepayments. While the loss component is often presented in terms of a CDR, in fact, it should really be called a *conditional loss rate* (CLR). But don't waste your time looking for CLRs in any materials on prepayments, losses or defaults. Virtually everyone uses the term CDR to cover both loss rates and default rates. Usually they are accompanied by a brief discussion pointing out differences between losses and defaults (just as I am doing here), but the charts and graphs all still use CDR.

Historically, most discussions of prepayment speeds in the home equity sector did not make specific reference to loss rates. Those were included in overall prepayment rates. With declining overall credit performance in home equities, it is more common to specify both voluntary and involuntary prepayment rates. However, in mortgage-backed securities issued by agencies, where losses are insignificant, the contribution of losses to overall prepayment speed is seldom specified separately.

REPORTING OF LOSSES

Rating agencies and other statistical services typically report loss data in two main ways — monthly losses and cumulative losses.

Monthly Losses

The monthly loss reported is usually monthly losses as a percent of the *remaining* pool balance. Monthly loss numbers are usually annualized. These monthly losses are equivalent to the CDRs discussed earlier. In sub-prime home equities, monthly loss rates (annualized) on seasoned loans typically run in the 1-2% range. In credit cards, that number is around 5-6%. In Jumbos, it can be zero for many months, but in general, averages a few basis points.

Cumulative Losses

The second major type of loss reporting uses cumulative losses (as opposed to monthly CDRs) over the life of a pool or deal as a percent of the *original pool balance*. Cumulative loss is not a monthly or annual number, so it cannot be compared directly to a CDR. It is simply found by dividing the total losses to date by the original balance of the pool. Note that with this measure, original balance is used rather than remaining balance. That contrasts with most other credit measures (such as delinquencies, foreclosures, and REO), which typically use remaining balance, as does the CDR (loss or default) rate discussed earlier.

While they are different measures, there is still a close relationship between cumulative losses and CDRs (i.e., monthly loss rates). A good approximation of total cumulative losses for a pool can be derived from the average CDR and the average life of loans in a pool. For example, a typical home equity pool can have CDRs ranging between 0% and 2%, which average around 1%-1.3% over the life of the deal. Since the average life of those loans is 3.5-4.0 years, total cumulative losses over the life of the pool will come in at around 4.0%-5.0%.

Remaining versus Original Balance

The loss measures discussed above differ in two respects. The first is the period covered — monthly versus cumulative. The second is that monthly losses are typically reported as a percent of the remaining balance, while cumulative loss is reported as a percent of the original balance. In Exhibit 1, we illustrate the relationship between loss measures based on those two different types of balances.

For the remaining balance data in Exhibit 1 we used a 15-year home equity deal and assumed a prepayment curve (i.e., a PPC) leveling off at 24% CPR. Balances are shown as a function of time in section 1 of the exhibit. The original balance (column B) is shown as a straight line, while the remaining balance (column A) shows the typical ski slope shape of an amortizing mortgage pool with a fairly high prepayment speed. Section 2 of the exhibit shows assumed dollar losses for each month, which are the same for columns A and B.

Section 3 of the exhibit shows monthly dollar losses as a percent of the balances — the remaining balance for column A, and original balance for column B. The section 3 curve in column A is typical of CDR curves used in most reports and loss projections. It rises for 2.5 years, levels off for 2 years, and then declines. Most mortgage-related products have loss curves with roughly similar shapes, but different maximum loss rates and different slopes. The PSA SDA curve used in the jumbo whole loan sector is similar. Only the 100% PSA SDA curve has a peak of 0.60% (not the 2.00% peak shown in section 1-B of Exhibit 1). And, in fact, the PSA SDA curve is for defaults, not losses.

Section 4 of the exhibit shows cumulative dollar losses, which is simply the sum of monthly losses shown in section 2. Section 5-B shows those cumulative losses as a percent of original balance. In our example, cumulative losses reach 4.59% (that's about average for 1996-1998 home equities). Section 5-A shows cumulative losses as a percentage of remaining balance. It is quite clear from Exhibit 1 why remaining balance is not used for representing cumulative losses. Shown as a percentage of remaining balance, cumulative loss becomes an infinite number as the remaining balance approaches zero.

Cumulative loss charts (rather than CDR charts) are often used in trying to compare losses between deals or vintages. Monthly CDRs from two deals can be volatile, which makes it difficult to tell which is performing better. This problem does not exist with a cumulative comparison, since cumulative data smooths out monthly fluctuations. And that is why we recommend using cumulative loss charts.

LOSSES AND SPEED

In preparing the graphs in Exhibit 1, we used two assumptions — the speed with which loans pay down (which determined the remaining balances in section 1-A), and the shape of the CDR curve. The monthly and cumulative losses presented in Exhibit 1 resulted from these assumptions. If either the CDR curve or the remaining balance curve were altered, then monthly and cumulative losses would also change.

Exhibit 1: Comparison of Loss Data Based on Remaining Balance and Original Balance

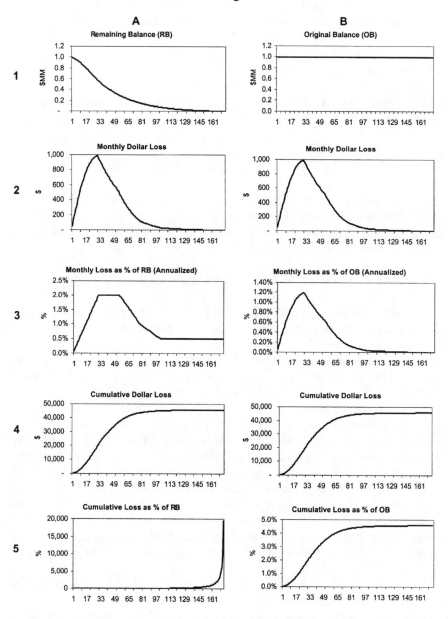

If prepayments are faster and the CDR curve holds constant, there will be fewer losses. In fact, faster prepayments usually do result in fewer losses, since more borrowers voluntarily prepay before they have a chance to default. But in reality, faster prepayments probably also alter the shape of the CDR curve. After all, CDR curves are based on historical experience, so they have a range of prepayment speeds and an average somewhere near current levels. If speeds are unusually fast or unusually slow, the CDR curve will shift, but most analysis assumes a constant CDR curve. That's probably not a bad assumption, since prepayment speed has greater potential for change than does shape of the CDR curve.

A THIRD WAY TO MEASURE LOSSES

The discussion of interaction between speed and losses brings up the point that there are three pieces to the loss picture. By starting with any two, the third can then be calculated. Another way of presenting these relationships is with the simplified equation below. For each month

$$\$ \text{ Loss Amount} = \$ \text{ Balance} \times \text{CDR}\%$$

For example, in constructing the graphs in Exhibit 1, I assumed a remaining balance curve and a CDR curve. These two curves then produced the monthly and cumulative dollar losses shown in sections 2 and 4 of Exhibit 1. I could have started with monthly losses in dollars and the remaining balance curves, and then calculated the CDR curve. Or I could have begun with losses in dollars and the CDR curve, and derived a remaining balance curve from that.

This way of looking at the loss picture helps clarify yet another approach to describing losses. I have discussed monthly CDR and cumulative loss curves. A third way is a frequency distribution of losses, an approach often used by the rating agencies. An example of such a distribution is shown in Exhibit 2, which is a loss distribution for home equity loans. The exhibit shows percentage of total losses that will occur each year. For example, year 1 will have zero losses. In year 2, 15% of total losses will occur, and so forth. By assuming a total loss number for a deal, this curve can be used to distribute those losses over time. That distribution (i.e., monthly losses) is one of the three factors needed to complete the curves in Exhibit 1. If one of the other two is assumed, the third can always be calculated.

In practice, a curve such as that in Exhibit 2 can be used to project total cumulative losses. For example, if we know that 60% of total losses typically occur by the 48th month, and losses on a particular deal or vintage reached 2.5% by the 48th month, we can project total cumulative losses of around 2.5%/60% = 4.2%.

Exhibit 2: Typical Loss Curve for Home Equity Loans

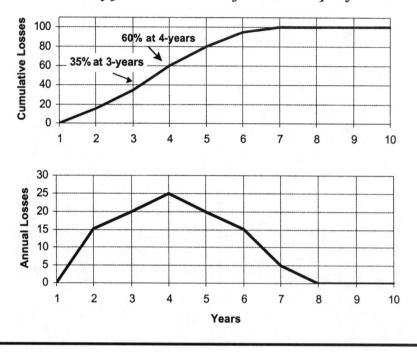

SUMMARY

The various approaches used to present ABS and MBS loss data can, at times, be confusing. The illustrations and examples in this chapter help show relationships between the different measures, and hopefully serve as a good reference point for a better understanding of how loss data are calculated and presented.

Chapter 13

Developing the Prospectus Prepayment Curve for Real Estate Backed Structured Products

Bradley Adams
Senior Vice President
Capital Markets Saxon Mortgage

Glenn Schultz, CFA
Director ABS Research
Banc One Capital Markets, Inc.

INTRODUCTION

B alancing the issuer's desire to maximize proceeds and the investor's desire to maximize relative value is central to determining the *prospectus prepayment curve* (PPC). The underwriter works to balance the interests between the issuer and investor. For example, issuers prefer a faster pricing speed when the yield curve is positively sloped. This is because a faster pricing speed shortens cash flows and increases the proceeds to the issuer. Conversely, investors prefer a slower pricing speed. The slower pricing speed extends cash flows and results in higher relative yields and "cheaper" bonds.

In this chapter we outline the development of the PPC from both the perspective of underwriters and issuers. The chapter is organized as follows. First, we examine the process undertaken by the underwriter to extract the PPC from the issuer's servicing tapes and the application of the PPC to deal execution. An analysis of Saxon Mortgage's servicing tapes and the pricing of Saxon Asset Securities Trust 1999-1 are used as a case study. Second, we outline the internal systems used by Saxon Mortgage to monitor and evaluate their prepayment experience.

DEVELOPING THE PPC RAMP:
THE UNDERWRITER'S PERSPECTIVE

Prior to deal execution the underwriter extracts the PPC from the issuer's servicing records. In the case of a new issuer the servicing tape is requested six -to - eight weeks prior to a deal execution. For existing issuers the servicing tape may be requested about four weeks prior to deal execution. A review of the collateral prepayment performance is undertaken for several reasons.

First, extracting the PPC is part of the due diligence process performed by both the rating agency and underwriter. An analysis of the servicing records provides an accurate PPC as well as an opportunity for the underwriter and rating agency to directly observe collateral performance and the issuer's adherence to stated underwriting principles.

Second, an accurate PPC is central to balancing the opposing interests of both the issuer and the investor. Finally, detailed loan level analysis can be communicated to the investor community, resulting in greater transparency at the time of pricing. The greater pricing transparency allows investors to access the implied option cost with a higher degree of certainty. Pricing confidence on the part of the investor community often results in improved deal execution for the issuer.

The steps involved in the extracting the prospectus prepayment curve are as follows:

1. *Delivery of the servicing tapes for each calendar month available.* For example, Saxon Mortgage has been originating home equity loans since 1996. So, monthly servicing tapes are delivered to the underwriter from August 1996 to present.

2. *Construct a database of the servicing tapes.* The analysis of the servicing tapes is an iterative process and performed in a powerful database environment such as SQL Server.

3. *Iterate through the database to extract the pricing PPC.* In this step the analyst aligns all loans in the servicing database by loan age regardless of origination date creating the static pool prepayment curve.

4. *Develop a loan level model used to determine the PPC for future transactions.*

Constructing a database of the servicing tapes requires the concatenation of each month's servicing report into a single series of records. The minimum data requirements to extract the PPC are outlined below:

Required Information	Required to Compute
Servicing Report Date	Loan Age and Scheduled Principal
Loan Origination Date	Loan Age and Scheduled Principal
Loan Original Balance	Scheduled Principal
Loan Rate	Scheduled Principal
Final Payment Date	Amortization Term and Scheduled Principal
Loan Current Balance	Single Monthly Mortality Rate and CPR

The servicing report date and the loan's origination date are used to calculate both the loan age and the scheduled principal. Loan original balance, loan rate, and final payment date are used to calculate the scheduled principal and amortization term. Finally, loan current balance is the beginning balance for each successive loan age group and is used to calculate the single monthly mortality rate and CPR.

Exhibit 1 shows sample servicing reports used to calculate the PPC. Once the servicing reports are concatenated as in exhibit 1 the next step is to determine the prepayment rate on a static pool basis. The steps for extracting the PPC curve from the servicing report database are outlined below.

First, compare the reported scheduled balance to a calculated scheduled balance. This is done primarily to check the integrity of the data. In addition, both the loan age and schedule principal are calculated and added to the servicing report database as shown in Exhibit 1.

Second, select the current coupon loans by seasoning (loan age). This is done irrespective of the loan origination date. The selection of current coupon loans by loan age is commonly referred to as "coupon mapping." Coupon mapping is used to remove the effect of premium and discount loans in the PPC calculation. Mapping the coupons in the servicing database requires the analyst to construct a vector of mortgage origination rates. The loan and mortgage origination rates are compared for each servicing report date. Loan rates within +/− 75 to −100 basis points of the prevailing mortgage origination rate for any given month are considered current coupon loans. These loans are selected according to the desired loan age bucket. The exception to the above is loans with the desired age in the final month of the servicing report. These loans are excluded in order to create a static pool. Exhibit 2 illustrates the results of this step for loans with one month of seasoning.

Third, select the same group of loans according to the interval (1month, 3months, 6months, 12 months) over which the prepayment rate is computed. PPC ramps are generally computed in monthly intervals. So, the next loan age interval selected is month 2.

Fourth, compute the single monthly mortality rate (SMM) as shown in Exhibit 2. In this example the SMM is 0.44% and the conditional prepayment rate (CPR) is 5.16%. It is important to note at this point that the calculated CPR is sensitive to the loan count in each month. As the loan count drops the relative impact on the calculated CPR of a single prepaid loan increases. CPR calculations are reliable for loan counts above 5,000 in any given month.

Steps 2 through 4 are repeated for each loan age group of interest. For deal pricing purposes the PPC ramp is derived for at least 24 months. If more data are available, the PPC is computed to the last available loan age group.

Exhibit 1: Sample Servicing Reports and Database Construction

Sample Servicing Report - December 2000

Loan Number	Original Amount	Current Balance	Origination Date	Interest Rate	Final Pmt. Date	Current Date
541234	100,000.00	99,746.29	11/15/2000	9.45	11/15/2015	12/30/2000
541235	150,000.00	149,168.61	08/15/2000	9.70	03/15/2020	12/30/2000
541236	110,000.00	109,896.94	10/15/2000	9.75	10/15/2030	12/30/2000
541237	115,000.00	114,897.83	10/15/2000	10.00	10/15/2030	12/30/2000
541238	120,000.00	119,391.46	10/15/2000	9.50	10/15/2015	12/30/2000
541240	95,000.00	95,000.00	12/15/2000	9.50	12/15/2030	12/30/2000
541239	85,000.00	0.00	09/15/2000	9.60	09/15/2020	12/30/2000

Sample Servicing Report - November 2000

Loan Number	Original Amount	Current Balance	Origination Date	Interest Rate	Final Pmt. Date	Current Date
541234	100,000.00	100,000.00	11/15/2000	9.45	11/15/2015	11/30/2000
541235	150,000.00	149,378.97	08/15/2000	9.70	03/15/2020	11/30/2000
541236	110,000.00	109,948.68	10/15/2000	9.75	10/15/2030	11/30/2000
541237	115,000.00	114,949.13	10/15/2000	10.00	10/15/2030	11/30/2000
541238	120,000.00	119,696.93	10/15/2000	9.50	10/15/2015	11/30/2000
541239	85,000.00	0.00	09/15/2000	9.60	09/15/2020	11/30/2000

Sample Servicing Report - October 2000

Loan Number	Original Amount	Current Balance	Origination Date	Interest Rate	Final Pmt. Date	Current Date
541235	150,000.00	149,587.65	08/15/2000	9.70	08/15/2020	10/31/2000
541236	$110,000.00	$110,000.00	10/15/2000	9.75	10/15/2030	10/31/2000
541237	$115,000.00	$115,000.00	10/15/2000	10.00	10/15/2030	10/31/2000
541238	$120,000.00	$120,000.00	10/15/2000	9.50	10/15/2015	10/31/2000
541239	$85,000.00	$0.00	09/15/2000	9.60	09/15/2020	10/31/2000

Concatenated Servicing Reports - Database

Loan Number	Original Amount	Current Balance	Origination Date	Interest Rate	Final Pmt. Date	Current Date	Loan Age	Scheduled Principal
541234	$100,000.00	$99,746.29	11/15/2000	9.45	11/15/2015	12/30/2000	1	253.7097218352
541235	$150,000.00	$149,168.61	08/15/2000	9.70	03/15/2020	12/30/2000	4	210.3651574744
541236	$110,000.00	$0.00	10/15/2000	9.75	10/15/2030	12/30/2000	2	51.7368270724
541237	$115,000.00	$114,897.83	10/15/2000	10.00	10/15/2030	12/30/2000	2	51.2979220377
541238	$120,000.00	$119,391.46	10/15/2000	9.50	10/15/2015	12/30/2000	2	305.4689205904
541240	$95,000.00	$95,000.00	12/15/2000	9.50	12/15/2030	12/30/2000	0	0.0000000000
541239	$85,000.00	$0.00	09/15/2000	9.60	09/15/2020	12/30/2000	3	119.7638345027
541234	$100,000.00	$100,000.00	11/15/2000	9.45	11/15/2015	11/30/2000	0	0.0000000000
541235	$150,000.00	$149,378.97	08/15/2000	9.70	03/15/2020	11/30/2000	3	208.6783408856
541236	$110,000.00	$109,948.68	10/15/2000	9.75	10/15/2030	11/30/2000	1	51.3198532646
541237	$115,000.00	$114,949.13	10/15/2000	10.00	10/15/2030	11/30/2000	1	50.8739722688
541238	$120,000.00	$119,696.93	10/15/2000	9.50	10/15/2015	11/30/2000	1	303.0696194366
541239	$85,000.00	$0.00	09/15/2000	9.60	09/15/2020	11/30/2000	2	118.8133278797
541235	$150,000.00	$149,587.65	08/15/2000	9.70	08/15/2020	10/31/2000	2	207.0050500642
541236	$110,000.00	$110,000.00	10/15/2000	9.75	10/15/2030	10/31/2000	0	0.0000000000
541237	$115,000.00	$115,000.00	10/15/2000	10.00	10/15/2030	10/31/2000	0	0.0000000000
541238	$120,000.00	$120,000.00	10/15/2000	9.50	10/15/2015	10/31/2000	0	0.0000000000
541239	$85,000.00	$0.00	09/15/2000	9.60	09/15/2020	10/31/2000	1	117.8703649600

Exhibit 2: Loan Age Selection Months One- to-Two and Conditional Prepayment Rate Calculation

Loan Number	Original Amount	Current Balance	Origination Date	Interest Rate	Final Pmt. Date	Current Date	Loan Age	Scheduled Principal
Averages of other Selected Loans	$25,789,397.00	$25,789,397.00	10/15/2000	9.75	10/15/2020	11/30/2000	1	$1,192,756.64
541236	$110,000.00	$110,000.00	10/15/2000	9.75	10/15/2030	11/30/2000	1	$51.32
541237	$115,000.00	$115,000.00	10/15/2000	10.00	10/15/2030	11/30/2000	1	$50.87
541238	$120,000.00	$120,000.00	10/15/2000	9.50	10/15/2015	11/30/2000	1	$303.07

Loan Number	Original Amount	Current Balance	Origination Date	Interest Rate	Final Pmt. Date	Current Date	Loan Age	Scheduled Principal
Averages of other Selected Loans	$25,789,397.00	$24,596,640.36	10/15/2000	9.75	10/15/2020	12/30/2000	2	$1,202,447.79
541236	$110,000.00	$0.00	10/15/2000	9.75	10/15/2030	12/30/2000	2	$51.74
541237	$115,000.00	$114,949.13	10/15/2000	10.00	10/15/2030	12/30/2000	2	$51.30
541238	$120,000.00	$119,696.93	10/15/2000	9.50	10/15/2015	12/30/2000	2	$305.47

Calculated Prepayment Rate For Month 1	
Current Balance	$26,134,397.00
Scheduled Principal	$1,193,161.90
Ending Balance	$24,831,286.42
SMM	0.44%
CPR	5.16%

Exhibit 3: Saxon Mortgage Fixed Rate Base PPC

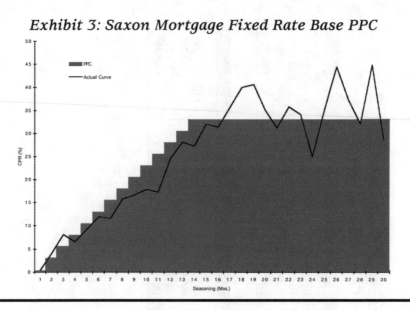

Finally, a loan level prepayment model is developed. The degree of sophistication that the loan level model assumes varies by underwriter. Transactions are generally priced using a loan age prepayment model for each collateral group. The collateral groups are referred to as "representative lines" (rep lines) or "loan cohorts." The loan age prepayment model specifies the number of months required to reach the maximum CPR. A loan age model where prepayments begin in month 1 at 2.40% CPR and increase to 24% CPR in the tenth month is specified as follows:

$$CPR = 24 \times \min\left(1, \frac{n}{10}\right)$$

where n = seasoning month.

PREPAYMENT MODELING AND
PPC ASSIGNMENT CONSIDERATIONS

Exhibit 3 graphically illustrates Saxon Mortgage's base PPC assumption. The PPC ramp was derived from loan level servicing reports covering the period August 1996 through February 1999. Exhibit 3 suggests that the appropriate PPC ramp for Saxon's fixed rate collateral begins at 0.4% CPR in the first month and increases 2.5% CPR per month for 13 months to a peak of 33% CPR in the fourteenth month. The PPC ramp in exhibit 3 is based on an analysis of Saxon's entire fixed rate servicing portfolio. A loan age model for Saxon's servicing portfolio based on the above is expressed below:

$$CPR = 0.4 + 32.6 \times \min\left(1, \frac{n-1}{m-1}\right)$$

where n = seasoning month and m = month of peak CPR.

The naive loan age model above ignores the effect of individual loan characteristics on the prepayment profile of the securitized pool of mortgages. As a result, transaction-specific PPC ramps may vary from Exhibit 3 based on the composition of the underlying collateral in each transaction. Factors influencing the probability of prepayment for any given loan may include:

1. Loan purpose.
2. Loan term (amortization).
3. Loan balance.
4. Borrower credit quality.
5. Impact of prepayment penalties.

In order to capture non-age correlated effects on prepayments most of the loan age models used for pricing are based on representative lines. For example, PPC ramps may be calculated from the servicing database based on loan amortization type, credit grade, and the presence of prepayment penalties. Assuming two major amortization types (15-year and 30-year), three credit grades (A, B, and C/D), and the use of prepayment penalties, a stratification of the servicing portfolio will result in 12 distinct loan age prepayment models used to price a single transaction.

Although it is possible to determine the appropriate PPC using loan age models based on numerous stratifications, a loan level prepayment model incorporating individual loan characteristics provides a superior estimate of the PPC ramp for transaction pricing. Exhibit 4 provides a flow chart of Banc One Capital Market's loan level prepayment model. It is a logistic model comprised of four sub-models and is used to estimate the aggregate prepayment rate for a pool of mortgages. Each loan is processed through the appropriate sub-model based on both loan term and loan age. The variables in each sub-model are original loan balance, loan purpose, borrower credit quality, and the presence of prepayment penalties.

Exhibit 5 compares Banc One Capital Market's estimated pricing speed, the actual pricing speed, and realized prepayments to October 2000. The exhibit shows that the SAST 1999-1 transaction was priced using a 24 HEP curve (home equity prepayment curve). Thus, prepayments are assumed to begin at 2.4% in the first month and increase 2.4% per month reaching a peak CPR of 24% in the tenth month. Banc One's loan level model projected that prepayments would begin at 6% CPR in the first month, 25% CPR in the tenth month, and 32% CPR in the fourteenth month. The prepayment model forecasted prepayment rates between 29% and 39% CPR between months 15 and 30. The higher prepayment estimates between months 15 and 30 are due to the inversion of the Treasury curve at the time of pricing (2/18/99). The inverted Treasury curve produced lower forward mortgage rates and higher prepayment assumptions. Due to burnout our prepayment estimates begin to drop off past month 30 and decline to between 20% and 25% CPR. The 25 HEP pricing assumption used for the SAST 1999-1 transaction is consistent with the results from Banc One's loan level prepayment model and balances both the issuer's and investor's interests based on the following inputs:

1. Loan level analysis of the servicing reports.
2. Estimated prepayments based on our loan level prepayment model.
3. Burnout considerations.

Finally, Exhibit 5 also compares actual prepayments against both the HEP pricing speed and loan level estimated prepayment rates. The exhibit shows that the realized prepayment rate has deviated from both pricing assumptions. The collateral did not ramp to a peak CPR according to either the HEP model or the loan level model. Furthermore, with the exception of months 15 and 19, peak prepayment rates are below both assumptions at the time of pricing. The difference between the actual and predicted prepayment rate is due to the increase in mortgage rates since the time of pricing. Exhibit 5 also provides a graphic summary of the 30-year agency mortgage rate from January 1, 1999 to 11/03/2000. The exhibit shows that since the time of pricing the mortgage rate increased from 6.49% on February 19, 2000 to a maximum of 8.44% on May 12, 2000. The higher mortgage rate resulted in a less pronounced ramping and a slower overall prepayment rate. The analysis presented in Exhibit 5 does not invalidate either the HEP or loan level PPC assumption. Rather, Exhibit 5 clearly shows that realized prepayments can differ from assumptions at the time of pricing depending on the future path of interest rates.

Exhibit 4: Flow Diagram of Banc One Capital Market's Home Equity Prepayment Model

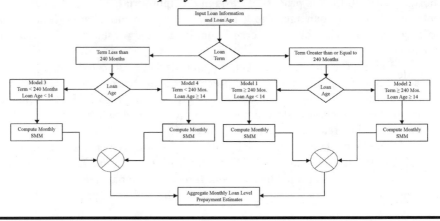

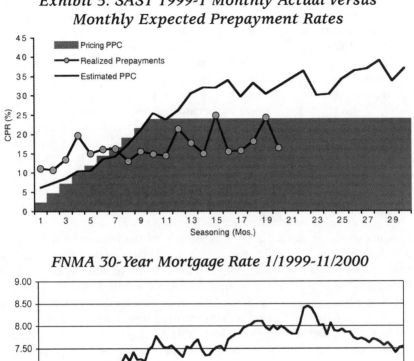

Exhibit 5: SAST 1999-1 Monthly Actual versus Monthly Expected Prepayment Rates

FNMA 30-Year Mortgage Rate 1/1999-11/2000

DETERMINING THE PPC RAMP:
THE ISSUER'S PERSPECTIVE

In order to determine the appropriate PPC ramp from the issuer's standpoint, Saxon Mortgage goes through a monthly loan level analysis of actual prepayment history. Saxon receives the servicing data from its affiliate Meritech Mortgage Services on the 18th of each month. Saxon, as master servicer, then goes through a thorough loan level reconciliation process in order to ensure accuracy for reporting and bond administration purposes. Once the prepayment calculations are finalized they are loaded into Saxon's system of record for tracking loan activity.

Historically, Saxon used the updated balances to create representative groupings of collateral in order to make the analysis less cumbersome. The representative lines are created to isolate loan characteristics that are deemed important in influencing prepayment performance. This process is similar to the stratification undertaken by the underwriter to build loan age prepayment models. Examples of the characteristics monitored by Saxon Mortgage are loan type, credit grade, prepayment penalty type, and loan-to-value ratio. Since the process was initially developed to support the valuation of Saxon's residual certificate holdings, the representative line categories are replicas of those used in residual valuation. The various prepayment curves are updated each month and compared to those used for valuing the portfolio of residuals. If there are variances that constitute a trend, the valuation assumptions are changed to eliminate the variance.

In 1999, Saxon modified its existing process to allow for loan level prepayment analysis. Rather than create the representative lines from each month's servicing data tape, Saxon now exports that data into a separate SQL server table appropriately named the CPR database. The historical 1, 3, 6, 9, and 12 month, and life to date CPR information for each loan populate the table. In addition, each month when the servicing report is brought in, the forecasted 1, 3, 6, 9, and 12 month, and life to date CPRs are calculated and stored in the same table. Using a software tool called BrioQuery, which allows Saxon to build in the SMM and CPR calculations as well as query the data at the same time, Saxon can analyze prepayment performance down to the loan level. With this query tool Saxon can attach the CPR database to another table storing origination data. This allows Saxon to examine and compare historical CPRs for any loan within any grouping or representative line. This gives Saxon the flexibility to very easily attach CPR performance to any loan or borrower characteristic, including those that may not be obvious candidates for influencing a borrower to prepay their loan.

With this robust analysis process in place, Saxon can use their own historical data to strongly recommend an appropriate pricing speed for the bonds they sell. More importantly to Saxon, they can use this information to improve front end pricing making the entire business model more profitable.

SUMMARY

Developing the PPC ramp used for transaction pricing is an intensive process beginning with a loan-by-loan examination of the issuer's servicing reports. Typically, the underwriter will develop a custom prepayment model. The prepayment model is either a loan level model or based on representative lines. In addition, the issuer will provide guidance to the underwriter based upon an ongoing analysis of the servicing portfolio. Ultimately, the underwriter will decide on the appropriate PPC ramp to price the transaction. The underwriter's pricing decision, with respect to the PPC ramp, seeks to balance the interests of both the issuer and the investor. Through the processes outlined above greater pricing transparency is achieved and transaction execution is improved for all parties involved.

Chapter 14

Securitization and Other Structured Finance Techniques for Equipment Leasing Companies

Jojy Vaniss Mathew
President & CEO
eBizTeka, Inc.

INTRODUCTION

F unding new lease originations and financing growth is often a critical issue for the success of any leasing company. Innovations in the financial markets are providing new funding techniques to equipment leasing companies. Term securitization facilities, conduit warehouse and securitization facilities, and forward funded securitization facilities are common ways equipment leasing companies are funding growth of their lease portfolios, and their leasing enterprise.

Asset securitization continues to be a preferred form of financing for many specialty finance companies. In the equipment leasing sector, many leasing companies use securitization as the primary funding tool. Larger leasing companies such as Heller, T&W, First Sierra, DVI, Case, LINC, Newcourt, and Copelco have been very active in bringing term and conduit securitization transactions to market. Many of the smaller leasing company players such as Centerpoint Financial, Captec, Icon, USA Capital, and Financial Pacific have also utilized securitization as an effective funding strategy. In keeping with the financing needs of equipment leasing companies, financial engineers at investment banking firms continue to develop newer and innovative securitization transaction structures to meet the needs of the leasing market.

In this chapter, equipment lease securitization and related financing techniques available to leasing companies are discussed.

WHY SECURITIZE?

Lease securitization has gained popularity among equipment leasing companies as a flexible lower cost funding source. Many leasing companies have established

171

their business model and infrastructure to allow them to securitize in recent years. Securitization offers many advantages to issuers and investors alike. Issuers benefit from lower cost of funding and the ability to access a new funding source. There has also been a keen interest among institutional investors to purchase bonds from equipment lease securitizations due to the attractive yields offered by lease backed bonds and the non-consumer nature of the collateral. Equipment leases are primarily originated to businesses and provide provisions limiting prepayment of the leases. Securitization provides advantages to both issuers and investors, and provides an effective medium of capital transfer. Issuers benefit from accessing new capital sources while investors benefit from new investment opportunities.

Benefits of Securitization for Equipment Leasing Companies

Direct Access to Capital Markets
Securitization provides equipment leasing companies direct access to the capital markets. Securitization allows the leasing company to borrow directly from the capital markets based on the credit quality of the lease portfolio being securitized and not the corporate credit worthiness of the leasing company. Utilizing the securitization structure, an unrated leasing company may be able to borrow at investment grade rates from the capital markets.

Source of Capital
Securitization offers a new source of capital to leasing companies. Leasing clearly is a spread oriented business and, therefore, funding is a key to the success of any leasing company. Being able to access funding sources at a lower cost of capital and originate leases at a higher yield creates a profitable niche for leasing companies. Securitization allows the leasing company to augment their traditional funding sources such as bank warehouse lines and other similar lending facilities. By issuing a securitized bond, the leasing company is able to borrow from other capital market participants such as insurance companies, money managers, and pension funds.

Lower Cost of Funding
Equipment leasing companies via securitization have an opportunity to borrow at competitive rates versus other funding sources available. Many leasing companies use pool sales or warehouse lines as their primary funding source. Securitization allows the leasing company to realize a lower discount rate versus pool sales or bank warehouse funding.

Even the Playing Field
Securitization creates an even playing field for the larger and smaller leasing companies. Securitization transactions provide competitive funding to both large and small leasing companies in the capital markets and provide access to the same capital sources.

Realize Cash

A securitization transaction provides a mechanism for the issuer to realize cash profits from its securitized lease receivable portfolio. In a typical securitization, the receivables are sold into the securitization and the issuer receives the proceeds from the bonds issued to purchase the receivables. Cash proceeds from the bonds that are placed are typically greater than the equipment cost that is financed in a warehouse line. The issuer is advanced the bond proceeds net of pay off to credit lines, reserves, and fees. The first loss position is often retained by the issuer and realized over the term of the deal.

Lock in Term Financing and Minimize Interest Rate Risk

By issuing fixed-rate bonds backed by lease receivables, the issuer has locked in term financing for the lease portfolio. The bond interest rates are set at closing and guarantees term financing to the issuer.

Portfolio Growth

Securitization allows a leasing company to turn over its lease portfolio and grow the business. The issuer is able to lock in term financing on a lease portfolio, freeing up its funding facilities and revolving warehouse lines. This allows the leasing company to originate new leases and grow its business. The securitization also compensates the issuer by a servicing fee for continuing to service the assets and becomes a new source of income for the leasing company.

Forces Efficiency

Executing a securitization transaction forces a leasing company to be efficient and thorough in its underwriting criteria, servicing practices, reporting capabilities, and collections procedures.

Build Market Reputation and Enterprise Value

An equipment leasing company utilizing securitization as an effective funding strategy develops a market identity among institutional investors and peers. As many of the smaller leasing companies look to grow and become larger public companies, securitization demonstrates to the equity markets that the company is established in its infrastructure, can borrow effectively in the capital markets, and has the ability to work with institutional investors. Securitization often adds an incremental enterprise value to leasing companies looking to go into the equity markets to raise capital.

Off-Balance Sheet Financing/Acceleration of Income

Securitization allows leasing companies to establish off-balance sheet financing and recognize income at the time of the securitization. While gain-on-sale accounting has been used liberally in recent years by leasing companies, most issuers have abandoned gain-on-sale accounting as of this writing. Gain-on-sale accounting has been disapproved by many of the capital markets participants and research analysts and has lost its appeal as of this writing. Most leasing companies are now taking the approach of recognizing income as it is received over the life of the leases.

Benefits for Investors

Attractive Spreads
Equipment lease ABS offers competitive yields to investors relative to other investment opportunities in the fixed income market. Many institutional investors have shown a strong appetite for equipment lease backed ABS, and especially rated private placement equipment lease backed ABS deals.

Matching Maturities
Tranches from equipment lease securitizations provide investment assets that match the duration of short-term liabilities of insurance companies and other institutional investors. Investors such as Aegon, ING, ITT Hartford, PPM America, and Great West Life are a few of the active players investing in equipment lease backed ABS.

Non-Consumer Collateral
Obligors of equipment leases are typically businesses. Many equipment leasing companies grade risk to these businesses in their underwriting practices and provide adequate yields for the lease collateral to compensate for risk at the various credit levels. Small ticket leases typically yield 12% to 16% or higher.

Diversified Collateral
Small ticket and mid-ticket securitizations offer investors collateral diversified by obligor, state, and equipment type. In many of the transactions, obligor concentrations are limited to 1% to 2%, state concentrations are limited to 15% to 20% for one state and 10% for a second state, with many of the other states under 5%. Equipment leases also offer institutional investors another asset class in which to invest.

Prepayment Risk
Due to the full payout, non-cancelable nature of equipment leases, equipment lease ABS present limited prepayment risk to investors. Relative to investments in other ABS types such as home equity and manufactured housing, and other residential mortgage collateral, equipment lease ABS offers an attractive alternative to institutional investors.

Structural Features
Equipment lease securitizations are often structured as senior-subordinate structures with the issuer often holding the first loss position. Cash reserve and liquidity accounts are often set up in these deals to provide timely cash flow to the bond investors. Inherent features of the deal structure in equipment lease backed ABS provides investors with an investment that has limited risk or principal loss.

Exhibit 1: Simple Lease Securitization Structure

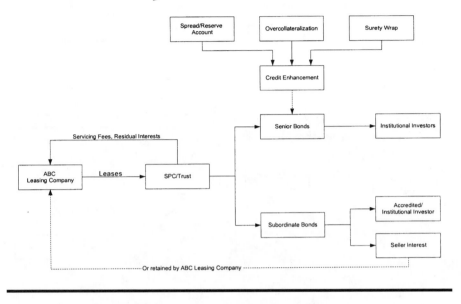

EQUIPMENT LEASE SECURITIZATION

Definition

Asset securitization is a capital markets financing technique whereby debt is issued to investors (via bonds) for an amount based on the cash flows from a discrete pool of cash flow generating pledged assets (collateral). Lease securitization involves transferring a pool of lease receivables and related security (collateral) to a *special purpose corporation* (SPC), which in turn issues lease backed notes (bonds) based on cash flows generated by the lease receivables. Investors in securitized debt rely only on the cash flows from the pledged assets to satisfy the bond obligations, and not the company's assets and revenue producing abilities. Exhibit 1 shows a simple securitization structure.

Rated bonds matching the cash flow characteristics and term parameters of the lease portfolio are structured and issued, allowing the leasing company to borrow directly from the capital markets at competitive rates. Transactions below $100 million are typically structured as private placements with institutional investors. The larger transactions are often executed as public transactions and involve tranching the bonds into various classes at different maturity and rating levels to take advantage of liquidity and pricing flexibility. There is an efficient market for public and private placement securitizations, and transactions as small as $25 million can be executed given a diversified lease portfolio.

Exhibit 2: Term Securitization Structure

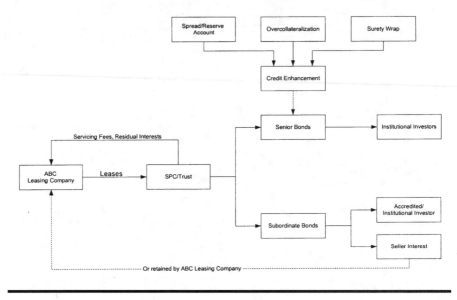

UNDERSTANDING SECURITIZATION STRUCTURES

Three types of lease securitization transaction structures are primarily used in the equipment leasing sector: term securitization, conduit securitization, and forward funded securitizations. *Term securitizations* allow the leasing company to issue equipment lease backed bonds based on an existing portfolio of equipment leases. The companies typically amass these assets in a warehouse facility. Leases from the warehouse facility are sold into a SPC, which in turn issues asset backed bonds to finance these assets. A *conduit securitization* allows the leasing company to sell a series of smaller lease pools into a securitization facility over a period of time. For example, the leasing company may sell $20 million initially and an additional $5 million per month over an additional 12 month period. A *forward funded securitization* provides financing for an initial portfolio followed by smaller quarterly portfolios similar to a conduit, but is structured similar to a term securitization and is placed directly with institutional investors. Institutional investors agree to finance the initial portfolio followed by subsequent portfolios sold quarterly into the deal over a specified period, typically 12 to 18 months.

Term Securitization

Term securitization is the most common form of equipment lease securitization structure employed in the market. Exhibit 2 illustrates a sample term securitization structure. While the larger equipment leasing companies employ public term securitizations, many of the smaller companies employ privately placed equipment lease term transactions.

Characteristics of Term Securitizations

Large Ticket, Mid Ticket, and Small Ticket Lease Securitizations Term securitization can be utilized as an effective funding strategy for any diversified equipment lease portfolio. Transactions have been put together in the large, middle, and small ticket sectors. Many of the leading equipment leasing companies use term securitization as one of their primary funding tools.

Lessor Has a Diversified Portfolio of Leases Ready to be Securitized Term securitization requires the leasing company to pool together a portfolio of leases before a transaction can be executed. Leasing companies put together these portfolios by utilizing warehouse lines, bank lines, and equity capital. Many conduit structures are also set up as warehouse lines, and the issuer can lock in term financing by moving the assets into a term securitization.

Private or Public Transaction, Depending on Size Public transactions typically involve additional transaction costs. They are not cost effective nor efficient for smaller leasing companies. Typical size requirements for private versus public are as follows:

- Private $25 million minimum
    smaller/first-time issuers
    target smaller group of sophisticated investors
- Public $75 to $100 million minimum
    large, well known, frequent issuers
    reaches a larger universe of investors

SPC Established In term securitizations, the lease assets are sold into a SPC established for the purposes of the transaction, and are isolated from the bankruptcy risk of the issuer. The SPC issues bonds to match the cash flow characteristics of the underlying lease assets. As the transaction is structured, a true-sale opinion is provided by the leasing company issuer's counsel and approved by the rating agencies to affirm the bankruptcy remote nature of the securitization. In the event of bankruptcy of the issuer, the assets are isolated from the issuer and continue to provide cash flow to pay off the bondholders.

Rated Transactions Term transactions are typically structured as rated transactions. Leasing securitizations are often structured to issue bonds at various rating levels ranging from AAA to B. Rating agencies determine advance rates and required credit enhancements based on the size, diversification, and quality of the lease portfolio. Historical portfolio performance statistics such as static pool losses, delinquencies, and obligor concentrations are closely evaluated to determine bond sizes and required credit enhancement levels.

Senior-Subordinate Structure Utilized A senior-subordinate deal structure is employed in almost all term securitization transactions. The subordinate bond is structured to provide credit enhancement to the senior bond by absorbing any losses from the underlying collateral.

Bond Insurance Wrap In some transactions, bond insurers such as MBIA and FSA provide a bond insurance policy for the senior bonds. By employing a bond insurance policy (a "wrap" as it is often called), the issuer is able to issue the bonds at an "AAA" rating, while the deal is structured to an "A" rating.

Priced to a Spread Over an Average-Life-Treasury The bonds in a term securitization are typically priced at the spread above the Treasury whose maturity matches the average life of the bonds in the deal. Based on the rating level of each bond, investors require appropriate spreads to compensate for the implied risk. In some transactions, the bonds are sized to various maturities and average lives to meet investor appetites for various maturities.

Prefunding can also be Utilized to Increase Deal Size A pre-funding structure can also be utilized in term securitizations to allow leasing companies to increase the deal size by an additional 20%. Rating agencies establish concentration and eligibility criteria at the time of closing to establish what types of leases can be sold into the transaction. Investors will fund the incremental 20%, which is deposited into a prefunding account. As leases are originated, the prefunded proceeds can be used to fund additional leases over a 3-month period. Prefunding allows the leasing company to issue an additional 20% in bonds and apply transaction costs against a larger transaction size.

Conduit Securitization

Conduit securitizations are another efficient way for leasing companies to fund their equipment lease portfolios. A conduit is an entity that finances receivables from multiple borrowers nationwide by issuing commercial paper (CP) in the capital markets. Conduit financing facilities are often structured similar to a rated securitization. Unlike a term securitization where all the assets have to be amassed prior to executing a transaction, conduits allow leasing companies to efficiently sell portfolios of leases monthly or quarterly into the conduit securitization facility. Conduits often commit to purchase portfolios from leasing companies over a number of months based on eligibility and concentration criteria. These types of transactions can be structured as a revolving warehouse or as a term note. When structured as a warehouse, conduits provide lease portfolio warehouse funding to companies, and charge the leasing company a spread over its CP funding and administrative costs. Transactions structured as term notes by conduits utilize swaps, caps or other interest rate derivatives in the conduit structure to lock in fixed term financing.

Characteristics of Conduit Securitizations

Exhibit 3 illustrates a conduit securitization structure. Below the characteristics of conduit securitizations are discussed.

Exhibit 3: Conduit Securitization Structure

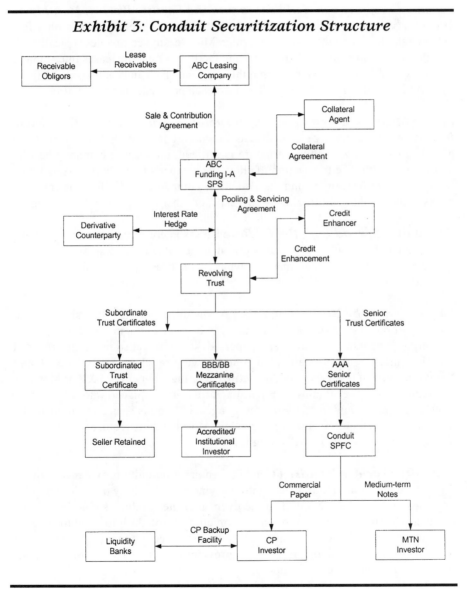

Transaction Builds Up Over Several Months Conduits allow leasing companies to sell an initial portfolio into the facility, followed by a series of monthly/quarterly sales into the facility. Leases are sold into the facility up to the facility limit. The initial portfolio that is sold into the facility must be significant enough to allow the conduit and the rating agencies to evaluate the make up of the aggregate portfolio.

Leasing Company can Sell Leases into the Facility Weekly, Monthly or Quarterly Conduits allow leases to be sold into the facility, based on a frequency established by the conduit provider. Most leasing companies typically sell into the conduit monthly and utilize a bank facility to fund the leases inter-month. Conduits establish a minimum on monthly amounts that can be sold into the facility. GAAP sale treatment can be utilized for each pool sale into the facility.

Can be Structured as a Revolving Structured Warehouse or Term Facility Conduits are primarily established as a revolving facility funded at the CP rate plus a spread. If a warehouse structure is utilized, the leasing company has the ability to structure the transaction to allow the company to move the assets into a term securitization. Some conduits also allow companies to fix funding rates for assets in the conduit by utilizing swaps, caps, or other interest rate derivatives.

Priced at a Spread over the CP Rate Unless interest rate derivatives are utilized, a conduit transaction is typically priced at the CP rate plus a spread. The gross spread charged by the conduit manager typically includes a program fee, a liquidity fee, a fee to the bond insurer if a wrap is utilized, and interest rate hedging costs.

Shadow Rated by Moody's and S&P A conduit facility is established to fund a variety of borrower assets and is required to be rated at the master conduit level for purposes of issuing commercial paper. Most asset backed conduits are rated A1/P1. While the older established conduits were rated primarily by S&P and Moody's, some of the newer conduits utilize a rating from either S&P or Moody's and one from Duff & Phelps or Fitch. Each transaction placed into a conduit is required to be shadow rated by the rating agencies, and is structured to meet the minimum credit requirements of the conduit. Most conduits require that the transactions be structured to an "A" rating level.

Liquidity Provider Required Conduits require a liquidity provider to provide liquidity to each transaction placed into the conduit. A liquidity provider provides back up funding to the conduit in the event that the conduit is unable to issue commercial paper. A surety provider is sometimes brought into conduit transactions to provide a bond insurance policy to guarantee payment of interest and principal to senior bondholders. A surety provider makes it easier to find a liquidity provider for conduit transactions.

Conduits are Structured Similar to a Term Securitization The senior bond in a conduit, often referred to as the *senior tranche*, is structured similar to a term securitization. The conduit structuring party evaluates static pool losses, delinquencies, concentrations, and other portfolio parameters to determine required subordination levels. Since most conduits are structured to an "A" subordination level, three times historic static pool levels are typically required to be retained by the issuer as subordination. Conduits allow smaller pools to be sold forward into the facility. Each pool that is sold into the facility is advanced based on the initial structure with regards to senior advance rates, and is required to comply with concentration (state, obligor, equipment type, term, yield) levels established at closing based on the initial pool.

Forward Funded Term Securitization

In keeping with the leasing company's need to warehouse and securitize leases originations, another structure has evolved in recent years blending features of a term securitization and a warehouse. A *forward funded securitization* is a recent innovation that allows an equipment leasing company to put together a securitization whereby an initial portfolio is sold into the securitization followed by a series of forward sales of smaller pools into the securitization. This structure is similar to a conduit, but is placed with an institutional investor instead of a conduit. Conduits provide floating-rate financing, while forward funded deals provide fixed-rate financing to issuers. One derivation of this structure allows the leasing company to negotiate a fixed spread at closing, sell an initial pool into the securitization at a fixed rate, and then over the next 12 months sell additional portfolios into the securitization quarterly where a fixed rate is set on each quarterly tranche as it is sold into the securitization at the then current Treasury rate plus the negotiated spread.

Characteristics of a Forward Funded Term Securitization
Exhibit 4 illustrates a forward funded structure. Below the characteristics of a forward fund structure are discussed.

Allows the Leasing Company to Sell an Initial Portfolio Followed by Quarterly Fixed Pool Amounts The issuer sells an initial pool into the deal at closing, followed by sales of additional smaller portfolios monthly/quarterly into the securitization for a fixed number of months/quarters, negotiated at closing. The investors will execute a note purchase agreement to fund additional quarterly amounts at a fixed spread over the average life Treasury index that matches the average life of each pool.

Structured as a Term Securitization A forward funded securitization is structured as a term securitization with the flexibility to issue additional notes. Multiple classes of securities can be created based on the initial pool. As each new pool is sold into the transaction, incremental amounts of notes are issued for each class.

Exhibit 4: Forward Funded Structure

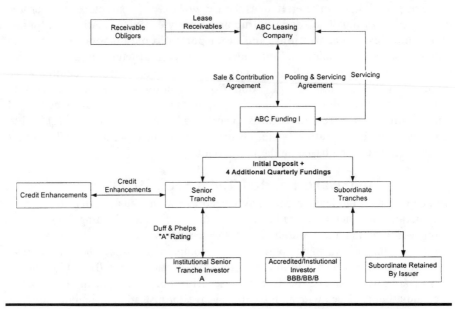

Typically Utilized by Well Established Companies This type of a structure is utilized by well established companies with a long track record of stable originations, servicing and collections.

Rating of Securitization Established Based on Initial Pool The initial pool has to be sufficient to allow the rating agencies and investors to evaluate and rate the transaction. The rating agencies utilize the initial pool parameters to determine the tranche sizes and establish concentration and eligibility criteria. Future pools are sold into the transaction based on concentration and eligibility criteria established at closing. As each pool is sold into the transaction, the rating agencies are involved in reaffirming the rating of the transaction.

Limited Hedging Requirements Since each future tranche is issued as a term note, the investors typically impose limited hedging requirements. As financing rates increase in the market, it is expected that the collateral yield requirements of the lease portfolio also increase. Therefore, when a new pool is sold into the securitization, the bond rate is set to the then current average life Treasury rate plus the negotiated spread.

Minimizes Transaction Costs The forward funded structure was created to minimize issuance costs for the issuer. This structure combines the features of a warehouse with term securitization to minimize costs for the issuer. When the leasing company establishes a warehouse with a lender and then completes a term securitization in the future from leases funded in that warehouse, the company incurs expenses for setting up the warehouse, and again incurs expenses for putting together a securitization in the future. The forward funded structure combines the warehouse and term securitization into one transaction and minimizes transaction costs by combining two steps into one.

REQUIREMENTS FOR SECURITIZATION FOR AN EQUIPMENT LEASING COMPANY

Securitization involves careful planning and organization on the part of the issuer. Smaller leasing companies looking to utilize securitization as a funding strategy need an infrastructure in place, before they can put together a competitive transaction. Every leasing company looking to utilize securitization as a funding strategy must evaluate the following issues in determining if they are ready for a securitization.

Standardized Contracts

A leasing company needs to have standardized underwriting and credit policies, and standardized lease documentation in place to be eligible to execute a securitization transaction.

Grading of Risk Via Underwriting

A leasing company needs to grade the risk of its lessees based on various criteria such as time in business, profitability, industry, etc. Uniform pricing standards are established to price deals based on credit quality of the lessee. Leasing companies in the small ticket sector often use scoring systems to grade risk, and underwrite each deal to meet the risk profile of the lessee.

Database of Historical Performance

Any leasing company looking to undertake lending or capital market transactions must put together statistics on historical performance on all leases originated and serviced by the company. The most common statistical analysis used by market participants such as rating agencies and investors includes static pool loss analysis, annual loss analysis, and delinquency analysis. Static pool loss analysis illustrates the performance of a lease portfolio originated in a particular year, over the entire life of that portfolio. Static pool loss analysis keeps track of gross losses, recoveries, and net losses for pools originated in each year. Annual loss analysis keeps track of losses in each year as a percent of the total lease pool in each year. Leasing companies must keep track of delinquency information for 0–30 days, 31–60 days, 61–90 days, and 90+ days.

Legal Structures and Documentation

A leasing company looking to securitize must have the capability to legally isolate each asset that is being securitized and move it into a bankruptcy remote special purpose corporation. The securitization SPC is required to have a first priority perfected security interest in all assets being securitized.

Must be Willing to Assign All Equipment and Residuals

Securitization structures require the issuer to assign all equipment and residuals to the securtization SPC, in addition to the receivables being securitized. In some transactions the residuals are monetized. Other transactions utilize residuals as additional credit enhancement.

Established Servicing and Collections Infrastructure

The company must be able to continue to service the lease portfolio. The servicing and reporting infrastructure of a leasing company must be at a mature stage for the company to participate in securitization. The company must have a servicing and collections staff in place to collect and service the portfolio that is being securitized. The company is responsible for reconciling collections, and is responsible for all securitization reporting. Receivables must be assigned to a lock box and isolated from the issuer. Transactions often require a collateral agent to take possession of all files. Each month the company is expected to put together reports for the trustee and investors that outline collections and distributions. Personnel, procedures, and systems must be in place before a leasing company can undertake a successful securitization transaction.

Experienced Management

A management team that is efficient at managing all aspects of the leasing business is evaluated thoroughly by the rating agencies and investors. Investor and rating agencies make site visits to meet the management team and evaluate the company's operations first hand. Background checks of the management team are often a requirement for securitizations put together by smaller leasing companies.

Equity

The leasing company must have adequate equity to continue to operate as an ongoing business concern, originate new business, and service the securitized lease portfolio. Rating agencies expect a minimum of $5 million in equity capital on the balance sheet of a leasing company looking to put together a securitization transaction. There have been several securitizations done by companies with less capital.

Stable Originations

Market players are hesitant to take part in securitizations put together by companies involved in seasonal or similar types of business, where the volume of originations are volatile month to month. Market participants expect stable originations and growth, and do not favor volumes to double and triple each year. This often leads to the stigma of relaxed underwriting criteria for the purpose of increased volume and growth.

Use for Capital

Investors expect leasing companies undertaking securitizations to have a clearly defined plan going forward once the securitization is completed. In many securitizations, the issuer shifts lease portfolios from warehousing facilities into the securitization. The company has to have stable originations and a clearly defined execution strategy to re-utilize the warehouse lines. Investors are hesitant to fund equipment leasing companies utilizing securitization as their sole funding strategy.

UNDERSTANDING THE PROCESS AND MECHANICS OF A LEASE SECURITIZATION

Equipment leasing companies meeting the basic securitization criteria described above can put together an efficient and competitive transaction. Leasing companies utilize bank, conduit and other warehouse lines to pool and age a portfolio of leases for securitization. To illustrate the mechanics and process of putting together a securitization transaction, the steps involved in executing a private placement equipment lease securitization transaction are described below.

Compile Necessary Company and Portfolio Information

The leasing company interested in putting together a securitization must first gather all the necessary information and put together an information package outlining the objectives of the securitization and the characteristics of the lease portfolio. Information required in the initial stages include:

- *Lease portfolio information* Lease level information listing obligor name, original receivable balance, remaining receivable information, payment, original term, remaining term, number of first and last payments, residual, state, zip code, equipment type, and industry segment. A spreadsheet file or database file with this information is necessary to analyze the equipment lease portfolio.
- *Company summary* Summary of company history, business plan, target markets, origination channels, servicing and collections infrastructure, historic portfolio summary, and strategic direction.
- Management biographies
- *Underwriting and credit policy guidelines* Manuals reflecting company's credit underwriting philosophy and practices.
- *Portfolio performance history* Static pool loss tables, annual loss tables, delinquency tables.
- *Financial statements* Audited financial statements for at least three years.

Interview an Investment Banking Firm to Manage the Securitization

Investment banking firms play a key role in the life cycle of a successful securitization. Investment banks are responsible for coordinating and managing the transactions from inception to closing. Certain investment bankers specialize in equipment lease securitizations, and such firms are a good choice for a leasing company seeking to arrange a securitization. Investment banking firms are responsible for:

- assisting the company gather the necessary information
- analyzing the lease portfolio
- creating a financial structure
- assembling a transaction team (legal, trustee, back up servicer, audit)
- modeling the transaction using structured finance software systems for rating agencies, investors, and other parties in the deal
- presenting the company and the transaction to investors
- presenting the company to rating agencies
- negotiating spreads
- coordinating all legal documents
- negotiating documents
- pricing transactions
- assisting the leasing company in understanding servicing requirements, and
- managing the closing of the deal.

A securitization transaction is a complex and sophisticated financing endeavor with many parties and steps involved in the deal. Enlisting the services of a competent investment banking firm is the key to a successful transaction.

Preliminary Term Sheet

Once an investment bank is chosen, that firm will put together a preliminary term sheet for the transaction. The deal is pre-marketed to institutional investors at this point to gauge their interest and to initiate pricing discussions. Investors will provide their input into structures, ratings required, yields required, subordination levels, etc.

Involve Rating Agency

Private placement deals in the equipment leasing sector are often rated by only one rating agency. Prior to its acquisition by Fitch, Duff & Phelps has been a very active player in rating equipment lease securitizations. Equipment leasing is an area of focus for Duff & Phelps and it is often willing to work with the smaller leasing companies in helping them arrange securitizations. Investment banking firms engaged to execute a transaction will choose the appropriate rating agency based on investor demand and rating requirements. The investment bank presents the information package put together by the leasing company to the rating agency, along with a proposed deal structure.

Engage Other Transaction Players

An investment bank will assist a leasing company in assembling the other parties involved in the transaction, who are as follows:

- *Trustee* A trustee experienced in managing equipment lease securitizations is hired to act as trustee for the transaction. Trustees also utilize their own counsel to review the transaction indenture and negotiate all trustee responsibilities.
- *Custodial agent* Most companies utilize custodial agents to handle all files when funding via a warehouse. The same parties can be utilized for the securitization.
- *Lock box agent* Payments from the lessees from the portfolio that is being securitized is isolated in a lock box. If the company has a current lockbox agent, they are contracted to manage the lock boxes for the securitization.
- *Transaction legal team* Hiring a competitive legal team is absolutely a must in putting together an efficient and smooth securitization transaction. The legal team is responsible for putting together all the transaction documents. Smaller issuers can usually use local counsel accustomed to working with their investment bank.
- *Audit* A procedure review and file review audit team is hired to evaluate the company and the portfolio. KPMG and BDO Seidman are active auditors for equipment lease securitizations, as well as other major firms.
- *Backup servicer* Rating agencies require smaller issuers to have a back-up servicer in place to back up servicing duties of the issuer servicer. The trustee often acts as back-up servicer.

Private Placement Memorandum

The transaction legal team puts together a private placement memorandum (PPM) at the direction of the investment bank. The PPM outlines the bonds offered, the collateral, the deal structure, and company information. As the PPM is developed, a preliminary PPM is provided to the investors. Investors respond back to the investment bank with comments, conditions, and requirements. The company is then brought into the loop to discuss the various investor demands. Revisions are made to the PPM reflecting the various discussions between the investors and the issuer. PPM is also provided to the trustee and the rating agencies.

Rating Agency Site Visit

Upon reviewing the company information and proposed deal structure, the rating agency will conduct a site visit to the issuer. The rating agency typically meets with management, reviews a few sample files, evaluates systems and personnel, and conducts a review of the infrastructure of the issuer. Updated PPM's will be provided to the rating agencies. The rating agencies utilize counsel to review the transaction documents. Documents are provided to the rating agency counsel for review. Upon review of the portfolio and the loss history of the company, a subordination level is established by the rating agency. Based on rating agency feedback, tranches and tranche sizes are determined by the investment bank and conveyed to all parties involved. Most equipment lease securitizations in the market are structured as senior-subordinate with a first loss position being retained by the issuer.

Investor Site Visit

With private placement deals, investors also make site visits to the issuer leasing company. Investors seek familiarity with the management, business practices, and infrastructure of the issuer. After the site visit, investors indicate interest in participating in the deal. Traders for the investment bank will start negotiating spreads and pricing indices for the bonds in the transaction.

Other Transaction Documents

As investors express strong interest in moving forward, additional revisions of the PPM are provided to the investors. Terms of the transaction are formulated between the investors and the issuer. The investment bank acts as an intermediary to resolve any issues and disputes. When the majority of the deal terms are agreed to, the transaction counsel will start putting together other transaction documents. Utilizing terms already agreed to in the PPM, articles of incorporation for the SPC, the indenture, sales and servicing agreement, back up servicing agreement, and other documents are compiled by the transaction counsel. The documents are provided to investors, the rating agency, the rating agency's counsel, trustee, and trustee's counsel.

Portfolio Review and Procedural Audit

The audit firm engaged to conduct a review of the portfolio will make a site visit to the issuer. Lease files from pool allocated to be securitized are sampled at random and evaluated for consistency with underwriting criteria, credit decisions, and necessary documentation. The audit firm has the responsibility of conducting file and procedures review for the investors. The investors may indicate to the audit firm additional requirements for the file review. The file review is conducted in a satisfactory manner to the investors. The results of the file review are provided to the investors.

Set Pricing

The transaction evolves, and as the investors express strong interest, the fixed income trading desk of the investment bank sets a pricing date. On the pricing date, the traders negotiate a spread over the yield on the average life Treasury index of each bond in the transaction. A spread is agreed to with the investors and the investors sign a commitment letter expressing commitment to the transaction. At this point the investors engage investor counsel to represent them in the transaction. All documents are provided to investor counsel participating in the transaction for review.

Final Structure Modifications and Rating Letter

Based on its review of the portfolio, portfolio statistics, the deal structure, and evaluation of the transaction by a credit committee, the rating agencies establish rating levels for the bonds in the transaction. Any structural changes are conveyed to all parties involved and incorporated in the documentation. Rating agency personnel and counsel will review all modifications to the documents. When all the rating requirements are met, the rating agency issues a rating letter for the transaction outlining ratings assigned to each bond class in the transaction.

Final Negotiations

Any outstanding issues are negotiated by the investors and the issuer. The investors and investor counsel may make additional demands limiting concentrations, requesting servicer advances, and attempting to negotiate a few additional terms in their favor. As final issues are resolved between the issuer and the investors, the transaction counsel incorporates all changes into the transaction documents. The trustee also will provide input into the indenture, servicing, and back-up servicing agreements.

Wiring Instructions

Wiring instructions are provided by all necessary parties for purposes of wiring funds at closing. The issuer will provide wiring instructions to investors for depositing bond proceeds. Parties involved in the transaction due fees will also provide wiring instructions to the issuer.

Establishment of the SPC

At closing, the collateral assets are sold into the bankruptcy remote SPC, which in turn issues bonds to investors to finance the purchase of the lease receivables. True-sale opinions are delivered by transaction counsel and are approved by the rating agency, trustee, and investor counsel.

Final Rates are Established

As the closing date approaches, a final pricing date is established by the investment bank's trading desk. On the pricing date, the final rate is established for each bond in the deal, based on the average life of each bond. Treasury securities and rates matching the average life of the bonds are established, and the bonds are priced to the matching Treasury rate plus the spread agreed to by the investors.

Closing

The closing of the transaction is organized by the transaction counsel to execute all necessary documents. Representatives of the issuer, trustee, and investors are made available to execute the necessary documents. Any final revisions are made to the documents and are executed by all parties. Funds are wired to the necessary parties.

Exhibit 5: Senior/Subordinate Structure

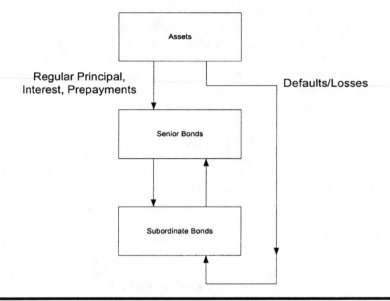

Post Closing and Servicing

On the first payment due date, principal and interest due to the investors are disbursed by the trustee based on servicing reports generated by the servicer. The investment bank provides any necessary assistance to the issuer.

UNDERSTANDING HOW THE DEAL IS STRUCTURED

Equipment lease securitizations are structured as senior-subordinate deals with rated senior bonds. Public deals are structured with investment grade bonds rated "AAA" to "BBB" in the credit spectrum. Subordinate bonds rated "BB" or "B" are also incorporated into many public deals, subordinated by an unrated first loss piece retained by the issuer. In many of the privately placed equipment lease backed deals, the senior tranche is rated "A." Bonds rated "BBB," "BB," and "B" are also incorporated into private placement deals, again subordinated by an unrated bond. In a senior-subordinate structure, losses are first allocated to the subordinate bonds, while the regular interest and principal payments are first paid to the senior bonds and then the subordinate bonds.

Equipment lease structures pay pro-rata interest and principal when the deal is performing adequately. In the event that the losses exceed certain thresholds, the deal structure is established to pay first to the senior bonds, and only after certain thresholds are met, the subordinate bonds. (See Exhibit 5.) Exhibit 6 illustrates a sample waterfall from an "A" rated private placement transaction.

Exhibit 6: Sample Lease Transaction Waterfall

Flow of Funds:	Monthly distributions from the SPC account will be made by the Trustee in the following priority: 1. Repayment of unreimbursed, uncollectable Servicer advances 2. Pay Servicing, Trustee, and Back-up Servicing Fee 3. Class A notes interest 4. Class B notes interest 5. Class C notes interest 6. Class A notes principal, pro rata 7. Class B notes principal, pro rata 8. Class C notes principal, pro rata 9. Excess amounts to Issuer In the event of a Trigger Event, the Flow Of Funds will occur as follows: 1. Repayment of unreimbursed, uncollectible Servicer advances 2. Pay Servicing, Trustee, and Back-up Servicing Fee 3. Class A notes interest 4. Class B notes interest 5. Class C notes interest 6. Class A notes principal, in full 7. Class B notes principal, in full 8. Class C notes principal, in full 9. Excess amounts to Issuer

Exhibit 7: Rating Agency Rating Multiples

Rating Level	Loss Multiple
AAA	5×
AA	4×
A	3×
BBB	2×
BB	1.5×
B	1×

Rating agencies size subordinate bonds to protect the senior bonds from any losses occurring from the underlying collateral. Rating agencies use a certain established methodology in determining the subordination levels. The most common criteria utilized by the rating agencies and investors are loss multiples. Rating agencies have established multiples for determining rating and subordination levels. (See Exhibit 7.)

The static pool loss performance of the company is evaluated in detail by the rating agencies to determine loss multiples. For example, assume ABC Company has a 3% static pool loss history. Based on the multiples established by the rating agencies as shown in Exhibit 7, the rating agencies require a 15% (5 × 3%) subordination level for a "AAA" transaction. If the senior bond is rated an "A," then a 9% (3 × 3%) subordination is required for the rating of the senior bond.

Exhibit 8: Bond Structure For A Sample "A" Deal

Bonds Offered	Bond Sizes
A	91% (100% − (3 × 3%))
BBB	3% (100% − (2 × 3%) − 91%)
B	3% (100% − (1 × 3%) − 91% − 3%)
Unrated	3% (100% − 91% − 3% − 3%)

For example, a company wanting to issue "A/BBB/B" deal will have the following tranches at a 3% loss level (see Exhibit 8). The BBB (3%), B (3%), and the Unrated (3%) combined provide the required 3 times loss coverage and the 9% subordination to the senior A rated tranche. Similarly the B (3%) and the Unrated (3%) provide the required 6% subordination to the BBB. In the event of losses from the underlying lease portfolio, losses are first applied to the Unrated bond. The Unrated bond is referred to as the "first loss position" and is retained by the issuer.

The other major criteria utilized by the rating agencies in establishing a subordination level is obligor concentration levels. For example, in a "A" transaction, rating agencies require the top 5 obligors to be covered by the required subordination levels. If the top 5 obligors cumulatively make up 10% of the portfolio, then only 90% can be advanced as the senior bond. Rating agencies thereby require a subordination of 10%. Diversifying the portfolio by obligor and state concentration levels will allow the issuer to issue the maximum amounts in senior bonds, allowing the issuer to maximize borrowing at the an "A" rating level and thus minimizing borrowing costs.

CONCLUSION

Equipment lease securitizations continue to thrive in the capital markets as a flexible, lower cost funding source for many equipment leasing companies. The characteristics of the lease collateral and the equipment lease ABS deal structures make equipment lease securitizations attractive to investors. Careful planning, execution, and an established origination, servicing, and reporting infrastructure will allow equipment leasing companies to successfully utilize securitization as a reliable funding source.

Ten years ago, the Equipment Lessors Association worried about the leasing business being composed of only minnows and whales due to funding costs. Securitizations have completely changed that scenario. Securitizations have allowed many minnows to become small whales as a result of competitive funding costs and the ability to enter the equity markets as well as the capital markets.

Chapter 15

Manufactured Housing Securitization

Paul N. Watterson Jr., Esq.
Partner
Schulte Roth & Zabel LLP

Shlomo C. Twerski, Esq.
Partner
Schulte Roth & Zabel LLP

Craig S. Stein, Esq.
Associate
Schulte Roth & Zabel LLP

INTRODUCTION

Securities backed by manufactured housing contracts are marketed as asset-backed securities (ABS) because of their underwriting, prepayment, default, and recovery patterns. However, securities backed by manufactured housing contracts share many of the legal characteristics of mortgage-backed securities (MBS). For example, some manufactured home financings are secured by mortgages or deeds of trust. Manufactured housing securitizations are generally structured as real estate mortgage investment conduits (REMICs) for tax purposes. The securities laws treat manufactured housing contracts as interests in real estate and, therefore, classify most manufactured housing securitizations with MBS transactions. The securities backed by manufactured housing contracts are typically tranched in ways more common in MBS transactions. The purpose of this chapter is to examine how the dichotomy between MBS and ABS affects the structuring and legal issues involved in securitizing manufactured housing contracts.

WHAT IS A MANUFACTURED HOME?

Manufactured homes are single-family residences constructed on a chassis at a factory and transported to a site in one or more components (single-section or multisection). Unit sizes range from about 400 square feet to more than 2,000 square feet.[1] Upon delivery to the site, the wheels are removed and the unit is placed on a concrete pad. Most manufactured homes are expected to remain at the site indefinitely; their wheels are simply a built-in means of transportation to the home site. The sites for manufactured homes are generally manufactured housing parks or private lots that are owned or rented.

MANUFACTURED HOUSING SECURITIZATION MARKET

In 1999, approximately $13.3 billion securities backed by manufactured homes were issued.[2] While Conseco (formerly, Green Tree) has been the largest issuer in this market, a number of other large finance companies are active issuers in this market.

In most of these transactions, the securitization is structured as a sale of the manufactured housing contracts by the originating finance company or financial institution, directly or through a special purpose subsidiary, to a newly formed trust. The trust then issues several classes of senior and subordinate certificates of beneficial interest in the trust, and a single residual class which in most cases is held by the seller or its affiliate. Additional credit enhancement may be provided by a reserve account or spread account. In a rare case, manufactured housing contracts (particularly land-and-home contracts, discussed below) and residential mortgage or home equity loans may be included in the same offering.

TYPES OF RECEIVABLES

Most manufactured housing contract receivables are installment sales contracts or installment loan contracts. The installment sales contract creates a security interest in the manufactured home. However, some manufactured housing contract receivables are "land-and-home" or "land home" contracts. Originators of land-and-home contracts require the obligor to execute a mortgage or deed of trust creating a first lien on the real estate on which the manufactured home is affixed to secure the manufactured housing contract.

A land-and-home contract is similar to a residential mortgage loan. The mortgage or deed of trust is recorded in the real estate records, title insurance usually is obtained, and, after a default by an obligor on its manufactured housing contract, foreclosure procedures similar to procedures for a residential mortgage loan may be commenced. A land-and-home contract may finance the acquisition of both the manufactured home and the land; in some contracts (a "land in lieu" contract), the obligor already owns the site and gives a mortgage on it to the lender in lieu of a downpayment on the manufactured home.

---

[1] "Manufactured Housing's Changing Landscape," Fitch Investors Service, L.P., July 15, 1996.
[2] *Asset Sales Report*, Vol. 14, No. 2 (January 10, 2000).

Most manufactured housing contracts are "three party paper" in which a dealer originates an installment sales contract to finance a consumer's purchase of a manufactured home and assigns the installment sales contract to a finance company, usually at the time of funding. However, an increasing number of manufactured housing contracts are being financed through direct origination by the finance company.

PROTECTION OF TRUST'S INTEREST IN MANUFACTURED HOUSING CONTRACTS

Chattel Paper: Perfection by Filing or Possession

Manufactured housing contracts are generally classified as chattel paper under the Uniform Commercial Code (UCC). Chattel paper is defined in Section 9-105(b) of the UCC as "a writing or writings which evidence both a monetary obligation and a security interest in or lease of specific goods." Each installment sales contract evidences the debt and the grant of a security interest in the related manufactured home.

Generally, UCC financing statements are filed to perfect the sale of the manufactured housing contracts to the trust. Under Section 9-308 of the UCC, "a purchaser of chattel paper ... who gives new value and takes possession of it in the ordinary course of business has priority over a security interest in the chattel paper" which was perfected by filing, if the purchaser "acts without knowledge that the specific paper ... is subject to a security interest." Thus, unless the trust has possession of the manufactured housing contracts, it is possible for the seller, through mistake or fraud, to transfer the manufactured housing contracts to a third party.

In order to evidence the trust's ownership of the manufactured housing contracts and to make it difficult for any purchaser to claim that it had no knowledge of the trust's interest in the manufactured housing contracts, the manufactured housing contracts can be stamped to reflect their sale to the trust. Alternatively, the trust could protect its interests by taking possession of the manufactured housing contracts. But it is customary in most securitizations of this type for the manufactured housing contracts to be held by the seller/servicer as custodian for the trust to enable it to perform the necessary servicing duties.

Additional steps may be taken to protect investors in the case of land-and-home contracts. The seller is more likely to deliver the land-and-home contracts to a third-party custodian, similar to the practice in MBS transactions.

Protection of Trust's Security Interest in Manufactured Homes

Under the laws of most states, manufactured homes constitute personal property, perfection of a security interest in which may be obtained by filing a UCC financing statement. In some states, manufactured homes are covered by certificate of title laws. In these states, perfection of a security interest requires delivery of the certificate of title or notation of the lien on the certificate of title of the manufactured home.

Because of the cost and administrative inconvenience involved, the practice in manufactured housing securitizations is not to amend the certificates of title of the manufactured homes to reflect the trust's lien, even though such amendment is required in some states to render the assignment of the originator/seller's security interest in the manufactured home to the trust enforceable against third-party creditors (including a trustee in bankruptcy) of the obligor under the contract. Instead, the originator/seller represents at closing that it has obtained a first priority security interest in the manufactured homes underlying the manufactured housing contracts. Investors rely on this representation and the good servicing practices of the servicer to protect the trust's security interest in the manufactured homes.

Land-and-Home Contracts: Filing in Real Estate Records

For land-and-home contracts the practice is different, because a mortgage or deed of trust is involved. First, the originator/seller records the mortgage or deed of trust in the real estate records. The mortgage or deed of trust is then assigned to the trust, together with the manufactured housing contract.

There are three basic approaches with respect to the assignment to the trust of the mortgage or deed of trust. One approach is to record the assignments of mortgage to the trustee in the real estate records. Another approach is not to deliver the assignments of mortgage at closing, but to establish triggers (for example, a decline in the credit rating of the seller) in the transaction documents which, if they occur in the future, will require the seller to deliver assignments of mortgage to the trustee for recording. The third approach, which is the most common, is to deliver assignments of mortgage to the trustee in recordable form, but not to record them at closing because of the cost involved. Instead, the transaction documents establish triggers which, if they occur in the future, will require the trustee to record the assignments of mortgage. Under the laws of many states, the recording of the assignments is not required to protect the interests of the trust.

Consequences of Change of Location of Manufactured Home and Permanent Attachment to the Site

There are two additional problems with manufactured homes that do not exist in MBS transactions. Like automobiles, manufactured homes can be moved to another state and retitled. This can result in the loss of the trust's lien on the manufactured home unless the servicer receives notice of the move and follows the proper procedure in the new state to protect the trust's lien on the manufactured home.

Another risk is that the manufactured homes can become permanently affixed to the real estate. Under the laws of some states once the manufactured home becomes "affixed" to the real estate, it becomes a "fixture" and, thus, becomes part of the real estate to which the manufactured home is attached. At the time the manufactured home becomes a fixture it becomes subject to the real estate title and recording laws, in which case perfection of the trust's interest would require recordation in the real estate records. Failure to record may result in the loss of the trust's lien on the manufactured home or the loss of the trust's first priority position against third parties (e.g., the obligor's real estate lender) that may have filed a mortgage in the real estate records. Manufactured housing contracts generally prohibit the obligor from attaching the manufactured home permanently to the site.

Filing of Continuation Statements

The UCC requires that a creditor file continuation statements every five years or lose its security interest in the manufactured home. Since manufactured housing contracts have terms of 25 to 30 years, this requires four or five filings to protect the trust's interest in the manufactured home. Revised Article 9 of the UCC provides that if the financing statement states that it is filed in connection with a manufactured home transaction the initial financing statement is effective for a period of 30 years. Revised Article 9 will become effective on July 1, 2001 in each state which has adopted it by then.[3]

TRANSACTION STRUCTURES

The structure of manufactured housing securitizations is driven primarily by tax considerations. Because of the Internal Revenue Code's "taxable mortgage pool" rules, most receivables secured by an interest in real estate can be securitized only in a multiple-class or tranched offering if a REMIC or financial asset securitization investment trust (FASIT) is used. A multiple class or tranched offering is desirable so that subordinated securities can provide credit enhancement for senior securities and so that the cash flows can be tailored to investors' average life requirements. This tailoring, in turn, broadens the investor base and improves the pricing of the transaction.

To qualify as a REMIC, each manufactured housing contract in the pool must be considered to be principally secured by an interest in real property. For these purposes, the Internal Revenue Code provides that a manufactured housing unit is to be treated as real property if it has at least 400 square feet of living space, is more than 102 inches wide, and is of the type customarily used at a fixed location. Most manufactured housing units meet this test and the contracts thereon are therefore secured by interests in real property, even if the manufactured housing contract is not secured by a mortgage, deed, or trust on the site.

---

[3] Currently 27 states and the District of Columbia have adopted Revised Article 9 of the UCC. See the National Conference of Commissioners on Uniform State Laws Official Website.

Under a 1996 IRS private ruling, an ANSI (American National Standards Institute) unit was also considered real property and a contract secured by such a unit was permitted to be included in a REMIC. An ANSI unit is at least 375 square feet, more than 102 inches wide, has the wheels removed, is anchored to the ground, and has additions attached to the unit. Contracts secured by units that are not treated as real property cannot be securitized as part of a REMIC.

A FASIT may hold a pool consisting of one or more types of debt instrument, whether secured or unsecured. Using a FASIT would allow the securitization of a pool containing contracts secured by any type of manufactured housing units, together with other types of qualifying receivables.

Because most manufactured housing contracts are considered to be interests in real property, most issuers have structured the securitization as a REMIC. Although some manufactured housing securitizations have been structured as grantor trusts, this structure is used infrequently because grantor trusts cannot have "fast pay/slow pay" or sequential classes of securities and can have only limited subordination of classes.

A trust that elects to be a REMIC (or a FASIT) is permitted to issue multiple classes of securities with senior/subordinate and fast-pay/slow-pay features. Usually, the trust issues senior classes of securities to investors and one or more junior classes that may be sold to investors or retained by an affiliate of the originator. The trust issues a single residual class in a REMIC (or a FASIT), which is usually retained by the originator/seller.

CREDIT ENHANCEMENT

In all securitizations, including those backed by manufactured housing contracts, there is the risk that obligors will default on the payments due under their contracts or will not make their payments on time. Credit enhancement seeks to minimize the risk that nonpayment by the obligors will cause a loss to the securityholders. Credit enhancement comes in many forms. It may be provided by the originator/seller or by a third party. The size of the credit-enhancement facility required to obtain the desired rating from the rating agencies for each class of securities is dependent on a number of factors, including the historical delinquency and loss experience of similar pools of manufactured housing contracts and the structure of the transaction.

Generally, qualifying credit enhancements may be included in a REMIC or a FASIT without adversely affecting the entity's tax status.

Senior/Subordinate Structure

The primary form of credit enhancement used in manufactured housing contract securitizations is the subordination of one or more of the classes of securities issued by the trust. These subordinated class(es) of securities serve as credit support for the more senior classes of securities issued by the trust. In a typical senior/subordinated transaction, the rights of the holders of the subordinated securities to receive distributions in respect of principal and interest are subordinated to the rights of the holders of the senior securities to receive such distributions. The subordination feature may also be accomplished by the allocation among the classes of securities of certain types of payments, losses or delinquencies on the manufactured housing contracts or the payments from reserve accounts or a guarantee.

The subordinated securities are sometimes held by the originator/seller. In this circumstance, the attorneys delivering the opinion that there has been a "true sale" of the manufactured housing contracts to the trust must consider whether the originator/seller has divested itself of the risks of loss on the pool of manufactured housing contracts.

Overcollateralization

Credit support may consist of overcollateralization whereby the aggregate principal balance of the manufactured housing contracts exceeds the principal balance of the securities on the closing date. Overcollateralization may be created after the closing date through the use of the interest collected on the manufactured housing contracts (in excess of the amounts necessary to pay the interest rate on the securities) to pay principal on the securities. Overcollateralization can be created in this way because the weighted average interest rate on the manufactured housing contracts is usually significantly greater than the weighted average interest rate on the securities. This "excess spread" is used to pay principal on the securities, thus creating overcollateralization as the principal balance of the securities is reduced faster than the principal balance of the pool of manufactured housing contracts.

Guaranty

Payments on a class of securities, deficiencies in principal or interest payments on the manufactured housing contracts, or liquidation losses on the manufactured housing contracts may be supported by a guaranty. The guarantor may be the originator/seller, an affiliate of the originator/seller or a third party financial institution. The guarantor may be required to make deposits to an account, make advances, or purchase defaulted manufactured housing contracts. The scope, amount, and allocation of payments made under and pursuant to a guaranty will vary from transaction to transaction. The rating on the class of securities supported by the guaranty will be contingent on the maintenance of the guarantor's credit rating.

Reserve Account

Credit enhancement for the securities or some classes of the securities may be provided by a reserve account. The purpose of a reserve account is to protect the trust from credit losses on the manufactured housing contracts. Funds on deposit in the reserve account may be withdrawn for distribution to holders of designated (or all) classes of the securities at times specified in the transaction documents.

Funds on deposit in the reserve account may be invested in eligible investment securities; and future funding of the reserve account may be secured by a letter of credit, guaranty, or demand notes. A reserve account may be funded at closing from the proceeds of the issuance of the securities, or the account may be funded from the "excess spread" generated by the manufactured housing contracts after the closing (in which case it may be referred to as a "spread account").

Subordination of Servicing Fee

The servicer typically receives its servicing fee prior to the securityholders receiving any distributions. However, in many manufactured housing securitizations, the originator/seller may agree that, so long as it or its affiliate is the servicer, the servicing fee will be subordinated and will be paid only if all payments then due to the holders of the securities have been made.

Other Forms of Credit Enhancement

Two other forms of credit enhancement frequently used in ABS transactions are not often seen in manufactured housing securitizations. In a few transactions, credit support has been provided by the issuance of a letter of credit from a third-party financial institution to support timely payments on the securities, to provide protection against losses on the manufactured housing contracts, to provide a source of funding for a reserve account or to secure the servicer's obligations. As in the case of a guarantee, the credit rating of the securities supported by the letter of credit will be tied to the credit rating of the issuer of the letter of credit.

Alternatively, a surety "wrap" may be obtained from an insurer to provide credit support for one or more classes of securities. This insurance product generally guarantees to securityholders the scheduled payment of interest and principal to which securityholders would be entitled. Again, the credit rating of the insurer will affect the rating on the securities.

LIQUIDITY ENHANCEMENT

Even if obligors ultimately make the payments due under their manufactured housing contracts, there is the risk that the timing of their payments may be such that the trust will not have sufficient funds on a distribution date to pay all amounts due to the securityholders. Liquidity enhancement seeks to minimize this risk by providing an alternative source of funds with which to pay the securityholders, pending receipt of the payments under the manufactured housing contracts.

Servicer Advances

The servicer typically agrees to help maintain a regular flow of scheduled interest payments to securityholders by making servicer advances to the trust. Such advances are usually made in the amount of the delinquency of each obligor on his interest payment (or, in some cases, his full scheduled payment) under his manufactured housing contract. The servicer is obligated to make the advance only if it believes that it will be recoverable from future payments by the obligor or through the proceeds of liquidation of the collateral. Such advances are reimbursed to the servicer out of late payments made by the obligor or the insurance proceeds or liquidation proceeds of the manufactured home; or, if the servicer determines that the advance is not recoverable from payments on other manufactured housing contracts in the pool.

Compensating Interest

If a manufactured housing contract is prepaid in advance of the final scheduled due date on the manufactured housing contract, the trust may receive less interest on such contract for a particular collection period than it would have otherwise received had such contract not been prepaid. The servicer may make a payment to the trust (but only to the extent of its servicing fee for such collection period) equal to the excess of the amount of interest that would have been due on such contract for the full collection period had the prepayment not been made over the amount of interest actually received for such collection period.

The amount paid by the servicer is sometimes referred to as compensating interest. The servicer often agrees to make this type of advance (as well as advances to cover suspensions of payments on contracts pursuant to laws protecting obligors performing military service) without any right to reimbursement.

Prefunding and Capitalized Interest Accounts

A manufactured housing securitization — whether structured as a REMIC, FASIT, grantor trust, or otherwise — may include a prefunding account. In such a transaction, the original principal amount of securities issued by the trust exceeds the principal balance of the manufactured housing contracts initially sold to the trust, and a portion of the proceed of the securities is deposited into a prefunding account. This account is used to purchase additional manufactured housing contracts during a short period, usually three months, after the initial closing date. In this instance, a capitalized interest account typically is established to protect against the negative arbitrage resulting from the investments in the prefunding account earning interest at a lower rate than the interest rate on the securities.

There are other circumstances in which a capitalized interest account may be required. For example, the monthly payments on some manufactured housing contracts sold to the trust may not commence prior to the date interest is due on the securities. A capitalized interest account may be established to cover the "lost interest" on these manufactured housing contracts.

SECURITIES LAWS

SEC Registration

Manufactured housing securitizations are treated to a large extent under the federal securities laws as MBS. Unless all classes of the securities are offered pursuant to a private placement exempt from registration under the Securities Act of 1933 (the "1933 Act"), the securities must be registered under the 1933 Act pursuant to a registration statement.

A stand-alone registration statement of securities backed by manufactured housing contracts typically was filed on Form S-11. This form is used for securities issued by issuers whose business is primarily that of acquiring and holding investment real estate or interests in real estate. Manufactured housing contracts are considered to be interests in real estate for this purpose.

Rule 415 under the 1933 Act, which permits shelf registrations of securities to be offered on a delayed or continuous basis, is limited to certain kinds of public offerings, including "mortgage related securities" and "asset backed securities." Securities backed by manufactured housing contracts can qualify for shelf registration under either rubric. A shelf registration for a manufactured housing securitization may be filed on Form S-11 or Form S-3 if the securities qualify as "mortgage related securities" under the standard discussed below.

Alternatively, a shelf registration may be filed on Form S-3 if they qualify as "asset backed securities" with "investment grade" ratings. An "asset-backed security" is "a security that is primarily serviced by the cash flows of a discrete pool of receivables or other financial assets, either fixed or revolving, that by their terms convert into cash within a finite period plus any rights designed to assure the servicing or timely distribution of proceeds to the security-holders."[4] A security is an investment-grade security if, at the time of sale, at least one nationally recognized statistical rating organization has rated the security in one of its generic rating categories that signifies investment grade; typically the four highest rating categories (within which there may be subcategories or gradations indicating relative standing) signify investment grade.[5]

SMMEA

If the manufactured housing contract-backed securities are rated double-A or better by at least one nationally recognized statistical rating organization and the contracts in the pool satisfy certain requirements, they will constitute "mortgage related securities"[6] for purposes of the Secondary Mortgage Market Enhancement Act of 1984 (SMMEA). As such, the securities will be exempt from many requirements under state blue sky and legal investment laws.

---

[4] Form S-3, general instructions parts I.A.4. and I.B.5.

[5] Form S-3, general instructions Part I.B.2.

[6] See Section 3(a)(41) of the Securities and Exchange Act of 1934, as amended.

Investment Company Act of 1940

As in most ABS and MBS offerings, a trust does not register under the Investment Company Act of 1940 (the "1940 Act") when it issues securities backed by manufactured housing contracts. Issuers of securities backed by manufactured housing contracts are excepted from the definition of an investment company under Section 3(c)(5)(C) of the 1940 Act. Section 3(c)(5)(C) of the 1940 Act provides that any person primarily engaged in the business of purchasing or otherwise acquiring mortgages and other liens on and interests in real estate is not an investment company under the 1940 Act.

Moreover, issuers of securities backed by manufactured housing contracts are exempt under Rule 3a-7. Rule 3a-7 exempts any issuer engaged in the business of purchasing, or otherwise acquiring, and holding "eligible assets" provided that the securities meet other requirements specified in the rule. Eligible assets are defined as financial assets, either fixed or revolving, that by their terms convert into cash within a finite time period. Manufactured housing contracts qualify as eligible assets, and the other requirements of Rule 3a-7 usually are easily met in a typical manufactured housing securitization.

CONCLUSION

Manufactured housing securitizations should be analyzed using both ABS and MBS concepts. An increasing portion of each pool of manufactured housing contracts is mortgages or deeds of trust and additional steps should be taken to protect the trust's interest in the mortgages or deeds of trust. Since most manufactured housing securitizations are structured as REMICs, a familiarity with MBS structures is helpful in analyzing the cash flow and class structure of the transaction and understanding the legal issues.

Chapter 16

Promoting Securitization in Emerging Economies

Bharat A. Jain, Ph.D
Associate Professor of Finance
Department of Finance
Towson University

INTRODUCTION

The success and explosive growth of securitization in the United States lead to bold predictions on the rapid global spread of the concept to both developed and developing countries. The U.S. model has been successfully applied in the United Kingdom and other parts of Europe, and both the volume of securitization and types of assets being securitized continues to grow. However, securitization has not yet reached its full potential and its role as a financing alternative remains limited or non-existent in many developed and emerging markets. For instance, many developed economies in Europe are only recently starting to use securitization for a limited set of assets. Nowhere is the rationale for securitization stronger than in Japan. Yet their securitization efforts thus far have been limited in scope despite aggressive prodding by U.S. investment bankers. Emerging markets are even further behind in the process of developing their securitization market.

The central focus of this chapter is to assess the opportunities for promoting the rapid spread of securitization in emerging economies. To address this central issue, this chapter focuses on the following related questions: (1) Can securitization volume grow to a point where it becomes an important source of financing in emerging markets? (2) Are current conditions suitable for the application of sophisticated forms of securitization? (3) What are some of the barriers to securitization and how can they be overcome?

The term "emerging markets" was first coined in the early 1990s. It has been used to describe economies in developing countries that took concrete steps to develop their capital markets. The process of capital market development was undertaken through a series of initiatives such as privatization, liberalization, stock market reform, elimination or relaxation of currency controls, and active encouragement of foreign direct investments. Countries such as Indonesia, Malaysia, Singapore, Thailand, Philippines, Romania, Russia, India, Poland, China, and Taiwan are considered among the more prominent emerging markets.

During the 1990s, these countries continued to focus on implementing significant reforms to increase the breadth and depth of their capital markets. The market capitalization of emerging markets increased from approximately $167 billion in 1986 to $2.1 trillion in 1997. It was becoming increasingly clear that emerging markets would be the likely engines of growth driving both developed and developing countries. The general consensus among the financial and investment community was that emerging markets presented an attractive opportunity for the introduction of an array of financial products and services.

The road to capital market development in emerging markets, however, has not been without its bumps. The widespread financial crisis witnessed towards the end of the 1990s clearly brought home the risks involved. A single isolated event such as the unexpected devaluation of the Thai currency triggered a global backlash and almost lead to a financial meltdown in several emerging markets. The consequences included a global banking crisis, competitive devaluations, sustained recessions, shrinking liquidity, and a restive population. The sheer speed and depth of the decline in emerging economies and its impact on the rest of the world took investors of all stripes by surprise and sent a chill through the global financial markets. Stock markets fell 40%-80% from their recent highs, yield spreads on bonds widened dramatically, liquidity vanished, and bank lending almost completely dried up. Inflows of offshore capital that flowed easily throughout the 1990s disappeared equally quickly at the first sign of trouble. Countries like Malaysia had to undertake drastic measures such as currency controls to prevent the further flight of capital. While most emerging markets have rebounded spectacularly from their lows, the recent crisis highlighted how fragile these newly developing financial systems are in reality.

It is clear that the development of emerging markets is still evolving and the ability to withstand shocks is still in question. An often cited reason for the recent crisis is that emerging economies rushed to open up and expand their markets without attending to the basic institutional infrastructure needs required to develop a robust financial system. It raises the question of whether these markets are ready for the introduction of sophisticated financial products. Typically, emerging economies are still bank centric with underdeveloped equity and bond markets. Banks are still the primary originators of almost all forms of lending with no real competition. A critical mass of domestic institutional investors is lacking. Venture capital and the private equity markets are either underdeveloped or non-existent. Firms seeking external financing have two choices — weak banks and illiquid capital markets. Banks, saddled with huge bad loans, usually to property markets are in no position to provide risk capital. The collateral on these loans have dropped to a fraction of the original value. There is a lack of commitment to find a solution to this problem and as a result there is little or no pressure on banks to find a way to quickly write off these bad loans. As a result, bank lending is confined to safe mature businesses and entrepreneurial firms are starved of capital. It is clear from the above discussion that emerging markets are saddled with structural problems that need to be systematically addressed to develop a robust financial system.

Given the above situation, it is only natural to ask whether emerging markets are ready for sophisticated financing alternatives such as securitization. However, it is some of these very adverse conditions that are ideal for securitization. Logically, a good starting point for addressing structural problems in bank-centric economies is to focus on the troubled banking sector. Clearly, there needs to be an overall movement for bank disintermediation. Securitization provides an alternative form of disintermediation that is more cost effective than that provided by banks. It increases the origination capacity of banks. It is an efficient method to create liquidity in the banking system. Additional benefits of securitization to banks include reduced risk and capital requirements. Investors gain access to a wide class of liquid instruments of varying risk return characteristics. Pooling of loans in tranches expands the market and helps attract a wider base of domestic and overseas investors. The beauty of securitization is that it can be implemented for almost any form of cash flow. Emerging markets can initially focus on natural securities rather than synthetic securities. Natural securities are debt instruments based on payment of principal and interest as seen in mortgages, auto loans, etc. In contrast, synthetic securities involve bifurcation of cash flows from natural securities to create a variety of investment options of different risk-return characteristics. As the market grows and investors become more educated about securitization, synthetic securities can be introduced.

It is clear that the U.S. model of securitization cannot be applied without modifications to the fundamentally different economic environment of emerging markets. Adaptation of the U.S. model to suit the financial systems of the local economies is needed. Since no guaranteed formula for this transformation exists, the process is likely to be incremental and based on reinforcing the successful elements and adaptation based on lessons from failure. A good starting point in this process is to gain an understanding of the economic environment in emerging economies and their level of preparation for the introduction of securitization. This will lead to an understanding of the structural changes required to create an enabling environment for the introduction of sophisticated financial products.

RATIONALE FOR SECURITIZATION IN EMERGING ECONOMIES

Is securitization really feasible in underdeveloped capital markets going through growing pains? Securitization in the U.S. has been highly successful and has provided both additional liquidity and created a variety of new instruments. Despite the phenomenal success in the U.S., securitization efforts in other economies have been slower than expected. The reasons include a variety of factors such as differences in consumer borrowing patterns, institutional infrastructure, investor base, and legal/regulatory environment. Another factor is the extent of involvement of central banks and the local banking system in promoting securitization.

It is clear that emerging markets represent a tiny segment of the overall securitization market. However, the current financial crisis has only strengthened the rationale for securitization in these economies. Securitization works well in economic environments where there is a shortage of funds due to withdrawal of traditional lenders, deficiencies in credit quality and a desire for yield among investors. The resulting credit crunch and the inability of traditional lenders to finance positive net present value projects create the ideal conditions for alternative sources of financing such as securitization to enter. Promoting securitization and other innovative mechanisms to allow for risk pooling and the creation of liquid instruments is especially important in markets where there is a critical need to create liquidity in the banking system. Another major problem in emerging markets is the lack of availability of housing finance. The demand for housing finance is huge in many emerging markets, but has remained underdeveloped due to limited origination capacity. Securitization can address the capital problem facing lenders and thereby spur home ownership. For all the above reasons, emerging markets appear to be ripe for securitization. In fact, a case can be made for securitization to develop faster in emerging markets due to the huge demands for financing and the lack of or inability of current institutions to meet the needs.

Securitization tends to benefit all market participants. It is an attractive option, both to healthy companies with high-quality assets, looking for off-balance sheet financing and ailing banks focused on getting rid of their non-performing and low-quality loans. It provides an opportunity to corporate borrowers with less than perfect ratings to raise capital on attractive terms. Originators benefit from the ability to sell assets easily and increased capacity to provide funds. Investors benefit from access to high-yield securities, liquidity, and diversification.

From the supply side it is clear that the rationale for securitization is strong in emerging economies. However, for the process to succeed, it is important that the appropriate foundation be laid to allow the demand side to develop. Investors tolerance for risk, especially with regard to emerging markets is understandably, extremely low at this time. Therefore, it is unlikely that securitizied assets originating from emerging markets will attract strong investor interest.

To create the demand for securitized products from emerging economies, it is important to raise investor confidence by addressing structural issues in capital market development. Enabling conditions for securitization include a viable banking system, strong legal framework, relatively high-quality assets, liquid swap markets, stable currencies, favorable tax treatments, credible rating information, strong corporate governance mechanisms, and a critical mass of investors with a high tolerance for risk. In addition, in order to implement securitization, a mix of institutions such as originators, investment bankers, poolers, credit rating agencies, insurers, and investors working together are required to create supply and demand. In the final analysis, given the current mood of investors, securitization in emerging economies is unlikely to succeed if only loans of the lowest quality are brought to the market. Efforts have to be made to improve quality of assets through institutional support and governance mechanisms. Basically, there is no substitute for a financial system that funnels capital into productive projects and punishes poor performers by cutting off the supply of funds. Otherwise, initiatives such as securitization are likely to be unsuccessful and turn into a fruitless search for liquidity.

ANALYSIS OF EMERGING MARKETS

The evolution and development of financial markets around the world has followed two distinct paradigms: stock market centric versus bank centric.[1] The stock market-centric system as seen in the United States and other countries is characterized by strong institutional infrastructure in the form of a mix of interdependent financial institutions such as pension funds, mutual funds, venture capitalists, insurance companies, and to a lesser extent banks that mobilize capital and are involved in corporate governance issues. The alternative bank-centric capital markets, such as in Germany and Japan, are dominated by banks with weak institutional infrastructure. In this system, banks are primary responsible for mobilization of funds and tend to play a central corporate governance role in monitoring managers.

Almost universally, emerging markets have adopted the bank-centric model. However, unlike Germany and Japan, they have struggled to effectively utilize this model for economic development. The recent global banking has thrown a spotlight on the limitations of the bank-centric model and raised some important institutional design issues. The issue of bank restructuring and reform is rapidly gaining prominence as the crisis has wrought havoc across a swathe of banks with loan losses rising, revenues down and pressure to cut costs. The need for a paradigm shift from a bank-centric capital market system to a stock market-centric system has become increasingly apparent. What is less clear is the extent of transformation required and the specific path to be followed in the design and development of institutions to support this transition. Therefore, the basic challenge is how to create a set of institutions that not only ensures the right balance in the composition of a nation's assets but also produce sustained and stable economic growth.

The discussion below provides both an assessment of the current situation and discusses potential solutions to develop a robust financial system capable of handling securitization and other asset backed securities.

Problems with the Banking Sector

For the most part, finger pointing for the emerging market crisis has been directed towards the inadequate and inefficient banking systems. A shared problem in

---

[1] Bernard Black and Ronald Gilson, "Venture Capital and the Structure of Capital Markets: Banks versus Stock Markets," *Journal of Financial Economics* (1998), pp. 243-277.

emerging markets has been an excessive reliance on the banking sector as a percent of GDP. This has severely distorted the balance between bank, equity, and bond market assets in the economy. Concentration of systematic risk through heavy intermediation by the banking system has eroded the underlying fundamentals of economic growth.[2]

In most emerging economies, the link between the traditional banking sector and financial markets has been weak. Further, governments were not keen to allow the banking sector to raise capital through the stock markets because they did not have the legal and regulatory enforcement mechanisms in place to ensure that such funds would be used for approved purposes. Thus, banks have operated, not as profit-driven companies accountable to independent shareholders, but as government influenced institutions. This has left banks locked into incestuous shareholding relations with clients. Further, the banking sector as a whole in emerging markets have had a high exposure to the property market. A real estate crisis has caused the value of the collateral to crash. Banks appear unable or unwilling to get the loans off their books. In many instances, property values have fallen dramatically to a point where banks are hesitant to offload them at such fire sale prices. Borrowers, on the other hand, are unable to pay the debt or maintain the properties. A paralysis of sorts has set in with no immediate resolution in sight.

The extent of the problem of non-performing loans can be seen from estimates of non-performing loans as a percentage of total loans for several emerging market economies. The estimates range from a low of 5% for Taiwan to a staggering 70% for Indonesia.[3] Being confronted with a problem of such magnitude is bad enough. However, what is even more disturbing, is the fact that these banks have still not written-off their bad loans, partly because a combination of lax regulation and accounting practices have allowed them to continue to disguise the problem. There has been no leadership from the government to force banks to recognize and deal with the problem. Although bank profits have declined dramatically, they have not been allowed to fail or consolidate.

All the above factors have resulted in a banking crisis of enormous proportions. Best guess estimates of the cost of resolving the banking crisis as a percentage of GDP are 25% for Malaysia, 20% for Thailand, 15% for Indonesia, and 5% for Singapore.[4] Securitization is one of the many options that can be utilized to help defuse the banking crisis. It provides a mechanism for banks to adjust their balance sheets and improve liquidity. Banks are likely to be under pressure from regulators and the markets to improve their capital adequacy. One method is to downsize assets through aggressive securitization. Banks in fact, can play a dual role in the securitization market, both as suppliers of assets to be securitized and as investors of securitized products.

---

[2] For example, in 1996 the credit to GDP ratio of selected emerging market countries was as follows: Brazil, 30%; Indonesia, 63%; Korea, 134%; Malaysia, 140%, and Thailand, 157%.

[3] As reported in *The Wall Street Journal* (April 3, 2000).

[4] World Bank.

Underdeveloped Equity Markets

Severely underdeveloped equity markets and lack of liquidity are typical problems in emerging markets. Primary market development has been a challenge since most efforts have proceeded without addressing the structural problems and basic institutional infrastructure needs. A healthy primary market is central to capital market development efforts and instrumental in creating products to sustain the market.

The typical approach has followed one of two paths. In countries where no stock markets existed, one was created rapidly without developing the necessary institutional structure. The problem of lack of products was addressed by rapidly privatizing state-owned enterprises with no attempts to restructure them or address fundamental problems. In countries where a market existed, attempts were made to increase listings. As a result, marginal promoters were allowed to go public. The focus was directed at creating product almost overnight to jump start the market and induce trading. Although successful in increasing listings, this approach led to widespread investor disillusionment due to poor post-listing performance of issuers. Investors who were allocated shares through mass privatization soon sold their allocations to a handful of funds leading to a concentration of ownership. In other markets, marginal firms that rushed to go public and list either remained unprofitable or failed. As a result, liquidity practically dried up and the opportunity for companies to tap the capital markets for financing essentially disappeared.

The importance of first addressing fundamental issues prior to developing stock markets must be clearly understood. Emerging markets have shown a tendency to approach the product supply problem without adequate attention to related issues required to support primary markets; such as disclosure, accountability, corporate governance, and institutional infrastructure. No enforcement mechanisms are available to ensure that promoters are held accountable to their commitments. Further, the market for corporate control did not develop due to weak institutional infrastructure and legal controls. Few attempts were made to develop the venture capital industry. As a result, young entrepreneurial firms were starved of capital. Start-up firms that could benefit from the nurturing and active participation of venture capitalists through their monitoring, advising, and strategic planning functions were forced to depend on inexperienced management. As a result, many of these firms never developed to a point where they become viable candidates for a public offering. While older mature firms orchestrated successful initial public offerings, their post-issue growth was slow. Since these companies were well past their growth stage, their post-IPO performance was considerably below investor expectations leading to disillusionment.

A weak primary market dries up secondary market trading and also prevents firms from raising additional equity through follow on offerings. Investors lose their appetite for equity products and seek refuge in bank deposits or other fixed-income products. Such conditions make it practically impossible to develop a strong local investor class for securitized products.

Need for Corporate Bond Market Development

The need to develop bond markets to complement the role of banks in financing long-term projects is of the utmost strategic importance. Emerging economies are recognizing the need for development of the domestic bond market to proceed in a systematic fashion. The results thus far have not fulfilled expectations, especially in the medium- and long-term corporate bond market. Although the overall corporate debt market has grown in recent years, it has fallen behind the growth in equity markets. One major reason is the lack of established institutional investors such as pension funds willing to participate in the corporate bond market. Retail investors are risk averse and prefer to stick with government securities. Independent rating agencies are either not present or in the early stages of development. Therefore, there has been inadequate attention to dealing with identifying, measuring, and managing credit risk, which has contributed to the problem. Transparency in the pricing of bonds is another important issue that has not been dealt with in a serious fashion. As a result, most investors have stuck to government securities.

WHERE DO WE GO FROM HERE?

From the above discussion it is clear that securitization cannot succeed in emerging markets unless structural problems with the banking sector, debt, and equity markets are addressed. Steps to address some of the above and other related issues to create an enabling environment for securitization are outlined below.

Development of a Government Securities Market

A strong government bond market provides an ideal learning ground to achieve pricing and trading skills without the distraction of credit risk. Market-based benchmark rates for medium- and long-term securities facilitate more accurate pricing and contribute to the development of a deep bond market. Further, market structure issues such as trading practices, registry, transfer and settlement, and accounting, can be established on firm ground.

Development of a Corporate Bond Market

The development of the corporate bond market as the engine of growth, is essential to emerging economies and should be assigned the highest priority. As the role of the government diminishes, the corporate bond market needs to take up the responsibility of providing funds for long-term projects. Both issuers and investors need to be educated on the benefits of fixed- and floating-rate notes. The necessary infrastructure to permit the distribution of issues and secondary market trading needs to be established.

Broadening the Range of Instruments (Issues and Maturities)

As capital markets evolve, the secondary market should develop from the basic equity and bond market to include a wide variety of asset classes of differing risk-return characteristics. The hunt for yield and diversification should lead to an explosion of instruments offering investors a smorgasbord of new risk classes. The securities market should be willing to take on credit risk. This should be the focus for moving the market to yet another level of maturity in its development process. As the market matures, financing alternatives such as securitization will become attractive.

Development of Risk Management Techniques

Sophisticated risk-management techniques are becoming increasingly important in emerging markets. The growth and innovation in financial instruments and derivative products have reduced boundaries between various risks. For instance, a bank can eliminate traditional risks by exchanging credit risk for market risk through an interest rate swap or mitigate both credit risk and market risk through contingent options. Such mechanisms should be explored for emerging markets.

Development of Credit Rating Agencies

Rating agencies play a critical and constructive role in the development of a market for securitization. The marketability of securitized products depends to a large extent on the strength of credit enhancements. Rating agencies provide a guarantee that the credit enhancement structure selected is consistent with the assigned rating. The presence of credible rating agencies permit a shift in focus from credit risk to other forms of risk. Strong ratings help reduce the cost to issuers and expand the institutional investor base otherwise restricted to investments in investment-grade securities.

Therefore, effective, independent, and credible credit agencies that develop models to evaluate and monitor outstanding credit risks, and provide critical information are an absolute priority as emerging markets move towards an increased level of maturity. Credit rating agencies should develop procedures consistent with international best practices.

Development of Institutional Investor Base

It is critical that steps be taken to broaden the composition of financial assets by institutional investors. Restrictions on pension funds and other institutional investors investing in securities backed by real estate or other assets need to be relaxed. Institutions, capable of providing venture capital and participating in debt and equity markets need to be developed. Also, there must be a conscious effort to allow pension funds and other institutional investors to participate in the debt and equity markets as well as in the venture capital market. Education of investors to the benefits of adding fixed- and floating-rate notes to their portfolio is an important contribution.

Application of Accounting, Reporting, and Disclosure Standards

Many emerging markets do not provide for independent auditing of financial statements which impact both the timeliness and quality of the data. Accounting practices should conform to international standards. Raising the bar on disclosure, holding promoters accountable to uses of proceeds stated in the prospectus, and allowing the market for corporate control to discipline poor-performing managers will help ensure post-listing performance and raise investor confidence. Listing requirements should be designed to prevent marginal firms from approaching the capital markets. A related and equally critical area is developing uniform underwriting standards.

It is vital that right from the beginning, emerging economies take steps to develop acceptable standards in credit practices and loan documentation. Creation of government or semi-government agencies similar to Freddie Mac or Fannie Mae in the United States will provide a major boost to the movement to securitize. Such institutions have the ability to set uniform underwriting standards and provide a measure of credit enhancement.

Enabling Securities Legislation

One of the major obstacles to securitization in emerging economies is the legal/regulatory environment. Legal changes are required prior to the introduction of securitization. The changes in the legal/regulatory environment to foster securitization and other similar instruments need to proceed at a rapid pace with strong support from the government. An obvious first step is to pass legislation permitting the issuance of securitized assets. A legal basis for the creation and functioning of trusts needs to be developed. New forms of trusts designed to meet the needs of local markets need to be developed. The concept of mortgages or enforcement of repossession either do not exist or are underdeveloped. Therefore, efforts are required by the government to establish a legal basis for some of the above and related issues to allow securitization to proceed on a fast track.

Development of the Home Financing Market

Securitization requires the continuous availability of product. Therefore, the volume of loan origination needs to be dramatically increased. Both the demand and supply side need development. To create demand, the government needs to become an active advocate of home ownership. It is beneficial to study the example of the British government during the mid-1980s in their role as strong advocates of home ownership and the steps they took to make it easy for renters to buy their houses. Similar programs need to be developed in emerging markets. This will generate a strong demand for home mortgages. On the supply side, additional sources of loan origination need to be developed. In addition to banks, entry of other players in the market should be encouraged. Securitization will help in freeing capital to increase the origination capabilities of banks and other players.

CONCLUSION

Financial crisis can become a driving force in promoting securitization. An argument can be made for a strong push to introduce securitization in emerging economies because of the magnitude of financing needs. However, implementing securitization in emerging economies can be a daunting task due to lack of institutional infrastructure, technology, and investor awareness. The main objective of this chapter is to start a debate on identifying and eliminating barriers to securitization in emerging markets. The need for securitization is clear, especially due to the banking crisis. What is less clear, is how to make it work in emerging economies. Securitization cannot proceed without first addressing the need for institutional infrastructure. The chapter discusses some priority areas that emerging markets need to focus on in order to develop a healthy market for securitization.

Overall, it is clear, that securitization in emerging markets needs to proceed in a phased and carefully planned fashion. First the appropriate institutional infrastructure should be in place before proceeding with securitization. Second, the initial focus of securitization should be on high quality rather than problem loans. Subsequently, the problematic loans can be selected as candidates for securitization. Third, securitization efforts should initially focus on natural securities before proceeding to synthetic securities. Finally, efforts to develop both a domestic as well as cross border market in securitization should proceed concurrently.

Appendix

Glossary of Frequently Used Terms in Asset Securitization*

Kenneth P. Morrison
Partner
Kirkland & Ellis

100 Holder Rule – An exemption from the Plan Assets Regulation that is applicable to equity securities which are offered in a public offering in which there are at least 100 initial purchasers who are not affiliated with the issuer or the underwriters.

*2a-7*** – Rule 2a-7 under the 1940 Act is a substantive regulation of money market funds' investment policies. It imposes certain requirements on investments held by money market funds, including a maximum remaining maturity of 397 days for any security held by the fund, a weighted average portfolio maturity of 90 days or less, limits on the rating of the investments held, including a requirement that all Asset-Backed Securities be rated by a nationally recognized rating agency, and a concentration limit by issuer. In calculating the concentration of a particular issuer, Commercial Paper Conduits are generally considered the issuer of their securities, although Rule 2a-7 requires a look-through to the obligor of the conduit's assets if such obligor constitutes 10% or more of the conduit's assets.

3a-7 – Rule 3a-7, adopted in 1992 by the SEC, provides an exemption from "investment company" status under the 1940 Act that is available for most securitizations.

---

* In preparing this glossary of terms, the author has assumed that the reader has a working knowledge of commonly used terms in corporate finance transactions (*e.g.*, basis points, GAAP, Rule 10b-5, SEC, trustee). This glossary sets forth brief explanations of commonly used terms more indigenous to asset securitization, without any attempt to be systematic or comprehensive. Readers seeking definitive explanations are urged to consult appropriate authorities. Readers seeking absolute truth may need to petition for divine intervention. Lawyers seeking to quibble with particular terms herein are urged to write their own glossaries. The author, of course, stands ready to provide further explication upon appropriate request.

** Statutes, regulations and the like that are often referred to in ordinary discussions without being preceded by an identifier (*e.g.*, Rule 2a-7 is often referred to simply as "2a-7") are listed herein simply by the numerical designation. On the other hand, provisions that are almost always referred to with an identifier (*e.g.*, FAS 140) are listed with that designation.

3(c)(1) – Section 3(c)(1) is a "private investment company" exemption from regulation under the 1940 Act. In general, it exempts investment companies with fewer than 100 holders of voting securities (although determination of the number of holders requires application of some difficult attribution rules).

3(c)(5) – Section 3(c)(5) exempted holders of paper arising out of sales or financing of goods, services and real estate (*e.g.,* finance companies and mortgage bankers) from investment company status under the 1940 Act. However, it does not exempt holders of other types of collateral, such as unsecured consumer loans, student loans, credit card cash advances, or corporate bonds, and thus is not available in many securitizations.

3(c)(7) – Section 3(c)(7) is a "private investment company" exemption from regulation under the 1940 Act that was enacted in the 1990s. In general, it exempts investment companies whose investors consist entirely of "qualified purchasers," irrespective of the actual number of holders. "Qualified purchasers," also known as "QPs," are individuals with total investments of at least $5 million, businesses with total investments of at least $25 million, and entities owned by such individuals or businesses.

1940 Act – The Investment Company Act of 1940, which imposes strict limitations on activities of investment companies (unless an exemption is available). A securitization transaction could not operate at all within these constraints. The 1940 Act was adopted for the purpose of regulating mutual funds and similar vehicles that are established for the purpose of investing in securities, but its broad definition of "securities" meant that most ABS structures were investment companies. Exemptions like Section 3(c)(1) and Section 3(c)(5) were available for many, but not all, securitizations. The adoption of Rule 3a-7 significantly reduced the impact of the 1940 Act on securitizations.

ABCP – Asset-Backed Commercial Paper.

ABS – Asset-Backed Securities.

Accumulation Period – In a Revolving Pool securitization, a period of time prior to the repayment of principal during which Principal Collections on the Receivables are set aside, or "accumulated," for later payment to the investors. Accumulation Periods can be used both for Bullet Maturity and Controlled Amortization structures.

Advances – See *Servicer Advances.*

Amortization Date – The first day of the Amortization Period.

Amortization Events – In a Revolving Pool securitization, certain events, somewhat analogous to events of default in a commercial loan, that will cause the commencement of an Early Amortization Period. Typical Amortization Events include insolvency of the Originator or the SPV, defaults in payments, non-performance of covenants and deterioration in the performance of the asset pool.

Amortization Period – In a Revolving Pool securitization, the period at the end of the transaction during which Principal Collections are no longer "reinvested" in new Receivables but are instead paid out promptly (usually monthly) to investors.

Asset-Backed Commercial Paper – Short term promissory notes (usually 30 days in tenor, and no more than 270 days) issued by a Commercial Paper Conduit.

Asset-Backed Securities – Generally refers to securitizations backed by assets other than commercial or residential first mortgages (although securitizations backed by home equity loans and loans on manufactured housing are generally considered to be ABS rather than MBS).

Automatic Stay – Section 362 of the Bankruptcy Code generally forbids ("stays") any person from and after commencement of a bankruptcy case from commencing or continuing any litigation or enforcing any judgment against the debtor, taking any action to obtain possession of, or exercise control over, property of the Bankruptcy Estate and collecting any claim from or setting off any debt against the debtor.

Back-up Servicer – The Rating Agencies will almost always require that some person not affiliated with the initial Servicer agree to become the Servicer in the event of a Servicer Termination of the initial Servicer. Frequently, the entity serving as trustee in the securitization will take on this responsibility. Usually, there is little attention given to whether the committed Back-up Servicer could effectively handle the servicing function. Occasionally, however, if the financial condition of the initial Servicer is uncertain enough, additional measures will be taken to ensure that the Back-up Servicer will be able to take over on short notice in a smooth transition. A "hot" or "warm" Back-up Servicer may be required.

Bankruptcy Estate – All of the debtor's legal or equitable interests in property at the commencement of a case under the Bankruptcy Code.

Bankruptcy Remote – A term used to describe an entity (typically an Special Purpose Entity) that has been established in a fashion intended to minimize the possibility that the entity could become a debtor in a bankruptcy or insolvency proceeding. Typical techniques used to enhance bankruptcy remoteness include one or more Independent Directors and a requirement that 100% of directors must approve any voluntary bankruptcy, No Petition Covenants from all identified creditors of the entity and strict limitations on the permitted activities and allowable indebtedness of the entity.

Basle Accord – An agreement reached in 1988 by banking regulators from 12 OECD countries (including the United States, Canada, Japan and the major Western European nations) regarding a common treatment of capital adequacy for international banks. The Basle Accord established the system of tier 1 and tier 2 capital, risk weights and credit conversion factors now used by banks and regulators to measure capital adequacy. Although the Basle Accord constituted significant progress in the coordinated regulation of international banks, it did not address the participation of banks in securitizations, and the various national regulators have been left to develop their own standards in this area.

Bullet Maturity – In a Revolving Pool securitization, a repayment of all or virtually all of the investors' principal in a single payment on a specified maturity date. If the failure to repay the full principal amount on the maturity date results in adverse consequences, such as an increase in interest rate or a liquidation of the securitized assets, the payment is said to be a *Hard Bullet*, and if such failure does not result in adverse consequences (other than the obligation to apply future collections to pay the remaining amount due), the payment is said to be a *Soft Bullet*. Contrast *Controlled Amortization*.

Business Trust – 1. Some states (notably Delaware) have statutes providing for the creation of "business trusts," which are legal entities the beneficial owners of which have limited liability for debts of the business trust. Delaware business trusts have been used as SPVs in a number of securitizations. 2. Under the Bankruptcy Code, a "business trust" is an eligible debtor. However, there is no definition of the term in the Bankruptcy Code, and the judicial construction of the term can be hard to reconcile. A 1994 Second Circuit case involving a trust that was formed in connection with an aircraft lease financing by Eastern AirLines and that issued trust certificates to investors held that the trust was not a "business trust" within the meaning of the Bankruptcy Code.

Cash Collateral Account – A form of Credit Enhancement in which funds are held in an account, subject to withdrawal in the event of losses on the assets in excess of available junior Credit Enhancement. Cash Collateral Accounts were (and are) used frequently in securitizations by Originators who do not wish to retain a Subordinated Interest in the securitization, such as banks who will not receive Off Balance Sheet treatment under Regulatory Accounting Principles if they retain a Subordinated Interest. Cash Collateral Accounts largely replaced letters of credit as a source of Credit Enhancement; now most issuers have replaced Cash Collateral Accounts with Collateral Interests.

Cash Flow CDO – Generally used to describe a type of Collateralized Bond Obligation or Collateralized Debt Obligation in which the Collateral Manager passively manages the pool of securitized assets, by liquidating the assets placed into the structure at closing. Contrast *Market Value CDO*.

CBO – Collateralized Bond Obligation.

CDO – Collateralized Debt Obligation.

Check-the-Box – A federal income tax regulation issued by the Treasury Department in 1996 that enables any domestic entity that is not a corporation to elect to be treated as a partnership for federal income tax purposes without the necessity of compliance with an arcane set of tax principles known as the "Kintner Regulations." Exasperated corporate treasurers, investment bankers and investors have been pleased by the adoption of the Check-the-Box initiative, as it saved countless hours of wrangling over Kinter Regulations minutiae, although the *PTP* and *FASIT* regimes mean that (thankfully for law firms) tax lawyers are still a fixture in securitizations.

Clean-up Call – The right of the Servicer to repurchase the remaining assets in the securitization when they have reached a low level compared to the outset of the transaction. Under FAS 140, a Clean-up Call is permissible so long as it entitles the Servicer to repurchase the transferred financial assets only "when the amount of the outstanding assets falls to a level at which the cost of servicing those assets becomes burdensome." In practice, the permissible level under FAS 125 was usually 10% of the original amount of the assets for corporations and 5% for banks. In securitizations of Revolving Pools (particularly with Master Trusts), the Clean-up Call is often styled as a repurchase of the investor interests rather than a repurchase of the actual assets.

Collateral Interest (popularly referred to as *Collateral Invested Amount*) – A form of Credit Enhancement used with increasing frequency in Master Trust securitizations of credit card receivables in which an additional tranche of investor interests is created and placed with one or more financial institutions. Typically, the Collateral Interest is rated "BBB" by one Rating Agency, is privately placed with an agent bank, and is used in lieu of (or in partial substitution for) a Cash Collateral Account.

Collateral Invested Amount – See *Collateral Interest*.

Collateral Manager – A person who manages the pool of assets securitized. This term is most often used in a CBO, CDO or CLO. The Collateral Manager may be the entity (such as a bank) that originated the assets in the pool, or it may be an investment management company that has acquired the assets in the secondary market for the purpose of effecting the transaction.

Collateralized Bond Obligation or *CBO* – In its purest form, a securitization of a pool of corporate bonds acquired by a *Collateral Manager* on the open market. A CBO is one of several forms of securitization of corporate debt obligations; also see *Collateralized Loan Obligation, Collateralized Debt Obligation* and *Market Value CBO*. Many CBOs in fact have collateral that includes not only corporate bonds, but also some corporate loans or other debt obligations.

Collateralized Debt Obligation or *CDO* – A securitization of a pool of debt obligations such as bonds, loans and asset-backed securities, which have been originated or acquired on the open market by a *Collateral Manager*, and which are typically commercial obligations (rather than consumer). CDOs have also been effected which consist partially or entirely of Asset-Backed Securities or other *Structured Securities*. Also used as a generic term to encompass securitizations which focus on a particular type of debt obligation, such as *CBOs* and *CLOs*.

Collateralized Loan Obligation or *CLO* – In its purest form, a securitization of a pool of corporate loans originated or acquired on the open market by a *Collateral Manager*. A CLO is one of several forms of securitization of commercial debt obligations; also see *Collateralized Bond Obligation, Collateralized Debt Obligation* and *Market Value CBO*. Some CLOs in fact have collateral that includes not only corporate loans, but also some corporate bonds or other commercial debt obligations.

Commercial Mortgages – Mortgages on Commercial Real Estate.

Commercial Real Estate – Income producing real estate properties, including multi-family residential properties, office buildings, shopping centers, and regional malls.

Commercial Paper Conduit or *CP Conduit* – Typically, an Orphan SPC that acquires receivables from one or more Originators and finances the acquisition with the issuance of highly rated commercial paper. The commercial paper rating is dependent on the presence of a Liquidity Facility and Credit Enhancement. Usually, the Liquidity Facility equals 100% of the conduit's rated capacity, but the Credit Enhancement (which generally comes from a combination of Overcollateralization and a third party surety bond, letter of credit or receivables purchase facility) is generally limited to a smaller percentage of the total facility. The "conduit" designation comes from the practice of passing through to the Originator(s) the interest expense on the commercial paper and the other expenses of the conduit. Generally, the conduit itself has little or no taxable income, although various fees are paid to the Sponsor, the providers of Credit Enhancement and Liquidity Support and other participants. See *Multi Seller Program* and *Single Seller Program*.

Concentration Limits or *Concentration Risk* – One of the principal benefits of most securitization structures is the diversity of the obligors in the pool (*e.g.,* a typical $1 billion retail auto loan pool will have perhaps 100,000 individual loans in it). Many pools of Receivables, however, will have one or a few significant obligors (*e.g.,* a typical trade receivables pool), which creates a risk, referred to as a "concentration risk," that a default or insolvency of a significant obligor will dramatically impact the pool. In such cases, the Rating Agencies will generally set a "concentration limit" on the permissible amount or percentage of Receivables from any one Obligor that will be considered eligible Receivables for purposes of the securitization. Often, the documents establish a series of concentration limits that increase as the creditworthiness of the obligor increases, so that Receivables from an unrated obligor might be subject to a 2% concentration limit while Receivables from an A-2/P-2 obligor might be subject to an 8% limit and Receivables from an A-1+P-1 obligor might have no upper limit. Finally, concentration risk based on factors other than the identity of the obligor can cause concern and impact a securitization's ratings or structure. An example would be geographic location (so that a pool of Receivables heavily weighted toward, say, asset securitization professionals could be at risk in the event of an earthquake in Arizona in February of any year).

Controlled Amortization – An approach to an Amortization Period under which a defined amount of Principal Collections are set aside each month for distribution to investors. The alternative is "uncontrolled amortization," under which the investors receive all of their allocated share of Principal Collections each month, regardless of amount. The Controlled Amortization arrangement reduces the investors' uncertainty over the amount of principal that it will receive each month (and need to reinvest) during the Amortization Period.

Credit Enhancement – A source of capital that takes a risk of loss (generally due to Uncollectibility) that is disproportionately greater than more senior positions in a securitization. Sources of credit enhancement vary substantially among transactions, but often include one or more of: Overcollateralization, Excess Spread, Reserve Accounts, Collateral Interest, Spread Accounts, letters of credit, Subordinated Interests, agreements to purchase defaulted receivables, financial guaranties and surety bonds. Credit Enhancement is sometimes categorized according to whether it is First Loss or Second Loss protection.

Days Sales Outstanding – A number used in trade receivables transactions to approximate the number of days of sales by the Originator that would be required to generate an amount of Receivables equal to the amount outstanding on the date of calculation. (For most trade receivables portfolios, this number seems to be in the range of 30-75 days.) Also sometimes referred to as "turnover days." See also "Portfolio Turnover."

Debt-for-ERISA – A term of art, rather than a strictly legal designation. Refers to the treatment of ABS as not causing the Plan Asset Regulation to be applicable by reason of the ABS constituting an instrument which "is treated as indebtedness under applicable local law which has no substantial equity features."

Debt-for-Tax – Refers to the treatment of ABS issued in a securitization structure (generally but not always a Master Trust) as indebtedness for federal, state and local income tax purposes, even though the form of the ABS is as a different type of interest (almost always a trust certificate). The treatment requires a "substance over form" analysis, which is always supported by an express agreement of all parties to treat the ABS as indebtedness notwithstanding the contrary form. See also *Partnership Fallback.*

Dilution – The occurrence of events unrelated to the creditworthiness of an Obligor which "dilute," or result in noncash reductions to the outstanding balance of, a Receivable. Examples include: for credit card Receivables, credits for returned merchandise; for dealer Receivables, credits for warranty defects; for trade Receivables, credits for cooperative advertising expense, volume purchase incentives and defective goods. There is typically some form of Recourse against the Originator for dilution.

Direct Credit Substitute – A term used mostly by the FFIEC to refer to a source of Credit Enhancement provided by a bank or thrift to a securitization of Receivables not originated by that bank or thrift. (In contrast, a similar Credit Enhancement provided by a bank or thrift for a securitization of Receivables that it originated is regarded by the FFIEC as "recourse.")

Disguised Recourse – A phrase bandied about by lawyers (but not reflected in the True Sale case law) that refers to the possibility that a form of Credit Enhancement (*e.g.,* a subordinate interest in a trust) retained or provided by a transferor of Receivables could be recharacterized as retained Recourse that would in turn result in a purported sale being recharacterized as a secured transaction.

Distribution Date – The term typically used to describe the day of each month or other fiscal period on which distributions of interest or principal will be made to investors. Sometimes called "*Settlement Date*" or "*Payment Date.*"

Early Amortization Event – See *Amortization Event.*

Early Amortization Period – An Amortization Period that commences in advance of the scheduled period for returning Principal Collections to investors.

EITF 88-22 – An abstract of a consensus (on issue no. 22 to arise in 1988, apparently) reached in 1989 by the Emerging Issues Task Force, which is an accounting body operating under the auspices of the FASB. This abstract concerned the appropriate treatment (sale v. financing) for credit card securitizations with differing allocations of Principal Collections during the Amortization Period. The consensus was that when "the percentage of principal payments allocated to the investors exceeds the investors' ownership interests in the receivables in the trust at the beginning of the" Amortization Period, then the transaction would not qualify as a sale even if it met the other conditions of FAS 77. The requirements of EITF 88-22 have not been carried forward in FAS 140, meaning that knowledge of EITF 88-22 will soon become a way to separate grizzled securitization veterans from raw recruits.

EITF 96-20 – A consensus of the Emerging Issues Task Force that addressed the conditions under which a Qualifying SPE under FAS 125 should be consolidated with the transferor. Previous practice, except in cases involving collateralized mortgage obligations, required consolidation unless the SPE had a significant amount of equity, a majority of which was owned by independent parties. However, under EITF 96-20, the ownership of the equity and the amount of the equity became irrelevant in a number of transactions, and transactions in which the SPE might previously have been consolidated with the transferor often were no longer be consolidated. So, for example, an Originator could achieve Off Balance Sheet treatment even if the Originator owned all of the equity interests in a Qualifying SPE, so long as the Qualifying SPE issues debt instruments to investors and the "isolation" criteria of FAS 125 were satisfied. EITF 96-20 has been incorporated into FAS 140.

ERISA – The Employee Retirement Income Security Act of 1974, a federal statute designed to regulate the establishment and management of ERISA Plans. Somewhat surprisingly to many initiates, ERISA contains many substantive limitations on the ability of ERISA Plans to make investments, including investments in Asset-Backed Securities. One such limitation arises if the investment in an Asset-Backed Security would cause the assets of the issuing trust to be treated as Plan Assets. Another limitation arises if the purchase of the ABS would constitute a Prohibited Transaction. The Department of Labor has regulatory jurisdiction over ERISA.

ERISA-Eligible – A term of art indicating that a security is generally eligible to be purchased by ERISA Plans. Often, this term is used for situations in which an exemption exists from the Plan Assets Regulation, which is usually the Debt-for-ERISA exemption. Pension plans and other ERISA Plans subject to ERISA hold trillions of dollars in investments, which means that the designation of an ABS as ERISA-Eligible can greatly expand the potential investor base. As a result, originators and investment bankers are always seeking ways to make ABS be ERISA-Eligible.

ERISA Plans – U.S. based pension, profit-sharing and other employee benefit plans, individual retirement accounts, and certain collective investment funds or insurance company general or separate accounts in which such plans and accounts are invested.

Emerging Asset Class – A term used to refer to a class of assets that has potential for securitization but has not yet been widely securitized. In part, classification as an emerging asset class lies in the eye of the beholder. The asset class has to have possibilities but can not have been too widely exploited yet.

Excess Servicing or *Excess Spread* – The interest or finance charge income generated by an interest bearing Receivable that is in excess of the amount needed to pay the interest expense on the ABS or MBS, the Servicing Fee and (depending on usage) to cover losses on Receivables.

FAS 77 – Statement of Financial Accounting Standards No. 77, *Reporting by Transferors for Transfers of Receivables with Recourse.* FAS 77 was issued by the Financial Accounting Standards Board in 1983, and it sets out the standards for "sale" treatment for GAAP purposes. As stated in the Summary to FAS 77, "This Statement specifies that a transferor ordinarily should report a sale of receivables with recourse transaction as a sale if (a) the transferor surrenders its control of the future economic benefits relating to the receivables, (b) the transferor can reasonably estimate its obligation under the recourse provision, and (c) the transferee cannot return the receivables to the transferor except pursuant to the recourse provisions." FAS 77 was superseded by FAS 125, effective January 1, 1997.

FAS 125 – Statement of Financial Accounting Standards No. 125, *Accounting for Transfers and Servicing of Financial Assets and Extinguishments of Liabilities,* adopted by the Financial Accounting Standards Board in June, 1996. FAS 125 superseded FAS 77, effective January 1, 1997. The basic structure established by FAS 125 has been carried forward in FAS 140, which supercedes FAS 125. The differences between FAS 125 and FAS 140 arise principally in the application of the structural tests established by FAS 125.

FAS 140 – Statement of Financial Accounting Standards No. 140, *Accounting for Transfers and Servicing of Financial Assets and Extinguishments of Liabilities,* adopted by the Financial Accounting Standards Board in September, 1999. FAS 140 supersedes FAS 125, effective for sales occurring after March 31, 2001 (except that certain new disclosure requirements are effective for financial statements applicable to fiscal years ending after December 15, 2000). FAS 140 provides that a transfer of financial assets will be accounted for as a sale to the extent that the transferor surrenders control over the financial assets and receives consideration other than beneficial interests in the assets in return. Surrender of control occurs if three conditions are met: (i) the transferred assets have been isolated from the transferor – put presumptively beyond the reach of the transferor and its creditors, even in bankruptcy; (ii) the transferee has an essentially unconstrained right to further pledge or exchange the transferred assets *or* the transferee is a Qualifying SPE and its holders have an essentially unconstrained right to transfer their interests in the special purpose entity; and (iii) the transferor does not maintain effective control over the transferred assets through an arrangement that entitles and obligates the transferor to repurchase the transferred assets or through a call option on the transferred assets (other than a Clean-up Call).

FASIT – Financial Asset Securitization Investment Trust.

FFIEC – The Federal Financial Institutions Examination Council, an interagency working group comprised of representatives of the four main federal bank and thrift regulatory agencies (the Federal Reserve Bank, the Office of the Comptroller of the Currency, the Federal Deposit Insurance Corporation and the Office of Thrift Supervision).

Financial Asset Securitization Investment Trust – A statutory tax regime for ABS that became effective on September 1, 1997. The FASIT provisions are modeled in certain respects on the REMIC provisions. It currently is an elective "safe harbor," so it does not necessarily displace existing tax characterizations. It also contains some problematic features that have sharply limited its attractiveness for many asset types. FASIT is generally acknowledged to be of marginal value, at best, to the securitization industry.

Financial Components Paradigm – A format proposed by Ray Perry in *Accounting for Securitizations* (in Accounting Horizons, September 1993) for accountants to account for securitizations, under which the securitization is treated as a sale if legal ownership of the Receivables is transferred to an SPE, with the originator "derecognizing" (*i.e.,* removing from its balance sheet) the transferred assets and "recognizing" (*i.e.,* putting back on its balance sheet) each interest in or relationship with the SPE. The Financial Components Paradigm is the conceptual backbone of FAS 140. Contrast the *Predominant Characteristics Paradigm*.

First Loss or First Loss Protection – Also sometimes referred to as *First Dollar Loss*. This term is used to refer to the source of Credit Enhancement that will bear the first losses due to defaults in the Receivables pool. The term is mostly used by the FFIEC in the context of trying to rationalize the risk-based capital requirements for banks and thrifts that participate in securitizations. However, the FFIEC has been somewhat unclear as to the specifics of this term; their May 1994 risk-based capital proposal relied heavily on the concept of first loss protection, but never defined the term.

First Priority Security Interest – In absolute terms, a security interest in an asset that is subordinate to no other lien claim on the asset. This is the sense in which the term is used in representations and warranties. In legal opinion terminology, however, an opinion that a security interest is of "first priority" is generally subject to numerous qualifications regarding possible security interests that would not be located through a search of the Uniform Commercial Code filing system.

Future Flow Securitization – This term refers to a transaction in which the rating is based on the likelihood of future cash flows arising from an activity in which the originator engages, in which there are few or no cash flows arising from existing Receivables. For example, in a future flow transaction involving feature films, the rating is based on the likelihood that a pool of feature length films (which may not yet have even been produced) will generate a sufficient amount of cash flow to repay the investors. Another example is a future flow transaction involving trade receivables from exports, in which the rating is premised on the ability of the originator to continuing producing a product for export (such as oil from Mexican wells) that will generate cash flows to be used to repay the investors.

Grantor Trust – A tax law term of art referring to a trust the income of which is taxed to beneficial owners under Sections 671 through 679 of the Internal Revenue Code. A grantor trust is not an "entity" for federal income tax purposes; rather, its beneficiaries are treated as holders of a ratable share of its assets (in contrast to partnerships, which are treated as entities, even though their income is allocated to the holders of the partnership interests). There are a number of Internal Revenue Code restrictions on the permissible interests issued by grantor trusts and the permissible activities of the trustee. The upshot of these regulations is that, for securitization purposes, Grantor Trusts are suitable only for Self-Liquidating Pools.

Implied Rating – A rating on a security that can be reasonably implied from actual ratings on other securities of the same (or, perhaps, a closely related) issuer.

Independent Director – A director of an SPC who is not also an officer, employee or director of, and does not have any other significant relationship with, the SPC's parent corporation or of another entity sponsoring the securitization.

Internet – A worldwide system of computers that are linked together for the purposes of legitimate research and cyberporn. The Internet has little to do with asset securitization, but no glossary used in the new millennium would be complete without a reference.

Investment Company – Under the 1940 Act, essentially a company that is engaged in the business of investing, holding or trading in securities that has more than 40% of its total assets (exclusive of government securities) invested in securities (exclusive of government securities and securities issued by non-investment company subsidiaries). Note that the definition of "security" is much broader under the 1940 Act than under the other securities laws, and is commonly understood to include Receivables.

Investment Company Act of 1940 – See *1940 Act.*

Liquidity Facility – A credit facility for the purpose of Liquidity Support provided by a group of commercial banks or other financial institutions ("*Liquidity Providers*"). A Liquidity Facility will almost always have a firm commitment to lend in order to repay maturing commercial paper or pay interest on other ABS, subject only to the conditions precedent that the SPV that is the issuer not be insolvent and that there is a sufficient "borrowing base" of Receivables. Under applicable banking regulations, the capital required to be held by a commercial bank against an undrawn Liquidity Facility will depend upon the maturity of the facility and the presence or absence of a borrowing base test.

Liquidity Providers – See *Liquidity Facility.*

Liquidity Support – In a securitization in which there is a risk of a timing "mismatch" (*i.e.,* that current collections on the Receivables will not be sufficient to make timely payments of interest or principal on the outstanding ABCP or other ABS), a source of liquidity must be established to bridge the mismatch. This liquidity can come either from funds invested in liquid assets (*e.g.,* a Spread Account) or from a syndicate of banks having a rating commensurate with the rating of the ABS. Unlike providers of Credit Enhancement, providers of Liquidity Support are not expected to bear the risk of Uncollectibility. See *Liquidity Facility.*

Low-Level Recourse – Recourse against a bank originator in connection with a securitization of financial assets for an amount that is less than the amount of risk-based capital (usually 8% of the total size of the pool) that the bank would be required to hold against those assets if it had not securitized them. If a bank has Low-Level Recourse, then the maximum amount of risk-based capital that it is required to hold against those assets is limited to the amount of the Recourse. The adoption of the Low-Level Recourse rule in early 1995 eliminated an inconsistency in the risk-based capital rules under which a bank could be forced to hold more risk-based capital against a securitized pool of assets than the maximum loss that the bank could suffer on the pool.

Market Value CDO – Generally used to describe a type of Collateralized Bond Obligation or Collateralized Debt Obligation in which the Collateral Manager is permitted to "actively" manage the pool of securitized assets – by buying and selling assets – so long as the "market value" of the assets, as measured through a series of tests approved by the Rating Agencies, meets the minimum established levels. Contrast *Cash Flow CDO.*

Master Owner Trust – A term that refers to a trust in a Revolving Pool securitization that is authorized to issue multiple series of notes or other debt instruments to investors. It is comparable to a Master Trust, except that it issues debt instruments rather than Trust Certificates. The principal benefit of utilizing a Master Owner Trust structure rather than a Master Trust is that debt instruments issued by a Master Owner Trust are generally going to be ERISA-Eligible, unlike most Trust Certificates.

Master Trust – A term that refers to a trust in a Revolving Pool securitization that is authorized to issue multiple series of interests to investors. Such a trust can issue new series to investors as the size of its assets grows or as existing series of investor interests enter their Amortization Periods and are repaid. Such trusts generally issue Trust Certificates that use a Debt-for-Tax structure. With the advent of Master Owner Trusts made possible by EITF 96-20, FAS 125 and FAS 140, Master Trusts are a dying breed.

MBS – Mortgage Backed Securities.

Monoline or *Monoline Insurer* – An insurance company whose business is limited to writing financial guaranty insurance, principally in respect of asset-backed securities and municipal bonds. The main Monoline Insurers in the United States ABS market are, in no particular order, Financial Security Assurance Inc. (often referred to as FSA), Capital Markets Assurance Corporation (CapMAC), Municipal Bond Investors Assurance Corporation (MBIA) and Financial Guaranty Insurance Corporation (FGIC).

Mortgage Backed Securities – Generally refers to securitizations backed by commercial or residential mortgages (although up to 1991 or so it would probably have been generally understood to refer just to securitizations backed by Residential Mortgages).

Multi Seller Program – Generally used in reference to a Commercial Paper Conduit that is established by a bank (or, occasionally, a financial guarantor or non-bank financial institution) to acquire interests in Receivables from multiple Originators (a/k/a sellers). Some Multi Seller Programs are limited to a specific type of Receivables (*e.g.,* trade receivables, health care receivables), but most are authorized to acquire interests in many types of Receivables.

Negative Carry or *Negative Spread* – The difference between the investment return earned on funds held in an account in which Principal Collections are held during an Accumulation Period, a Cash Collateral Account or other securitization account as compared to the coupon rate on outstanding Asset-Backed Securities.

No Petition Covenant – An agreement by a party (typically a creditor) not to file an involuntary bankruptcy petition against another person (typically a debtor). It is typical in securitizations for all parties other than shareholders to agree to No Petition Covenants in favor of entities intended to be Bankruptcy Remote SPVs.

Non-consolidation – See *Substantive Consolidation.*

NRSRO – Acronym for "nationally recognized statistical rating organization," a term used frequently by the SEC when referring to Rating Agencies in regulations which utilize ratings issued by the Rating Agencies.

Obligor – The person obligated to make payment on a Receivable.

Octagon Gas – Octagon Gas v. Rimmer (In re Meridien Reserve, Inc.), 995 F.2d 948 (10th Cir. 1993), a much disparaged decision by a federal appeals court that wrongly interpreted the Uniform Commercial Code to hold that a person who *sold* accounts nonetheless retained an interest in those accounts when such person became a debtor in a bankruptcy proceeding. The holding has been roundly criticized and the Permanent Editorial Board of the Uniform Commercial Code has adopted a Commentary to the effect that *Octagon Gas* is wrongly decided. Revised Article 9 overrides the Octagon ruling.

Off Balance Sheet – Shorthand for accounting recognition of a transfer of receivables as a sale to a non-consolidated entity under the applicable accounting rules. See *FAS 77*, *FAS 125* and *FAS 140*.

Originator – The entity that generates Receivables, by means that include making loans, selling goods or services on credit, and providing financing for the acquisition of goods or services.

Orphan SPC – An SPC that is not owned by or, under applicable accounting principles, consolidated with the Originator or the sponsor of the securitization.

Owner Trust – A tax law term of art originally referring to a trust that is treated as a partnership for federal income tax purposes, but now generally used to refer to offerings in which the trust issues debt instruments. Frequently, so-called "owner trust" offerings are effected through the use of a Delaware Business Trust. However, many other owner trust offerings are effected using simple common law trust arrangements. Owner trust structures can be used effectively for securitizations of either Revolving Pools or Self-Liquidating Pools. See also *Master Owner Trust*.

Overcollateralization – A popular form of Credit Enhancement in which outstanding ABS or MBS are supported by Receivables having a principal amount (or, for non-interest bearing or low-interest bearing Receivables, a discounted value) greater than the principal amount of the ABS or MBS.

Partnership Fallback – Most Debt-for-Tax structures were originally structured with a "partnership fallback" for federal income tax purposes, which means that the ABS would be characterized as interests in a partnership in the event that the Debt-for-Tax treatment was not accorded. As a partnership (other than a Publicly Traded Partnership) is treated for federal income tax purposes as a "flow-through" entity on which no income tax is imposed, such treatment will enable the investors to achieve essentially the same result as if the Debt-for-Tax treatment was respected (although some categories of investors, notably foreign persons, could be disadvantaged). The alternative to partnership taxation is generally taxation on the same basis as corporations, which would result in a tax being imposed on the income of the entity, thereby perhaps diminishing the assets available to repay investors. The advent of Check-the-Box means that Partnership Fallback is automatic for trusts and other unincorporated associations, although the potential partnership must still be structured to avoid PTP status.

Pass-Through – Generally refers to a structure or an investment in which an investor owns an equity interest (*e.g.,* a trust certificate representing a beneficial interest in the trust, even though it may well be rated AAA) in the issuing vehicle and receives a ratable share of Principal Collections during the Amortization Period. Contrast *Pay-Through.*

Pay-Through – Generally refers to a structure or an investment in which an investor owns a debt interest (*e.g.,* a note or bond issued by a trust or a corporation) in the issuing vehicle and receives a share of Principal Collections during the Amortization Period that is less sensitive to the actual level of collections. Although this term was in vogue in the early days of securitization, it is now somewhat anachronistic. Contrast *Pass-Through.*

Plan Assets – Assets owned by an ERISA Plan. Under the Plan Assets Regulation, assets owned by an entity in which an ERISA Plan has an equity investment can constitute Plan Assets, which means that the entity's assets will be subject to the Prohibited Transaction rules.

Plan Assets Regulation – A regulation promulgated by the Department of Labor under ERISA which deems assets of an entity (*e.g.,* a trust that has issued ABS) in which an ERISA Plan acquires an "equity interest" to constitute Plan Assets, unless certain exemptions are available. If the assets of the ABS trust are treated as Plan Assets, then the Prohibited Transaction rules will be applicable and will likely make it impossible for the ABS trust to operate. The most common exemption from the Plan Assets Regulations used in ABS offerings is the Debt-for-ERISA exemption, under which the interest of the ERISA Plan is not considered an equity interest. A second exemption, when the interest of the ERISA Plan is treated as an equity interest, is the 100 Holder Rule.

Portfolio Turnover – An approximation of the number of times that a Revolving Pool of Receivables will "turn over," or effectively replace itself, in a year. Usually equal to 365 divided by Days Sales Outstanding.

Predominant Characteristics Paradigm – An approach to accounting for securitizations that is said to base the "sale" or "financing" determination on whether the sale or the financing characteristics of the transfer of Receivables appear to be predominant. Contrast *Financial Components Paradigm.*

Pre-funding – Generally understood to refer to the technique of an Originator raising more funds against the issuance of ABS backed by a Self Liquidating Pool than the value of the Receivables in the Self Liquidating Pool at the outset. The excess funds are held in a "pre-funding account" and used periodically to acquire from the Originator additional eligible Receivables as they are originated. Typically, the arrangement contemplates a pre-funding period of a relatively short duration (*e.g.,* six months); if insufficient new eligible Receivables have been originated during that period, then the excess funds in the pre-funding account are returned to the investors.

Principal Collections – With Receivables that are interest-bearing, this term generally refers to the collections in respect of the principal amount owing by the Obligors. In some securitizations, the sponsor or seller has the right to designate a portion of collections that would otherwise constitute Principal Collections to instead be finance charge collections. The purpose of such a provision is to increase the "yield" on the Receivables.

Prohibited Transactions – ERISA and the Internal Revenue Code prohibit ERISA Plans from engaging in specified transactions with persons that are "parties in interest" under ERISA or "disqualified persons" under the Internal Revenue Code. Violation of the prohibited transaction rules can result in prohibitive excise taxes and other penalties for such persons. If an ERISA Plan acquires ABS and the Originator, the SPV, the issuing trust or any of their affiliates are deemed to be "parties in interest" or "disqualified persons" with respect to that ERISA Plan, then a prohibited transaction could result.

Publicly Traded Partnership or *PTP* – A tax regime that taxes certain partnerships and other entities that would otherwise be taxed as partnerships (see *Check-the-Box*) as though they were corporations. Avoiding PTP status is important in virtually all securitizations. The Internal Revenue Service in 1995 released final regulations regarding PTP status.

Qualifying SPE or *QSPE* – Under FAS 125 and FAS 140, a "qualifying special purpose entity" is a trust, corporation or other "legal vehicle" that is limited to performing the activities involved in the securitization and that has "standing at law distinct from the transferor" and that has essentially no ability to take discretionary actions. In accountants' parlance, a QSPE must be "brain dead" or on "automatic pilot." In most securitizations, it is the trust (rather than the special purpose subsidiary) that is the QSPE.

RAP – See *Regulatory Accounting Principles.*

Rating Agency – Standard & Poor's Ratings Services, Moody's Investors Service, Inc., and Fitch, Inc. are the main agencies that rate ABS and MBS. Until its acquisition in 2000 by Fitch, Duff & Phelps Credit Rating Co. was also one of the Rating Agencies. See also *Fast Ticket to Investment Banking.*

Real Estate Mortgage Investment Conduit – A designation added to the Internal Revenue Code in 1986 applicable to entities (which may be corporations, partnerships, trusts or other entities) that hold loans secured by real property and issue multiple classes of interests. If such an entity complies with the detailed REMIC rules, it will be entitled to pass-through tax treatment. Effective in 1992, the REMIC provisions became the exclusive pass-through treatment for vehicles issuing multiple classes of real estate backed securities. If such a vehicle fails to comply, it will be taxed as a corporation.

Receivables – The right to receive payment in the future of an amount of money. In securitization, this term is generally understood to mean that the person to whom the money is owed does not have to perform any action in order to maintain its right to receive the money. Note that most securitizations have involved Receivables, but there have been several transactions that have securitized assets that might more commonly be thought of as "inventory" or "natural resources," such as standing timber and oil and gas reserves.

Recourse – Generally understood to mean the right of a transferee of Receivables to charge back to the transferor all (or a portion, if recourse is limited) of the amount of Receivables that are uncollectible. For a thought-provoking article taking a fresh look at this fascinating topic, see Pantaleo (Reporter), K. Morrison (and a gaggle of other lawyers***), *Rethinking the Role of Recourse in the Sale of Financial Assets*, 53 Bus. Law 159 (1996). See also *True Sale.*

Regulatory Accounting Principles – Accounting principles specified by U.S. bank and thrift regulators which are set forth in the instructions for the so-called "Call Reports," which are Consolidated Reports of Condition and Income that are filed by banks and thrifts with the main regulatory agencies. Currently, federally chartered banks follow GAAP when preparing Call Reports. However, pursuant to the risk-based capital rules, if there is Recourse (other than *Low-Level Recourse*) against a bank Originator in connection with a securitization of financial assets, the bank generally would be required to hold capital for the full outstanding amount of the assets securitized. The OCC and other bank regulatory agencies are currently considering revisions to the regulatory capital treatment for securitizations with Recourse.

REMIC – Real Estate Mortgage Investment Conduit.

*** These other lawyers can generate their own publicity; the don't need a mention here. Actually, it is believed that so many reprints of this article have been sent out by the various authors that every person in America who is possibly interested in the topic has already received at least one copy.

Reserve Account – A form of Credit Enhancement in which investment securities are held in an account for use in the event of a shortfall in the collections available to pay scheduled interest or principal to investors. A Reserve Account is generally understood to provide support for shortfalls due to defaults (uncollectibility) and, often, timing mismatches between collections and payments to investors (liquidity); a *Spread Account*, by contrast, is generally understood to exist principally for the purpose of remedying liquidity problems.

Residential Mortgages – Generally understood to refer to first mortgages on owner- occupied single family residences.

Revolving Pool – A pool of Receivables in which collections are, for some period of time generally referred to as the "revolving period," reinvested in newly originated Receivables rather than being paid out to holders of interests in the entity owning the Receivables. Very short term Receivables (*e.g.,* trade Receivables, dealer Receivables and health care Receivables) are always securitized in Revolving Pools, as are almost all credit card receivables. Contrast *Self Liquidating Pool.*

Second Loss or *Second Loss Protection* – Also sometimes referred to as *Second Dollar Loss.* This term is used (again, mostly by the FFIEC) to refer to the source of Credit Enhancement that will bear the losses due to defaults in the Receivables pool once the First Loss Protection is exhausted. As with First Loss, the FFIEC has been somewhat unclear as to the precise parameters of the term.

Self Liquidating Pool – A pool of Receivables in which collections are periodically paid out to holders of interests in the pool rather than being reinvested in new Receivables. Mortgage loans and retail auto loans are examples of Receivables that are generally securitized in Self Liquidating Pools.

Servicer – The party who is responsible for continuing to collect payments on the Receivables, notify delinquent Obligors, foreclose on collateral (if any), perform data processing functions, prepare periodic reports to investors and Rating Agencies and take other actions to service the Receivables. Usually, but not always, the Servicer is also the Originator or an affiliate of the Originator.

Servicer Advances – In order to provide additional liquidity, in many transactions, the Servicer will agree to advance on each Distribution Date payments on Receivables due in the prior month that were not timely received. Such payments are generally limited to amounts that the Servicer reasonably believes can be collected in the future to ensure that such payments do not constitute Recourse.

Servicer Termination – Most securitization transactions contain provisions for terminating and replacing the Servicer in the event of a material default by the Servicer in the discharge of its duties.

Servicing Fee – The fee paid to the Servicer with respect to an ABS transaction. Typically, the fee is expressed as a percentage of the outstanding balance of the Receivables or the related Asset-Backed Securities and is a payable as part of the Waterfall. See *Servicer.*

Shadow Rating – An informal rating given by a Rating Agency to an interest in Receivables or an ABS, frequently for purposes of assessing the impact of such interest or ABS upon a third party. For example, when a Monoline Insurer issues a policy that supports a pool of Receivables, the rating of the ABS will be equal to the rating of the Monoline Insurer (AAA/Aaa), and the implicit creditworthiness of the Receivables pool will not be directly relevant to the rating. However, the Rating Agencies will give a Shadow Rating to the pool, because the creditworthiness of the pool will affect the amount of capital that the Rating Agencies will require the Monoline Insurer to hold against the pool in order to maintain the insurer's AAA/Aaa rating.

Single Seller Program – Generally used in reference to a Commercial Paper Conduit in which all of the Receivables have been originated by a single Seller or group of affiliated Sellers. Contrast *Multi Seller Program.*

Soft Bullet – Generally used to refer to an ABS the principal of which is expected to be repaid in a single lump sum on a "targeted" date, but which is not absolutely required to be paid until a later "final maturity" or "legal final" date.

SPC – Special Purpose Corporation.

SPE or *SPV* – Special Purpose Entity or Special Purpose Vehicle.

Special Purpose Corporation – A Special Purpose Entity that is a corporation.

Special Purpose Entity or *Special Purpose Vehicle* – An entity that is established with a limited purpose, which is generally the acquisition and financing of Receivables. The entity, which may be a corporation, partnership, limited liability company or trust, depending on the transaction, is generally not authorized under its certificate of incorporation, articles of partnership or similar organizational documents to incur liabilities or engage in business except in ways that are necessary or advisable in connection with the securitization(s) in which it is to be involved.

Spread Account – See *Reserve Account.*

Structured Securities – Generally, securities that rely substantially on structural features that reduce the dependence of repayment on the creditworthiness of the originator. ABS are a principal category of Structured Securities. Other types of securities are also often considered to fall within this designation, such as credit derivatives and synthetic securities.

Subordinated Interest – An interest in a securitization that is subordinated in priority of payment to one or more other classes of interests. The Subordinated Interest may or may not bear a risk of loss that is disproportionate to its ratable investment in the securitization, depending on whether there are additional classes of interests or sources of Credit Enhancement that are subordinate to it.

Substantive Consolidation – A doctrine under federal bankruptcy law under which a creditor or trustee of a bankrupt debtor can seek to consolidate the assets and liabilities of another entity (which may or may not at the time be in bankruptcy proceedings) with those of the debtor. This doctrine is analogous in certain respects to the corporate law doctrine of "piercing the corporate veil" and is most often applied to substantively consolidate subsidiaries of a bankrupt entity.

Sub Prime Receivables – Generally, refers to Receivables from consumers with questionable or no credit histories. As a result, such consumers present a higher risk of non-payment and the Receivables bear a higher rate of interest. By definition, the overall credit quality of a pool of Sub Prime Receivables is likely to be poor in relation to a more traditional pool of Receivables subject to a securitization. Thus, more Credit Enhancement and other structural protections will be required.

Titling Trust – A Bankruptcy Remote trust established for the purpose of holding title to motor vehicles that have been leased. State certificate of title laws require retitling of a motor vehicle every time it is sold and notation of all liens on the certificate of title. In a securitization of auto leases (unlike auto loans), it is necessary to transfer the economic ownership of the vehicle as well as the stream of payments under the lease. It would be prohibitively expensive and cumbersome for the Originator or Servicer to retitle a vehicle and note each lien on every certificate of title upon the closing of a securitization, so the practice of titling newly leased vehicles directly into these trusts has developed. A securitization of the leased vehicles and the leases is then effected by means of a transfer or pledge of a divided beneficial interest in the titling trust rather than an outright transfer of the vehicles themselves.

True Sale – A transfer of Receivables in which ownership of the Receivables has been effectively conveyed to the transferee under applicable state law, so that in the event of a bankruptcy of the transferor, the Receivables would not be deemed property of the transferor's Bankruptcy Estate. If a transaction were not a True Sale, it would be characterized as a secured loan, with the result that the transferee would still have an ownership interest in the conveyed assets. The determination whether a transfer of Receivables constitutes a True Sale is different from the determination whether the same transfer constitutes a sale for GAAP (see *FAS 77, FAS 125* and *FAS 140*). For law firms asked to deliver a "Would" Opinion that a True Sale has occurred, the presence or absence of Recourse, and the extent of the Recourse, is considered an important issue. There are few cases that are on point, and none of them involve limited Recourse.

Trust Certificates – A certificate representing a beneficial interest in a trust. Such interests are considered "equity interests" under state law and, therefor, notwithstanding credit ratings of up to AAA/Aaa, are considered not to be "debt" for purposes such as ERISA classification (generally a bad result, because it makes a key regulatory exemption unavailable) and the Trust Indenture Act (generally a good result, because it obviates (i) the need to qualify the Pooling and Servicing Agreement under that Act as an indenture and (ii) the substantive provisions of that Act).

Turnover Days – See *Days Sales Outstanding.*

Uncollectibility – The inability to collect payments due on a Receivable due to a credit- related default by the Obligor.

Waterfall – Shorthand term for the often lengthy section(s) in a securitization document that detail the order and amounts in which collections will be applied to various uses, including (depending on the deal) interest, principal, Servicing Fee, trustee fees and other transaction expenses, losses on Receivables and deposits into Reserve Accounts. Typically, funds are applied monthly, although in a Revolving Pool securitization, reinvestment in Receivables and other amounts may be applied daily.

Weak Link Approach – A Rating Agency methodology that posits that a transaction cannot receive a higher rating than its lowest rated source of Credit Enhancement or Liquidity Support. If, for example, an A-1/P-1 rating is desired for commercial paper, then an A-1/P-1 rating will be necessary for each bank in the Liquidity Facility and each provider of Credit Enhancement. A downgrade of any such entity to A-2 or P-2 would, if such entity is not replaced, result in a downgrade of the commercial paper to A-2 or P-2.

"Would" Opinion – Shorthand term for a legal opinion that concludes (usually after a great deal of reasoning, many assumptions and qualifications and visible anguish) that a court considering an issue would reach a certain conclusion. The Rating Agencies have established "would" opinions as the standard for True Sale and Non-Consolidation analyses. A great deal of heat, but little light, has been generated over the question of what the distinction is, if any, between a "should" opinion and a "would" opinion.

Worst Case Scenario – The assumption, commonly employed by the Rating Agencies in evaluating a proposed securitization, that the Originator will become insolvent prior to the scheduled repayment of principal to the investors. Most securitizations are designed to withstand the a bankruptcy of the Originator, and the Rating Agencies will generally assume that the bankruptcy has occurred when evaluating the performance of the Receivables pool.

Wrapped – Asset-backed securities are "wrapped" if they are fully guaranteed as to timely payment of interest and ultimate return of principal by the stated maturity by a Monoline Insurer. Generally, the financial guaranty will also cover any payment which is made to securityholders and subsequently recoverable and is sought to be recovered as a preference payment by a trustee in bankruptcy.

Yield Supplement Account – Funds maintained to provide protection against interest shortfalls resulting from the Receivables in a securitized pool bearing interest at a rate lower than that required by the deal, *i.e.*, the sum of the coupon rate on outstanding ABS, the Servicing Fee and any other fees to be paid from interest collections.

Index

DATE DUE

DEMCO 38-297